WRITING FOR LOVE AND MONEY

# WRITING FOR LOVE AND MONEY

## How Migration Drives Literacy Learning in Transnational Families

Kate Vieira

OXFORD
UNIVERSITY PRESS

OXFORD
UNIVERSITY PRESS

Oxford University Press is a department of the University of Oxford. It furthers the University's objective of excellence in research, scholarship, and education by publishing worldwide. Oxford is a registered trade mark of Oxford University Press in the UK and certain other countries.

Published in the United States of America by Oxford University Press
198 Madison Avenue, New York, NY 10016, United States of America.



CIP data is on file at the Library of Congress
ISBN 978-0-19-087732-3 (pbk.)
ISBN 978-0-19-087731-6 (hbk.)

1 3 5 7 9 8 6 4 2

Paperback printed by Webcom, Inc., Canada
Hardback printed by Bridgeport National Bindery, Inc., United States of America

*For the families separated across borders*

*Ás famílias separadas além das fronteiras*

*Veltīts ģimenēm, kuras šķīrušas attālums*

*Посвящается семьям, разделённым границами*

*A las familias separadas por fronteras*

*Присвячується родинам, які розділені кордонами*

# CONTENTS

# PREFACE

It is a haunting moment in U.S. history to be completing a book about separated migrant families. As of June 2018, more than 2,300 children have been forcibly separated from their parents at the U.S. border with Mexico as part of the Trump administration's policy to deter migrants and asylum seekers. Children taken from their guardians are sleeping in cages. The youngest are housed in "tender age" facilities, where they cannot be physically comforted.[1] Each morning's news brings fresh horror. An infant is ripped from her mother's arms as she is breastfeeding.[2] Children attempt suicide.[3] Wails for mothers and fathers reverberate across the Internet.[4]

"Como ubico mis hijos?" a flyer given to parents by the U.S. Department of Homeland Security/Immigration and Customs Enforcement (ICE) asks. "How do I locate my children?"[5] In the flyer, these questions are followed by three "actions" parents can take, actions that are presented logically, as if it is a reasonable thing to have one's children kidnapped at gunpoint. "If calling from an ICE detention facility," one bullet point under Action 1 reads, "call using speed dial #9116 on the free call platform." In subsequent "actions," there are more *ifs*. There are more *thens*. There is more syllogistic violence.

I feel the panic heat my neck, and my nerves fly loose. *How do I locate my children? The ones you have taken.*

The flyer, it is worth noting, does not promise reunification. In fact, a journalist interviewing a former head of ICE reported that hundreds of children will likely never find their parents again, despite court orders.[6] Perhaps sensing the outcome, a distraught father separated from his family hanged himself in a cell in Texas.[7]

The United States is causing a humanitarian crisis, the consequences of which are as yet untold. The president of the American Association of Pediatrics, after visiting a children's detention center, detailed the irreparable damage this imprisonment can cause to children's brain chemistry and subsequent development.[8] Scholars of education, history, psychology, sociology, and other fields, in a letter signed by hundreds of faculty with expertise in human development, named the practice unconscionable and called for immediate reunification.[9] The UN human rights chief echoed the American Association of Pediatrics in labeling the treatment child abuse.[10] Amnesty International called it torture.[11]

This book, to be clear, is not about families forcibly separated at the U.S. border. Nor does it primarily address children. In fact, though one chapter is set in the United States, the book does not center on U.S. migration trajectories. This book is instead about how under unjust economic policies, families who are separated across borders in South America, Europe, and North America communicate. It is about how migration creates the emotional demand for communication, spurring new kinds of literacy learning. It is about how family members write—and learn new ways of writing—to sustain relationships. It is about how people remain close when they find themselves far.

In completing revisions of this book in the United States in this nightmare year, I am aware that the children kidnapped from their families by my government do not have the option of communicating with their families in the ways I have documented here. They have tried. We have heard the anguished recordings of their calls for their parents. In response to which there are often no texts from afar, like the ones described in this book, that hold the potential to set hearts at ease.

Still the stories of transnational familial separation that are at the core of this book can, I hope, help readers appreciate what happens when family members, spurred on by unjust policies, by legacies of colonization, by fear for their lives, or by the honorable human desire for something more, something better, say goodbye. Listening to these stories, I have often thought of my own white enough, documented, middle-class, single-mom hustle. The birthday parties. The price of milk. From where I sit, I can only imagine the historical conditions, the years of planning, can only imagine, *God,* the nauseating risk, for parents to dare to approach the United States border. From where I sit, it would be unethical not to imagine. Especially now, when familial separation is not only a byproduct of unjust policies but is in fact the policy itself.

I believe that imagining others' realities can be an ethical act. To that end, this book, as an ethnographic undertaking based in the practice of life history interviews, offers stories of transnational families' love. My analysis of these stories aims to name and honor this shared love and the ways people learn—in trying conditions—to sustain it. To that end, I hope this book does a small part in affirming our shared humanity. Migrants, it bears stating explicitly, are human beings.[12]

While in recent days the policy of separating children from their parents has ended, the consequences for those parents and children—and for *their* children—will be lasting. I am not a psychologist. But it is clear that many families who shared their stories with me found writing to be an emotional salve. In fact, work in neuroscience and in writing studies has suggested that writing is one means that people can use to sort through the layers of trauma and the consequences of the evil they have endured.[13]

It is up to us, as educators, administrators, social workers, community members, family members, and others, to support this process. In doing so, we can learn from educators working in creative literacy programs with youth marginalized by the state.[14] And we can learn from our brothers and sisters in Latin America, like those in Colombia, who have been helping children develop narratives and poetry to overcome the trauma of their country's decades-long civil war and to construct a peaceful future.[15] The job of adults, these scholars and activists teach, is to accompany children, to hear and hold their stories, to help turn their cries for their mothers and fathers into a collective call for peace.

Madison, Wisconsin, July 2018

## SAUDADE

*Allison Chaplain*
*Tem dias em que parece que acordamos*
*com saudade*
*Outros é a saudade que acorda com*
*a gente*
*Mas em ambos os dias, tem saudade*
*e tem a gente*
*Tem gente que saudades sente e*
*que saudades deixa*
*Outros simplesmente, deixam a gente*
*e saudades levam*
*Em meio a tantas saudades e*
*tantas gentes*
*A gente que só sente gente*
*Com saudades e saudades*

*(dedicada a su matriarca)*

This poem first appeared in *Poéticas Periféricas: Novas Vozes da Poesia Soteropolitana* organizado por Valdeck Almeida de Jesus, Galinha Pulando Press, Victoria da Conquista—BA, 2018.

## *THE COMMITTEE SPEAKS OF LANGUAGE*

*Dylan Weir*

*It began with our hands. Picking gnats*
*from each other's hair. Moved to our mouths*

*and into the classroom. Pledge allegiance. Say*
*please. A dog carrying its litter's loose neckskin*
*between its teeth. It looks like love. It sounds*
*like a baby breastfeeding. The first written words*

*will be a record of who has paid their taxes.*
*We raised our heads. We taught you how*

*to eat out of the trash can. To pass the hat*
*when it's time to clap. What a reckless thing,*

*telling children they can change the world.*
*Let's burn our passports. Let's unscrew our tongues.*

This poem first appeared in the 2018 edition of *North American Review*.

## PUENTES

Elsa Isabel Bornemann

Yo dibujo puentes
para que me encuentres
Un puente de tela
con mis acuarelas . . .
Un puente colgante
con tiza brillante . . .
Puentes de madera
con lápiz de cera . . .
Puentes levadizos
plateados, cobrizos
Puentes irrompibles
de piedras, invisibles . . .
Y tu . . . ¡Quien creyera!
¡No los ves siquiera!
Hago cien, diez, uno . . .
¡No cruzas ninguno!
Mas . . . como te quiero . . .
dibujo y espero.
¡Bellos bellos puentes
para que me encuentres!

This poem first appeared in *El Libro de Los Chicos Enamorados,* Buenos Aires, Fausto, 1987.

# ACKNOWLEDGMENTS

I wish to thank the University of Illinois Center for Latin American and Caribbean Studies for funding fieldwork in Brazil; the University of Wisconsin, Madison, research competition for funding fieldwork in Latvia; the Spencer Foundation for funding analysis and drafting of Latvia fieldwork; the Vilas Associates Award for funding fieldwork in Wisconsin; and the Susan J. Cellmer Distinguished Chair in Literacy for assisting with the funding for final revisions.

I am also deeply grateful for having received a Spencer/National Academy of Education Postdoctoral Fellowship during 2015–2016, which allowed me to conceptualize and draft the manuscript in its entirety. As part of this fellowship, I had the privilege to be mentored on different aspects of this project by a series of powerful and wickedly smart women scholars: Kris Gutiérrez, Maisha Winn, Shirley Brice Heath, Carol Lee, Elizabeth Moje, and Sarah Dryden-Peterson. Your collective social and scholarly commitment has set me straight when my own wavered.

And speaking of wicked smart powerful women scholars, a huge thank you to Ellen Cushman, Christina Haas, Deborah Brandt, and Caroline Levine for their support, especially in this project's early stages. Catherine Prendergast, I don't know what I would do without your sensible and incisive reads of both my work and my life.

I am grateful to Kaia Simon and Rebecca Lorimer Leonard for reading and responding with heart, expertise, and, bless you both, such *patience* to the whole manuscript in its messy early stages; to scholars Eileen Lagman, Elisa Findlay, and Mariana Pacheco for crucial conversations about writing, money, and migration; to the undergraduate students and graduate TAs in English 204, Writing and Money, for pushing my thinking on the relevance of literacy and economics for U.S. college students; to anonymous reviewers for their careful conceptual insights; to my most dedicated readers, my parents, for calling me to account when I got swallowed in jargon; and to my composition and rhetoric family in the University of Wisconsin's English Department for their support of this project even when it took me both geographically and academically far from home. Sharp and tireless research assistants aided in the development of this manuscript from beginning to end: Madina Djuraeva helped with the analysis of Latvian data, Margaret Bertucci Hamper with chapter 3, and Catherine Marotta and Timothy Cavnar with information hunting, editing, and formatting. Praise for the genius maps goes to Casey Kalman and Tanya Buckingham of the University of Wisconsin's cartography lab. Finally, thank you to the team at Oxford University Press, especially Hannah Doyle and Hallie Stebbins, for their enthusiastic support throughout the publication process. All of you have made this book infinitely better. All errors are exclusively my own.

This work would not be possible without the generosity of research participants on three continents, who submitted to my questions, my prying eyes, my digital recorder, and my imperfect Portuguese and Russian with such patience and grace. It has been a privilege to be invited into your lives and stories and homes. A heartfelt *obrigada* to Rafael Fernandes de Arruda Leme and Raquel

Corazza for helping me locate research participants in Brazil and for ferrying me to homes and schools to meet with them. A huge *spasibo* and *paldies* to Ilona Ustinova, Galina Pitkeviča, and the entire Voitov clan for connecting me with research participants and so much more in Latvia; to Alla and Alexei Suboč for the generosity and humor that sustained me and my daughter during data collection; to Kristine Pitkeviča for her honest reactions to my emerging findings and for crucial insights into Latvian culture, language, and history; and to Svetlana Veligura for linguistic, cultural, and so many other kinds of support. Thank you to the many caregivers, especially my mother, who nurtured my daughter while I was researching and writing. And deepest gratitude to Amália, my fellow fieldworker, who at the tender ages of three (Brazil), five (Latvia), and seven to eight (Wisconsin), accompanied me with an unflagging sense of adventure and fun on these journeys.

Finally, a brief word on money and love in the writing of this book. Writing this kind of book is, of course, my job. But more than that, I offer it as a humble return on the investment public institutions have made in my educational development, from kindergarten to PhD to the post-PhD teaching and research positions I have had the privilege to hold. Scholarly books are public documents through and through. They are sponsored by a society's financial commitment to literacy, with the hopes that the academic creation of knowledge—the slow, painstaking, and in many ways small work of building from and adding to legacies that have come before—can promote more informed public decisions, a better functioning and perhaps more just society. This is the spirit in which I make this particular contribution to our much larger collective work.

At the same time, I also wrote this book for love. In some ways, it is an elaborate love letter to the diverse communities in Latvia, Brazil, and the United States that shaped my young adulthood, to people whose stories I hold dear and have molded to fit these pages.

But let me confess that I also wrote this book for you, readers, whom in the composition process I have come to envision as people I also love. I wrote this book on a once-new laptop issued to me by a land grant university. Its battery is now shot and its pink hard shell is now cracked. Take this book. I remit it.

# Introduction

## *Literacy Learning in Immigrants' Homelands*

This book tells the story of how families who are separated across borders write—and learn new ways of writing—in pursuit of both love and money. Over the past two decades, global economic inequality has continued to promote the growth of labor migration. According to the UN, 244 million people currently live outside of the countries of their birth.[1] And many more remain in homelands. The human drama behind these numbers is that migration often separates parents from children, brothers from sisters, lovers from each other. While migration can promote economic growth for struggling families via financial remittances, it can also take an emotional toll.[2] Migration, often undertaken in response to problems of the pocketbook, also poses problems for the heart.

Based on field research and interviews conducted between 2011 and 2016 with transnational families in South America, Europe, and North America, these pages show how migrants and their family members turn to writing to address these problems. That is, they write to sustain meaningful relationships across distance and to attempt to better often impoverished circumstances. While policymakers are often concerned about "brain drain," a phenomenon in which emigration lessens homelands' intellectual resources, the stories people shared with me suggest that immigrants' departures, even en masse, do not leave homelands wholly educationally hobbled. Instead, migration can actually promote experiences of literacy learning in transnational families as they learn new ways of writing to reach the two life goals that globalization consistently threatens: economic solvency and emotional intimacy.[3] This book reveals how.

It does so not primarily from the perspective of migrants, of those who go elsewhere, but instead largely from the perspective of the family members and loved ones who stay. Policymakers, teachers, and researchers (including me) have long grappled with the literacy learning of immigrants in host countries, asking how they best learn new languages, how they draw on home-country literacy practices in their writing, and how they might use literacy for upward mobility and social change under often difficult conditions. But with some notable exceptions, relatively little is understood about what happens to the literacy learning of the millions who remain behind when loved ones leave for elsewhere.

Much of the research that exists on homeland learning addresses formal educational attainment. Some worry that outmigration reduces the overall educational level of homeland communities, as young people deal with the potential trauma of familial separation and as crucial expertise is "drained" from homelands toward wealthier countries.[4] Others have documented how formal educational attainment can increase when family members migrate, because migrants send back both money, "remittances," that can be used for tuition and school supplies, as well as other kinds of social support for academic success.[5] Still others have examined how migrants may increase their formal educational skills in anticipation of moving or in the process of migrating, contributing to "brain gain" upon their return, particularly with scientific or technical knowledge.[6] This crucial work, across education, economics, and migration studies, offers needed transnational analyses of educational challenges in homeland communities, often beset by the lack of opportunity that motivates migration in the first place.

But what these scenarios miss is the kind of learning that takes place outside of formal institutions, in the less visible, but no less educational, transnational networks of families separated across borders. This kind of learning is born of a desire not necessarily for formal skills, though skills are often attained along the way, but instead for something more elemental, for something more necessary, for something more at the root of human experiences—what this book identifies as love and money. This kind of educational desire is often activated in the profoundly human and fundamentally economic practice of literacy, a practice that, as ethnographic studies of transnational writing have shown, can connect family members across distance, can symbolize their deeply held aspirations, and whose value often hinges on the unequal global economic conditions that promote labor migration.[7] When we focus only on formal educational attainment, we miss the array of deeply felt out-of-school literacy learning experiences that migration can set into motion, what I am calling "migration-driven literacy learning."

Let me explain migration-driven literacy learning via a brief anecdote: It was in my previous research with undocumented immigrants in the United States that I first became curious about the literacy learning of those who remained in homelands.[8] I was interviewing a young man whose three children had stayed in Brazil with his parents while he and his wife labored in the United States to send back money for their children's educations. "My father always wanted us to finish school," this man told me, "and now this is our hope for our children." Familial separation was the price of upward social mobility.[9]

But in addition to the heart-wrenching calculation underlying this father's dream to provide for his children's formal education, there was something else educational going on, something else that impinged on literacy, something else that had to do with love. This man described to me his longing for his children, what Portuguese-speakers call *saudades*. To allay his *saudades*, he said, and here he gestured to a computer set up in his living room where we were speaking, he wrote to them regularly. Typing, however, had become difficult. During an accident at his construction site, his hand was injured by a colleague, leaving it immobilized in a cast. Still, in our conversation, he motioned as if his fingers were flying over the keyboard.

At the time, I was primarily interested in how he used literacy to navigate the challenges, injustices, and in his case the physical repercussions of undocumented status in the United States. Later, however, I continued to think of his hand, stiff in its cast, making the motions of typing out messages to those he loved. I thought of the limits of the body. And I thought of writing. His writing, it occurred to me, was not only local. It did not only address his current political situation within the United States. Nor did it stay put in his computer in his apartment in the working-class neighborhood of the former mill town in Massachusetts where he and his wife had emigrated. Rather, it traveled to his family in Brazil.

What, I wondered, did it do there? The literacy that this man sent to his children seemed to me to be a kind of remittance, albeit not a financial one. Years later, as I embarked on research for *Writing for Love and Money*, I eventually came to identify it as a "writing remittance," which, across many more ethnographic encounters, I came to define as the communication hardware, software, writing practices, and literacy knowledge that migrant family members often circulate across borders. How were such writing remittances taken up by those who remained in homelands? What were migrant and nonmigrant family members learning about literacy through these cross-border exchanges? To what extent, I wanted to know, could migration itself promote experiences of literacy learning—not just for those who left but also for those who stayed?

I wrote this book to find out.

In the process of describing the transnational phenomenon of migration-driven literacy learning in this book, I will not argue that emigration boosts *formal* educational attainment in migrants' homelands.[10] Instead, my focus here is on what people learn about literacy, and learn to do with literacy, in everyday familial contexts of lives lived across borders. To that end, I hope to capture the kinds of literacy experiences that often escape formal assessment.[11] Building from the ethnographic tradition in literacy studies, I describe literacy practices that occur outside of concerted institutional efforts to teach them, practices that I saw people develop to negotiate the interpersonal and economic demands of a moment of rapid globalization and technological change.

I hope to paint a picture here, then, of how people use literacy not only to respond to unjust economic circumstances but also to intervene in such circumstances, as they reconfigure family relationships and economic desires across borders. From within and across the globalized literacy learning hives of their families, the people who shared their stories with me are actively creating meaningful transnational lives.[12] My aim is to shine a light on these experiences.

## LIVING LITERACY

At the heart of arguments about brain drain are questions of the value of immigrants' and home communities' knowledge and skills, including literacy. Institutions such as the United Nations and World Health Organization have regarded literacy as a part of human capital, defined as an attribute that allows people to produce economic value. In most human capital views of literacy, literacy is measured by standardized tests and certificates of formal educational attainment. Such views, however, are limited. They underestimate both the volatile nature of literacy's value across time and space and the creative power of the human beings who use it.

First, literacy cannot be abstracted from people's lives. It is a human activity. One of the failures of conventional approaches to brain drain, especially in relation to literacy, is the implication that skills can be separated from the flesh and blood people who embody them.[13] Migrants, however, are more than houses for skills, more than tools that produce labor.[14] They are people. As such, in what sociologists of migration have called the development of "lifelong human capital" and in what education scholars have called "life-long, life-wide, and life-deep" learning, migrants and their families practice literacy in relation to past experiences, future desires, community obligations, and core values and beliefs.[15] Any kind of knowledge work is a human undertaking. And migrants, it bears repeating at this political moment, are human beings.

Wrangling with a resource like literacy requires human beings' full creative power, for literacy's value shifts across time and national borders, making its profitable use by migrants contingent on their abilities to adapt it to changing circumstances.[16] Across time, literacy's standards are ever changing. Its ante is often upped. For example, a high school diploma doesn't offer the same kinds of job opportunities it used to in the United States, and the ability to write an email, a new technology in the 1990s, is now a necessity in many workplaces. As a result, people who have earned a formal degree can be rendered illiterate in their lifetimes as the standards of literacy pass them by, leaving literacy's promise—that its attainment can lead to economic stability—unfulfilled.[17] Put another way, what was valuable literate human capital in 1990 is not necessarily valuable literate human capital in 2018. The result is that for literacy to be of use to everyday readers and writers, it has to be updated.

Likewise, literacy's value fluctuates across *space*. Much research has shown that what counts as a valuable literacy in one national or local context does not count as valuable in another. Diplomas, accents, skills, languages, and practices that function well in one country are often devalued economically and/or are taken up for quite different purposes in another.[18] Standardized assessments of literacy required for entry into a host country, for example, may not reflect the multilingual and socially situated literacy resources migrants and their families actually mobilize in workplaces and personal lives.[19] Thus, formally attaining literacy in school may not translate into the upward mobility that so many transnational families are seeking.[20] Literacy's economic potential lies instead in how people can entrepreneurially adapt it to new, unfamiliar, and often unjust circumstances.[21]

One's literacy, then, is not simply a tool one can retrieve from somewhere in the base of one's brain or from underneath the diaphragm where one may have been storing it, to sell for a wage. It is more of a living organism, sensitive to its context, growing and moving in relation to available water and light. It pulses through people's bodies, relationships, and activities. Given this complexity, I think of literacy as less of a discrete measurable skill in a human capital toolbox of skills and more of a sociohistoric trend—a trend that circulates across people, texts, institutions, time, and of course borders.[22]

To the extent that literacy is a skill, its successful use lies in how people find access to it (and access to literacy is far from equally guaranteed), gauge its potential value at any given sociohistorical moment, and use it for what matters to them. Using literacy successfully in transnational contexts is like catching a wave. It takes awareness, judgment, timing. It takes a good amount of moxie. It takes a blood red heart thumping against a cage of ribs.

Which brings me to writing.

## WRITING ACROSS BORDERS

Writing is both the paper or digital evidence of how people have grappled with the shifting sociohistoric trend that is literacy and the activity of that grappling. To return to the metaphor above, it's the foaming crest of literacy's wave. As Deborah Brandt has put it, "Writing is the means by which literacy as a skill is transacted."[23] And as Charles Bazerman points out, because writing is visible, because it is a public outward-facing act that "project[s] meaning and shared orientations at a distance," writing has consequences.[24] It moves a reader or it doesn't. It goes viral or goes unnoticed. It gets the grant or it fails. As a Shakespearean scholar colleague told me once, anytime a letter shows up in a Renaissance play, it might as well be a gun. It sets a plot twist in motion. For families separated across borders, the economic and interpersonal stakes of transnational literacy are often concretized in acts of writing—acts that can sustain love, that can make money, or that can, for various social, rhetorical, and technological reasons, fail to achieve these goals.

Reading and writing are of course related, but writing, more so than reading, is linked to money, love, technology, and travel—the very aspects of transnational life that are at the center of the stories families in this study shared with me. Readers will hear more about these connections in chapter 1, but let me offer a brief synopsis here.

*Money*: While reading has historically been tied to religion and morality, writing has a more economic historical legacy—one linked to mercantilism, commerce, and production.[25]

*Love*: Writing is also a fundamentally relational act, by which writers imagine an audience, direct their communication toward that audience, and therefore engage in a process of meaning making that involves others.[26]

*Technology*: The rise of new writing technologies via mobile phones and computers has contributed to a historical moment in which writing is reaching ascendancy over reading.[27] This shift from reading to writing entails an array of print and new media literacy practices in which people are even reading as writers, leading to characterizations of young people's emerging literacy identities as "readers becoming writers becoming global citizens."[28]

*Travel*: A crucial part of the technology of writing, of its very materiality, is that it can communicate at a distance, via the post or Internet or cellular networks.[29] In the case of migrant families, writing often travels more easily than do bodies.[30]

These associations and affordances allow writing to serve multiple transnational functions.[31] It is at once (a) a resource or skill that people adapt and leverage for economic and other ends in transnational contexts; (b) a dialogic practice in which people engage to communicate across borders; and (c) a delivery system through which people send and make meaning across distance. Calling on these uses, transnational family members in this study wrote, and learned new ways of writing, for love and for money.

A transnational perspective helps explain why and how: When people migrate physically, they nonetheless often maintain financial, political, and familial relationships with their home communities—relationships that transform both host country and homeland.[32] Migrants and their family members, it bears repeating yet again, are human beings, with social obligations and complex sets of relationships. There is rarely just a gaping hole where a family member used to be. Rather, migrants often remain involved. They often remit money, cultural practices, and ideas, all of which set into motion changes in homelands, which are then refracted, adapted, and circulated back to migrants in what anthropologist Peggy Levitt has called "social remittances" and in what economic sociologist Viviana Zelizer has called a transnational circuit of exchange.[33] One of the aims of this book is to extend this understanding of transnational circulation to writing.

As readers will see, one family member's departure often activates writing's circulation—via text chains, emails, video chats, and sometimes (still!) letters encased in envelopes and delivered by airplane, automobile, or hand. And such circulation can promote more writing, and more learning, in response. In fact, writing is a unique kind of "social remittance" in that it is at once a means and an end of interpersonal transnational exchange. Seen this way, writing forms an integral part of transnational mobility itself, as families use new ways of writing to live their lives across borders. Writing is both an activity and a material object, both a skill and a technology, both a resource and a machine.[34] For this reason, as people move, even if physical brains appear to be drained, writing continues to flow, knowledge continues to accrue, literacy continues to be practiced and, in that practice, learned.

In exploring how migration drives literacy learning in transnational families, this book, then, does not offer the results of tests of people's literacy before and after migration. Rather, it documents how family members, spurred on by global political and economic changes, adapt their use of it. To that end, I detail here how people experience literacy when families use writing to do what families, transnational or not, often do: love each other through times of hardship and change.

## TO BRAZIL, LATVIA, AND BACK: AN ITINERARY

With this broad understanding of literacy packed in my carry-on, with a curiosity about the kinds of informal literacy learning migration might promote, and with a commitment to naming and valuing transnational families' writing practices, I set out in 2011 to understand how migration shaped the writing experiences of ordinary people separated across borders—those everyday emailers and language learners and blog writers and video chatters and letter composers, those through whom literacy flows as they address the absence of loved ones. Over the course of five years, I spoke with forty-nine different immigrants, potential immigrants, and their family members (many multiple times), on three different continents (South America, North America, and Europe), in three different languages (Portuguese, English, and Russian), in person (during eight concentrated weeks of research in Brazil and Latvia and over the course of a year and a half in the United States), and online (at a more leisurely pace via Skype and email). I sat in their homes, met with them in their workplaces, observed them video-chatting and composing, and listened to their stories. I will say much more in chapter 2 about these communities, their generous members, the scholarly and personal routes that led us to be part of eachother's lives, and the methodological details of our work together. For now, though, I offer a broad outline of the shape my itinerary took.

To understand how migration shaped transnational families' writing experiences, I used a comparative case study approach, tracing migration-driven literacy learning both across differently positioned geographical sites and also across people's lives as they described them to me in oral history interviews.[35] I first examined migration-driven literacy learning in two homelands: one a largely economically struggling community in Daugavpils, Latvia, and one a largely middle-class community in Jaú, Brazil. Each community is located in an ordinary, midsize town, a four-hour bus ride from its state's capital, and each has sent emigrants to the United States and elsewhere. But that's where the demographic similarities end. At the time of my research, Latvia's emigration rate (-4) was high—comparable to many places with long-standing conflict.[36] Many Latvians were harnessing their educations in order to leave. In Brazil, by contrast, many were riding the larger national trend of middle-class growth, so emigration rates were relatively low. Most residents planned to stay.

This contrast allowed me to understand how migration-driven literacy learning was experienced by people differently positioned in relation to the forces of globalization.[37] In Brazil, because migration was not widespread, I dug in to individual experiences of writing remittances to show how meanings of love and money resonated from the technologies of transnational communication with which people across social classes wrote and learned. For example, a Brazilian mother who described herself as lacking literacy learned to use the laptop remitted by her son, a migrant in Japan, to log on and video-chat with him—an educational labor of love undertaken via hardware that came to reverberate simultaneously with her son's presence and with his absence. In Latvia, because migration permeated the community, I explored migration-driven literacy practices more broadly, homing in on the political currents that promoted such learning in the social life of the community as a whole. Across these sites, and in different ways, migration was driving experiences of literacy learning, as people wrote and learned to write for love and for money.

In order to understand migration-driven literacy learning across not only space but also time, I conducted oral history interviews. The historical perspective I gleaned from these interactions was key to understanding how literacy's uses in the past resonated with and shaped its uses in the present.[38] For example, as video chat became more common in Brazil, letter writing to distant loved ones took on the sheen of nostalgia, signaling deep emotional labor. And as Latvians moved from a Soviet past of Russian-language literacy to the proliferation of languages in the European Union, they sought to rapidly accumulate languages to both reunite with distant family members and to steady their economic footing. For example, one mother in Latvia trained her eleven-year-old daughter in French, English, Russian, Latvian, and German to prepare her to join her sister abroad. "It breaks my heart," the mother said, "but there is nothing for her here."

In listening to such stories of people's literacy lives, I was attuned to how migration-driven literacy learning shifted as people's technological and political circumstances changed.[39] As in other contexts of regime change, not only were people moving across borders, but borders were also moving across people, with implications for how and what people were writing and learning about writing.

Finally, I realized that my understanding of migration-driven literacy learning would be incomplete without the perspective of immigrants themselves. (For this insight I thank an emergent research design, in which my early findings and questions led me to new field sites and areas of inquiry.) So beginning in 2015 I began research in a third field site—a community of immigrants in the midwestern United States. Here I had the privilege to spend time with two transnational families, both spanning three generations, and both of whom generously invited me into their homes and answered my questions about the role writing remittances played in their longer literacy histories. If my work in Brazil allowed me a material and emotional lens on migration-driven literacy learning, and my work in Latvia offered insight into broader sociohistoric aspects of it, the community in the United States revealed how immigrants could experience their participation in these circuits, and what the implications of such participation might be for their literacy use and learning, particularly in a U.S. context of race- and class-based educational stratification and political persecution.

I learned that remitting U.S.-based literacy practices and technologies to homelands could reinforce existing commitments to literacy learning. For example, one woman I spoke with saved money to buy a tablet loaded with apps to help her cousin's son in Mexico learn to read. This transnational investment in "writing remittances," though costly financially, deepened the grooves of their family's transnational literacy learning network, promoting intergenerational writing practices. In this bidirectional exchange, literacy came to act less like money and more like love: the more people gave, the more they got.

In what follows, readers will delve more deeply into these stories, meeting these members of transnational families and many more, all of whom were learning literacy under conditions of family separation and across shifting technological and political terrain. This book tells the story of how such learning is experienced and why it matters.

## WHY DOES MIGRATION-DRIVEN LITERACY LEARNING MATTER?

Migration-driven literacy learning matters in four ways.

First, it recasts migration not as an educational problem to be solved, but instead as an educational resource to be supported. Just as mass migration and war may have contributed to widening the web of print literacy in the late nineteenth and early twentieth century (as readers will see in chapter 1), I hope to show here how current transnational migration may be facilitating the spread of many new kinds of literacies. In detailing the family networks through which literacy education reaches beyond state borders, this book reveals the everyday processes through which *local* learning becomes *transnational* learning, and *transnational* learning becomes *local* learning. Such learning implicates a literacy that is technologically savvy, emotionally attuned, globally conscious, and entrepreneurially at the ready—in other words, a literacy made for our current historical moment.

Second, it highlights writing's crucial emotional role in transnational family life. For many, the act of sending literacy remittances seemed to help families negotiate, in communion with others, the potentially chaotic trauma of separation. At once a potentially meditative process and a means of interpersonal connection, literacy remittances formed a space of transnational reckoning. They gestured, with hope and with love, towards an integration of host country and homeland identities, of past and future, of self and family.

Third, migration-driven literacy learning offers some insights for teachers and policymakers who are hoping to globalize and digitize their classrooms. As migration has risen 33% since 2000, and as market and civic demands for critical digital literacy rapidly rise, this book provides starting points, grounded in everyday people's realities, for how teachers and policymakers can build on the family-based migration-driven literacy learning that is already occurring in community sites.[40] That is, I hope that we might take hints from familial literacy learning, democratizing such learning so that it is available to youth and adults both in their communities and in their schools.

And finally, because I am a scholar with a kind of single-minded fascination for this widespread social phenomenon called *literacy*, I hope this examination of migration-driven literacy learning reveals something new about literacy itself. That is, I hope to document how literacy is both a deeply felt internal resource and an economic engine; how people's words shuttle across borders to one another and in the very process are vacuumed into larger economic and political trends; and how for many, transnational or not, literacy—and writing in particular—is fundamental to both sustaining love and earning money.

If educators and researchers look at literacy in the way I am suggesting here, as a sociohistorical trend whose potentials people activate, via writing, in transnational contexts, we can ask different questions and find new answers about how migration shapes people's literacy lives. On one hand, we can explore the bigger picture of how the rapid global movement of people across borders—a hallmark of the contemporary moment—can promote the uptake of new kinds of writing. At the same time, we can home in on the microrealities of the learning that is experienced when, for example, a niece learns to write an email to her distant aunt. Taken together, we can begin to draw some connections between the intimate details of familial communication and the broader sweep of history, allowing us to better grasp how literacy matters not just for transnational families but for all of us, who are reading and writing across changing economic, emotional, technological, and political landscapes. Such a view of literacy, I believe, might help us practice literacy better. It might help us teach it better. Examining the everyday writing lives of transnational families can help us see learning where it is often overlooked, and therefore value it and support it.

## THREE STORIES

To meet these goals, this book tells three related stories. One story traces migration-driven literacy learning in three different locales: in one place marked by moderate emigration (in Brazil), in another marked by mass emigration (in Latvia), and in another marked by immigration (in the United States). The second story is of literacy itself: how literacy's materiality impinges on both economics and emotions (Brazil); how literacy shape-shifts across both time and space (Latvia); how literacy accrues value, forming a mobile "fund of knowledge," as it circulates (United States). The final story tells of learning in homelands and host countries: in homelands, migration can drive digital literacy learning (Brazil and Latvia) and language learning (Latvia), and in host countries, remitting literacy can enhance its ideological purchase, promoting investment in it as a means for upward social mobility (United States). Taken together, these three stories complicate traditional notions of brain drain, showing how the exigencies of migrant labor and the desire to express familial love conspire to promote experiences of literacy learning across borders.

To tell these stories, I've organized this book as follows: chapter 1 draws from the social history of literacy to detail what is new about writing for love and money in transnational families; chapter 2 describes the three locations in which I conducted research and what I did there; chapter 3 examines how migration drives digital literacy learning experiences in Brazil; chapter 4 documents how migration drives digital and multilingual literacy learning experiences in Latvia; chapter 5 details migration-driven literacy learning experiences from the perspective of two multigenerational migrant families in the United States; and the conclusion explains how writing for love and money matters both for transnational learners and for others who are writing and learning under conditions of globalization. The afterword is an homage to transnational mothering.

*Chapter 1*

# What's New about Writing for Love and Money?

A Latvian mother takes a computer literacy class for pensioners in order to keep in touch with her son, who has migrated to Belgium. A young Brazilian man uses a webcam remitted from his sister in France to both communicate with her and to become the go-to tech guru of his neighborhood, ultimately opening his own international IT business. A teenager in the United States writes letters to her younger sister in Mexico, teaching her some words in English, in the hopes that one day the family will reunite stateside. Love and money infuse these brief scenes of contemporary migration-driven literacy learning, as family members write to keep in touch with loved ones separated by labor migration, and as they learn and teach literacy practices that they hope may reap material and emotional rewards.

In some ways, these examples of writing for love and money are time-stamped as early twenty-first-century phenomena. They occur, after all, in the context of recent changes in digital technologies that, as in the Latvian example, can leave pensioners scrambling to keep up and that, as in the Brazilian example, can gift some with potentially remunerable knowledge. They also occur in the context of relatively recent political changes. The U.S. teenager's separation from her sister is the byproduct of increased Mexico-U.S. border security over the past decades, which has made migration more deadly and more costly, increasing the length of time families are separated and leading many to depend on writing to communicate.[1] Likewise, that the Latvian pensioner's son is working in Belgium is a result of Latvia's accession to the European Union in 2004, which opened Western Europe's borders to workers from some former Soviet republics, for whom the 2009 global recession made work in the West less of a choice and more of a necessity. In other words, the above accounts, culled from fieldwork in quite different corners of the earth, have the economic, political, and technological *now* written all over them.

Yet migration-driven literacy learning is not new: consider, for example, the turn of the twentieth century, when, for example, many immigrants from Europe to the United States were learning to write letters.[2] For them, the regularization of postal routes via steamship seemed to collapse time and space, making communication feel instantaneous—perhaps something like people experience with Internet technology today.[3] While the transnational literacy institution of the postal system differs from that of the Internet, both promise to connect loved ones across borders—if only those loved ones could learn to communicate in ways that traveled.

Drawing such historical parallels—and others—is instructive. Literacy practices do not exist only in the ethnographic present. They draw force from repeated patterns of literacy's use in the past, accumulating social significance over time and providing insights into current practices that exclusively contemporary views can miss.[4] On one hand, a historical view helps explain *individual* literacy practices: our literacy practices are linked to how our mothers or teachers taught us to hold a pencil; the kind of pencil that was or was not available to us; our neighborhood, with its varying levels of racial diversity or homogeneity or legacy of equality or inequality, in which our school was zoned. At the same time, a historical view can also help illuminate *societal* literacy practices: literacy, across many societies and moments in time, has been tied up in some of the same institutions—bureaucracy, economy, religion, family. And many of these institutional meanings and uses of literacy persist.

So when historically minded researchers and educators see hints of these "domains" in contemporary literacy activities, we know to pay attention.[5] We know that there may be some deeper meaning, deeper cultural significance brewing underneath the surface of what appears to be a routine practice—for example, signing a credit card receipt (economic domain) or sending a text (relational domain). Such awareness can promote more informed, and ultimately more just, literacy education. As co-authors and I have elsewhere written, "Whether we are cognizant of it or not, when we intervene in people's literacy development as educators, administrators, researchers, and writers, we are also intervening in history, aligning ourselves with particular ideologies and distancing ourselves from others."[6] With this understanding, historically inflected ethnographic research about literacy seeks to shed light on current practices through attunement to the resonances of the past.

In order to collectively attune ourselves to some of these resonances, this chapter weaves together selective scenes in the social history of writing for love and money with recent ethnographic examples of it. What, this chapter asks, is new about writing for love and money?

## MONEY

For many transnational families, the pursuit of money often motivates individual migration, leading many migrants to report that they emigrated "in search of a better life." Such decisions take place against a backdrop of stunning global wealth inequality. A 2013 UN report pointed out that while a full 72% of the world's population lives in what they call "low-income countries," such countries produce only 1% of the world's wealth. "High-income countries," on the other hand, which house only 16% of the world's population, produce a whopping 55% of wealth. The upshot, the authors of the study argue, is that the country that one calls home determines, to a large extent, one's financial prospects, which helps to explain the prevalence and economic logic of international labor migration.[7] Economic disparity alone, of course, does not account for all migration. If it did, entire countries would be emptied of people.[8] Nonetheless, across an economically inequitable international field, money proves a powerful motivator for many to try their luck elsewhere.

Such "luck"—or the ability to earn enough money to make migration worth the investment—is tethered to literacy in ways that reflect this economic injustice. Ethnographic studies of such diverse sites as postcommunist Slovakia, the Mexico-U.S. border, Central Africa, and the Philippines have revealed that the economic consequences of neoliberalism often curtail migrants' abilities to trade their literacy training for fair compensation.[9] For example, literacy ethnographer Eileen Lagman has shown how Filipina migrant service workers often hide their advanced educational backgrounds from their host-country employers, and instead accentuate the low-level, rote, skill-based literacy required in their jobs.[10] As literacy is carried across unequally positioned countries in the bodies of laborers, its value often depreciates.

Other examples abound. Literacy scholar Catherine Prendergast has shown how in postcommunist Slovakia, English is valued as long as few know it, and even that specialized knowledge is devalued when Slovakians migrate to wealthier English-speaking countries, such as the United Kingdom or the United States.[11] And linguistic ethnographer Jan Blommaert has shown how in Central Africa, multilingual literacy might set one apart from compatriots, but one's discourse still might be unintelligible to wealthy interlocutors in Europe.[12]

Likewise, my own work and that of others has revealed how in the United States, many migrants who are undocumented face obstacles in trading on their literacy skills for work because they don't have the papers required to apply for well-paying jobs.[13] The financial return on individual immigrant literacy often varies with the economic standing of the country from which they hail relative to the one to which they migrate.[14]

This is because literacy is more than an individual resource. It is also an economic and bureaucratic one, long used by governments and oligarchs to organize wealth and consolidate power, making the literate labor of ordinary people valuable in some circumstances and expendable in others, regardless of such labor's sophistication. Literacy is popularly thought of as having more to do with expression and meaning making than with money and finances, yet literacy is deeply imbricated in economic transactions, making economics one of the central domains of literacy activated in migration-driven writing.[15]

First, literacy has fueled economic growth in many societies. For example, in ancient Mesopotamia, one of the (many) birthplaces of writing, a complex inscription system involving clay tablets was developed to document who did and did not pay taxes.[16] As the temple economy grew more complex and began to spread over distance, so too did writing, moving from the imprinting of clay tablets to more abstract numerical and literate symbols that eventually evolved to include the date, identification of the taxpayer, and even some scenes of punishment for those who did not pay. This writing-based bureaucratic structure allowed the temple economy to manage agricultural production and thus grow, making writing "infrastructural" to society.[17]

Second, just as literacy can contribute to economic growth, so too does literacy require economic investment. Writing in particular requires raw materials, specialized human labor, and the technological development to make that writing happen. For example, the rise of literacy in medieval England depended on wax to seal envelopes (materials), scribes (labor), and quills (technology).[18]

Third, as an economic resource, literacy's financial value is often dictated by laws of supply and demand. In the example of medieval England above, where wax and ink were in short supply, fewer people could be trained to be scribes, making the work of writing, crucial to the king's increasingly bureaucratic reign, more valuable.[19] On the opposite end of literacy supply and demand, in situations in which literacy became widespread, such as in the wake of state investment in public education in modern Europe (or perhaps in the wake of a glut of undergraduate students with college degrees in the contemporary United States), literacy became less remunerable as an individual skill because there was, for the first time, a surplus of it.[20] As the Filipina migrants in Lagman's study learned, regardless of objective measures of literate skill, one's literacy is only as financially valuable as the market—itself a globally, racially, and gender-biased construct—allows.[21]

The fallout of such trends is unequal returns on literate investments, especially as literacy standards change, lifting some and leaving others behind. Based on a study of oral histories of literacy collected in Wisconsin across the twentieth century, literacy scholar Deborah Brandt called this uneven process of literacy's spread "sponsorship," whereby corporations and other distant agents invested in the literacy practices of particular people in order to extract that literacy later and gain by it.[22] Dependent on the vagaries of capitalist production imperatives, systems of literacy sponsorship can work to entrench inequalities. In some ways, it seems that the economic cards have long been stacked against ordinary readers and writers who would like to leverage their literacy for upward mobility in any country.

But literacy's social history also teaches that just as larger economic forces—the temple economy, corporations, colonizers, and oligarchs—can shape what writers earn from their writing, so too can savvy and strategic writers leverage their literacy skills to make money. And here I don't necessarily mean J. K. Rowling, Stephen King, or other best-selling writers. Consider a few selective examples of how ordinary people have leveraged writing for economic gain in unfavorable circumstances: indigenous communities in Peru used *khipu,* a meaning-making system involving knotting, to counter the power of the Spanish alphabet.[23] In keeping their own records using *khipu,* some could negotiate with Spanish colonizers for payment, essentially challenging the dominance of the alphabet as the purveyor of absolute truth. And consider, too, enslaved African Americans in the antebellum U.S. South: in a context in which the punishment for learning to write could be dismemberment, many brave enslaved people quietly and at great risk learned literacy. Such work allowed some people some advantages, such as the ability to author passes for travel to the North.[24] And in yet another quite different context, consider a 2011 study of online poker players, in which expert authors leveraged both their reputations and Internet savvy for maximum cash for selling high-priced poker strategy manuals.[25] I put these contexts together not to compare the incomparable, but to show that under varying historical conditions, writing can be an advantageous undertaking for those who can, at sometimes great risk and in circumstances of grave injustice, plug themselves into particular markets, institutions, or sets of social conventions.[26]

Transnational families are doing just this. From their often marginalized position at the raw end of global economic inequality, they are exchanging literacy along relational networks and leveraging their knowledge and practice of it in ways that have the potential to pay off. While the literate labor of those from low-income countries may be expendable from the perspective of global neoliberalism, the resourceful members of migrant families, painfully aware of how the value of their resources and skills shifts across borders and historical moments, also often find themselves in a unique position to exploit them.

## LOVE

Of course, as any letter writer, emailer, texter, love-poem writer, or Facebook-poster knows, writing cannot be reduced to its economic value. It is also an intimate act of connection and expression, often among those who are distant from each other.

Distance from loved ones over both space and time is a fact of life for many transnational families. For some, particularly for those migrating undocumented between the United States and Latin America, long-term separation is a commonsense response to increased border enforcement: 2015 was the deadliest year for migrants in recorded history; migrants crossing the U.S.-Mexico border in 2017 were dying at a faster rate than in previous years; and the inhumane U.S. immigration policies of familial separation put into practice in 2018 have as yet untold consequences.[27] It makes sense that those who risk entering the United States undocumented might leave children and other loved ones behind and make few return trips.[28] But even for those, like the Latvian migrants featured in this book, who have the privilege of authorized travel to locations within the European Union and for whom inexpensive Ryanair flights make frequent visits a possibility, Eastern Europe's persistent economic depression can make reunification a fantasy that remains unrealized. For example, one Latvian woman resettled in Latvia after laboring in a U.K. factory for seven years to earn enough money to put her daughter through college—at which point her daughter left Latvia to pursue better opportunities abroad. Despite the family reunification policies enacted by many countries (and which are under threat as of this writing in the United States), reunification is often a possibility only for those with both the privilege of legal documentation and local educational and job prospects. Ultimately, the economic and political relationship between sending and receiving countries often conspires to keep families apart.

Enter writing—a practice that doesn't solve the economic and political problems that cause family separation but that people nonetheless use to negotiate it. In the classes I teach on theories of literacy, I often riff on the concept of dialogism, a theory that describes how writing makes meaning in the crucible of interpersonal communication.[29] I start by drawing two stick figures on the board, one labeled "writer" and the other labeled "reader." And then I draw a heart between them. Inside the heart, I write the words, "the text." The text-heart, I explain, is the place where writers and readers come together. To this meeting they bring their literacy knowledge and their social backgrounds, which they use not only to decipher and interpret but also to *feel* the words.[30] Literacy theorist Louise Rosenblatt has described this "transaction" between reader and writer in terms that are downright sexy: "Instead of an interaction, such as billiard balls colliding, there has been a transaction . . . in terms of reverberations, rapid oscillations, blendings, and mutual conditions."[31] Writing, in sum, is one site where people often attempt to make good on a deeply felt human desire: to commune.

As part of this relational work, writing can offer a material space to navigate the emotions associated with bodily separation. Bodies are sites of what theorists have called "affective practices," such as narrative or dance, through which emotions' social meanings are both managed and—because emotions are essentially communicative—shared.[32] In the bodily absence of loved ones, emotions have often been physically offloaded onto material sites of literate production, such as letters. Consider the following examples: historian Patrick

Fitzgerald, having culled data from nineteenth- and early twentieth-century archived letters of Irish immigrants, revealed how strong emotion caused migrants to, in their words, "lift up my pen," to write letters to family members remaining in Ireland.[33] Likewise, literacy ethnographer Niko Besnier has described how, for family members of labor migrants on the island of Tuvalu, letters released the emotional excess provoked by separation.[34] And in my own previous research, Portuguese immigrants to the United States told me how letters could be cathartic, how in writing letters they could, in the words of one elderly woman, "empty their souls."[35]

In addition to managing emotions in transnational family life, writing across distance can also make the absent other seem present. As literary theorist Roland Barthes writes of the "preposterous situation" of writing to someone who has departed, "You have gone (which I lament); you are here (since I am addressing you)."[36] Letters thus often become, according to historian David A. Gerber's work on nineteenth-century British immigrants, a "transnational meeting place."[37] Nor are such "meeting places" confined to letters. Consider the nineteenth-century Italian peasant described by literacy historian Martyn Lyons. Having lost her husband of forty-six years, and lacking paper on which to write, she inscribed her loss and loneliness on the bed sheets they once shared, thereby channelling her late husband's absence into a material and discursive presence.[38] Writing, in sum, can hold out the promise of intimacy between distant writers and readers, even those with no forwarding address.

Writing for love is not limited to paper (or, in the above example, sheets). Digital writing across borders serves a similar purpose: ethnographers Mirca Madianou and Daniel Miller, for example, have coined the term "polymedia" to account for the range of media—from cassette tapes with recorded voices to synchronous video chat to letters to texts—that transnational families choose to employ depending on what they would like to communicate and how they would like to configure transnational familial relationships.[39] Such communicative choices underlie what sociologists Loretta Baldassar and Laura Merla have called the "circulation of care," whereby love is enacted across borders, often via digital literacy, without the necessity of physical proximity.[40]

Of course, while writing may make possible the circulation of care for separated families, it is not a panacea for the pain so often wrought by distance. For some, writing, including via digital communication technologies, is an insufficient expression of transnational love in contexts of long-term separation, which can foster intergenerational resentment.[41] And for others, the use of digital communication technologies can be inhibited by the punishing work schedules that often accompany low-wage labor, the difficulty of scheduling moments to talk across time zones, restricted access to the technology itself, and limited digital literacy skills.[42] In sum, writing to sustain familial relationships across international borders requires access to both communication channels and to the means to learn how to use them.[43] Writing across borders, perhaps especially in the emotionally charged, technologically shifting, and often physically demanding context of labor migration, is imperfect. In the most privileged of conditions, Skype calls get dropped, time zones get confused, and one sends texts one wishes one could snatch back from the ether. But still. Migrant families continue to write.

In transnational families, writing is always an act of communication, is often an act of longing, and sometimes, though it's not common to use the *l* word in scholarly circles, an act of *love,* which may be the most powerful motivator for literacy learning (or for anything, for that matter) there is. Consider the supposedly illiterate Italian soldier sent to the front during World War I who taught himself to write in order to compose over eighty love letters to his wife.[44] Or consider the adult children who migrated to the United States from Great Britain in the late nineteenth century who taught their parents to address envelopes for correspondence at a moment when the postal system was just standardizing its routes.[45] Or consider any of the great epistolary novels.[46] Distance between loved ones has driven writing to such an extent that historian David Henkin has argued that in the nineteenth-century United States letter writing preceded mass literacy.[47]

Distance can even promote the spread of entirely new systems of writing: as literacy historian Ellen Cushman has documented, the inventor of the Cherokee syllabary, Sequoyah, delivered letters in the new script and sat with readers to decode them, uniting the roles of social leader, literacy educator, postal worker, philologist, and artist.[48] Similarly, studies of contemporary migration have shown how migration can promote an uptick in digital literacy use in families that span the U.S and Mexico, Italy and Australia, and China and the United Kingdom, among others.[49] Bodies don't travel easily to and from such locations. But the infrastructure of a postal system (or the Internet or cell towers) allows paper (or emails or texts) to connect where physical contact is impossible. Two stick figures united by a virtual or paper heart.

In some ways, then, literacy can reshape space and time, with the result that distant loved ones can meet on paper or screen. However, as readers saw in the discussion of money, space and time can also reshape literacy, foreclosing and opening particular opportunities to leverage literacy productively, depending on one's geographic, economic, and historical context.[50] In this sense, migration-driven literacy learning operates at the intersection of writing's potential for helping transnational families meet their goals and of its limits. Writing, then, cannot autonomously resolve the difficulties of familial separation amid economic injustice. What is clear, however, is that writing is integral to the ways many transnational families have long negotiated these challenges.

In fact, families have often used writing in ways that simultaneously mediate both love and money, materially and discursively linking them, and thereby co-constructing their meanings across borders.[51] For example, in the classic early twentieth-century work of epistolary sociology, *The Polish Peasant*, many of the letters to and from Polish immigrants in Chicago both professed love and requested money.[52] Money did not infect the more lofty sentiments of love, but rather, aided by the letter itself, contributed to love's expression. Likewise, in a contemporary example, Madianou and Miller describe synchronous video-chat events in which families in the Philippines and the United Kingdom gather around the computer screen while those in the Philippines unwrap presents sent from abroad, thereby linking labor, remittances, and love via digital communication technologies.[53] In such swollen pedagogical moments of familial transnational communication, like the ones readers will soon encounter in more detail, literacy's associations with love and money thicken, inflecting how and why people learn it and use it.[54]

## SO WHAT IS NEW ABOUT MIGRATION-DRIVEN LITERACY LEARNING?

So what precisely is new about migration-driven literacy learning? This chapter has told of writing's enduring entanglement in love and money across selected historical and contemporary periods and cultures. Given the longstanding and widespread nature of this relationship, the relevant question is perhaps not so much what is new and what is old, a question that implies a kind of generalized and decisive break with the past, but instead what has changed and what has remained the same—and for whom? Put another way, what legacies of writing for love and money do people activate or discard given their particular historical moments, their particular geo-political contexts, their particular relationships, goals, and lives?

Answering this more nuanced question is tricky, because contexts of migration are often characterized by change. Consider, for example, the contexts taken up in this book: For Latvian community members in this study, not only have family members moved, but the very borders of their country have also shifted underneath their feet, as Latvia moved from the Soviet Union to Independence (1991) to the European Union (2004). And while Brazilians hadn't seen such drastic political changes in the years leading up to this study (the fall of their military dictatorship occurred in 1985), the shifting valuation of the Brazilian *real* certainly shaped outmigration. What's more, Brazilians, like many others, witnessed rapid changes in literacy technologies across their lifespans, from paper to synchronous video chat, which transformed for many what it meant to be literate. Finally, for many U.S. immigrants, state borders also changed in their lifetimes, with new legislation and policies, such as the Deferred Action for Childhood Arrivals, known as DACA, shaping both educational paths and connections with homelands.

As previously firm borders crumble, as previously porous borders are enforced with steel, as markets rise and fall, as the worth of one laborer's hour of work from one country is valued or devalued in relation to the worth of the labor of others, as more and more people log on to the Internet, as prices for digital literacy technologies rise and fall, and as families continue to bid each other farewell in order to, as one Latvian participant lamented, "earn one's piece of bread,"as the world shifts around all of us and as many of us shift around the world, the particular ways everyday members of transnational families write and learn to write for love and money also change.

But how?

This is the question this book seeks to answer.

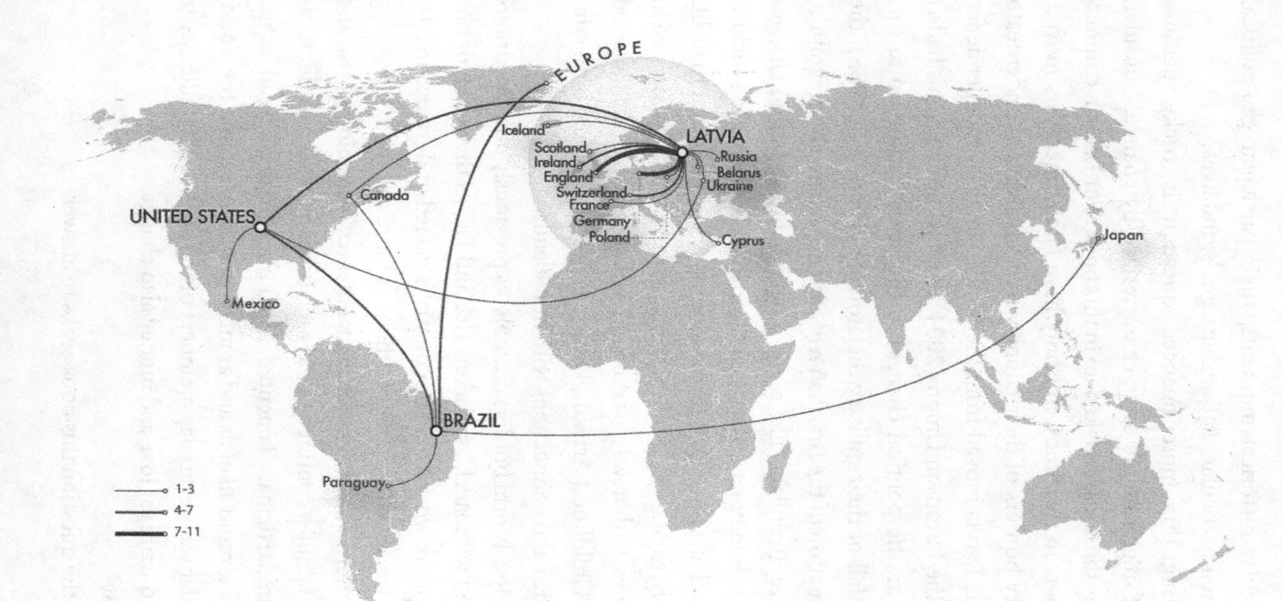


Map 2.1 Migration and literacy trajectories of participants and/or their family members in Brazil, Latvia, and the United States

Chapter 2

# Writing for Love and Money on Three Continents

To put the question more specifically: How do transnational families' experiences with migration-driven literacy learning shift across their lifespans, in relation to changing political borders, economic circumstances, and technologies? This is a question with a lot of moving parts. But at its core, the humming engine of this question, the piece that drives the rest of its clauses and complications, is the concept of migration-driven literacy learning. In this project, my primary research aim was to move from the hunch about migration-driven literacy learning that was born in my previous research with migrants to develop, in this study, the richest conceptual understanding of it I could.

To do so in a way that honored the social complexity of both literacy and its users was methodologically challenging. I needed to see more than what was apparent in one geographically bounded location, more than what was revealed in one temporally bounded moment in time, and more than what was experienced by just one group of people. I needed to get at writing for love and money from a number of angles.

In this chapter, I tell the story of how I attempted to do so. Here I reveal the costura, the stitches, that form the underside of what may appear to be this book's otherwise neatly hemmed seams, of how I examined migration-driven literacy learning across lives and across continents.

## COMPARING CASES

In grappling with the complexity of the research question, I was helped by comparative case study research, which as defined by education researchers Lesley Bartlett and Frances Katherine Vavrus, "compares and contrasts phenomena and processes in one locale with what has happened in other places and historical moments."[1] Bartlett and Vavrus describe three axes of comparison across place and time that allow researchers to examine multiple dimensions of the phenomenon they are studying: transversal (across history); vertical (across scale); and horizontal (across sites). Adopting this approach allowed me to see migration-driven literacy learning across people's lifespans (transversal); among people differently positioned in relation to the forces of globalization (vertical); and across differently positioned communities in Brazil, Latvia, and the United States (horizontal).

Working comparatively helped me peel back layers of migration-driven literacy learning and, rather than leaving them in a pile on the floor, organize them meaningfully along the axes described above. To be clear: I was not attempting to holistically account for the cultures of these individual sites, nor was I attempting to set these sites parallel to each other in order to control for variables. Communities, after all, do not have fixed cultures of literacy—for cultures themselves are sets of activities in constant formation.[2] Borders shift, people move, and histories, collective and individual, rarely stay still. Even if I wanted to, I could not have flattened out or fixed literacy's particular meanings in each of the communities that hosted me. Still, comparing cases helped me to follow conceptual threads from one site and one person to the next, weaving them into a larger theory.

To respect the contingent and volatile nature of both literacy and globalization in this process, I used what is called an "emergent research design." In each individual location, after each interview or field note, I consolidated my understanding of migration-driven literacy learning, thought about which questions remained, and made methodological decisions for the future.[3] In this way, in Brazil, I was able to dig into migration-driven literacy learning's technological, material, and emotional aspects; in Latvia its broader social and historical aspects; and in the United States, its context of stratified access to literacy. Taken together, this exploration helped me move towards a multidimensional understanding of migration-driven literacy learning.

## RESEARCHING ACROSS LIVES

To get at the "transversal" or historical aspect of migration-driven literacy learning, I used a lifespan approach to ethnographic research.[4] As part of this approach, I defined literacy historically, as a trend that circulates across time and space via people, texts, technologies, and larger political and economic institutions, such as capitalism. For readers who came to Ancient Mesopotamia, medieval England, and precolonial Latin America with me in the previous chapter, this definition, I hope, makes conceptual sense; literacy travels with people, technologies, and societies, and it also connects them.

I used this historical definition in part because it was how the people I interviewed understood literacy. For many who were born pre-Internet, literacy was intimately tied to the reading and writing of print. And they extended these print-based notions of literacy to their experiences with the multiple modes available via digital technologies.

One woman, for example, reported being rendered "illiterate" by her discomfort with newer digital technologies, contrasting such "illiteracy" with her professional print-based training as an accountant who wrote reports and figures by hand. Such historical legacies of print hovered over even seemingly print-absent communication technologies (such as video chat) in the form of log-ins, messaging (the go-to interface when video failed), and the interface of the keyboard. Print-based literacy historically "accumulated" in these new sites, even as such sites also involved using synchronous visual and aural modalities made possible by the Internet.[5] Which is a long way of saying that for the purposes of this book, I see the use of video chat as a literacy because people *experienced* it as a literacy—a literacy that resonated with their longer literacy histories. This historic and emic definition allowed me to track how "older" and "newer" incarnations of literacy interacted in transnational families.

To get at these experiences across people's lifespans, I conducted literacy history interviews (LHIs). A unique research tool, the LHI elicits memories of how people have used reading and writing. As such, they provide insight into what Deborah Brandt has called the "macro-force of literacy" that appears in stories of individual literacy experiences.[6] Put concretely, Latvians' memories of, say, standing in line at a Soviet post office to send a telegram to a family member in a far-off republic speaks both of their personal relationship to writing (they were sending a telegram to a sister for her birthday) and to their placement within a larger social and political context (the state-controlled interrepublic communication institution of the post office and the political system that dictated in which republics particular citizens would work and live). While interviews and memories can be unreliable, I was less interested in the objective "telling of truth" and more in the "truth of the telling," that is, in how people's subjective experiences manifested in the stories they shared.[7] In sum, LHIs helped me understand both particular slices of literacy's history as well as how people made sense of that history in a moment of rapid technological and global change.

They also helped me take into account how people were differently positioned in relation to sociohistorical forces, giving me access to the "vertical" axis of comparative case study research. By attending to LHIs through the lens of differential access to power, I was able to see, for example, how social class shaped how people wrote for love and money in Brazil. That is, each individual interview gave me insight into individual pasts, but when analyzed together, they allowed a picture of which kinds of experiences were shared, which weren't, and how these experiences were hooked in to people's social positions.

By engaging with people's experiences of the past, I was better able to delineate what mattered about their present, as they wrote amid shifting economic currents to sustain and reconfigure family relationships. To this end, I also conducted ethnographic fieldwork, talking with participants, taking notes on their reading and writing, interacting with them, and following up with questions in formal and informal interviews. While such work was focused on the ethnographic present, the practices and activities taking place in real time, I also was alert to echoes of the past. In this way, I attempted to capture how historical shifts played out in people's literacy lives—that is, how the movement not just of people but also of borders and historical events shaped their experiences of writing.

## RESEARCHING ACROSS CONTINENTS

In order to get at the most robust understanding of migration-driven literacy learning I could, I explored how everyday people in transnational families wrote and experienced writing in three different communities, namely, in two homeland communities (Jaú,

Brazil, and Daugavpils, Latvia) and in one community of migrants (Wisconsin, United States).

In order to further this chapter's goal of turning the study inside out to reveal its seams, here I describe both the personal circumstances that led me to engage with these particular communities and the methodological rationale for turning to them for this study. After all, it is not only research participants' literacy activities that are positioned in relation to the forces of globalization, not only research participants who write and travel for love and money. Researchers' particular locations and passions are also part of the story. Far from detracting from (outdated) ideals of ethnographic objectivity, my personal history with these communities quickened my sense of urgency and responsibility to understand, in as wide a context as possible, how migration-driven literacy learning operated.

To be clear, while I was connected to these communities by love, by chance, and by choice, I did not share most participants' social conditions. As someone who experiences white privilege, who is three generations removed from immigration (from the Azores and Lebanon), who is middle class, and who makes a living with her daughter by her side, I came to each ethnographic encounter with a host of privileges. One of the many dangers of such privilege in ethnographic research is the ease with which it lets the privileged discount others' realities. I attempted to check such potential violations through working closely with key participants in many (though not all) processes of data collection and analysis and through conscious attempts to clock power dynamics. Still, I am participating in a tradition—writing about others—that is rife with the potential for abuse.[8] To curtail such abuse, scholars have developed robust frameworks for "humanizing" research agendas that emphasize participants' agency and desires.[9] Such models are my guide.

## *Jaú, São Paulo, Brazil*

I first encountered Jaú in 1999, when, as a twenty-two-year-old Peace Corps English-teaching volunteer in Latvia, I dumped my meager savings on an overseas flight to visit my then boyfriend, a Brazilian citizen. On the four-hour bus ride from the São Paulo airport to Jaú, the windows revealed a long avenue marred by traffic alongside a river, and then, little by little, the urban landscape quietly opened to green. I remember all of a sudden understanding the phrase *God's green earth*. The dirt was red and the sky was blue, hues so primary they could not be real. I was in love. With my boyfriend, yes, but also with what I had seen of Jaú. I would return to Brazil at regular intervals over the course of fifteen years, letting the clipped accent of my limited heritage Azorean Portuguese widen into the open vowels of the Brazilian countryside. Each time I visited, I played slightly different roles: girlfriend, wife, daughter-in-law, mother, and finally researcher. It was in this last role that I returned to Brazil in 2011, accompanied this time by my three-year-old daughter, to explore migration-driven literacy learning.

Jaú is a medium-size town in the interior of São Paulo, Brazil, with a modest rate of outmigration. While Brazil as a whole has been a notable sending country of immigrants since the 1980s, and there are just under 2 million Brazilians living abroad, many of Jaú's residents do not migrate.[10] Judging from the rate of automobile ownership (one car for every two residents), Jaú at the time of my research was riding the larger national trend of middle-class growth.[11] Its relative prosperity made labor migration relatively rare, though as readers will see in the next chapter, class divisions in this community meant that people experienced differential access to writing for love and money.

What highlighted migration-driven literacy practices in Jaú was not that everyone left, but that most tended to stay. Felipe, for example, whose brother migrated to the United States, grew up in Jaú, where both of his parents were born. He married his high school sweetheart, then moved into a house across the street from her parents, who had built the house there for that purpose. (His wife's brother lived next door in an identical house.) Felipe often visited his father at lunchtime, and weekend activities often included extended family gatherings, where his brother was missed. Residents thought of Jaú as quiet, friendly, and safe, a town securely ensconced in Brazil's interior heartland—a collective belief that made the absence of one member of the community noteworthy and highlighted individual experiences of migration-driven literacy learning.

Here, then, I dug into the nuances of these individual experiences by conducting nineteen LHIs, some by Skype when I was in the U.S, and some during fieldwork in 2011. I found that to address the longing for those who had migrated, what Portuguese speakers call *saudades*, migrants had remitted technologies of communication, such as laptops and webcams. I saw how people's emotional relationships to these remittances textured their experiences of literacy learning, which helped me to develop emerging theories about how the practices of writing for love and money interacted with the changing role of literacy technologies in transnational lives.

But I was left with a question: What might migration-driven literacy learning look like in communities where migration was more widespread, more of a fact that pervaded social life? Answering this question would require work in a different field site.

### *Daugavpils, Latvia*

I first encountered Latvia when I arrived at the Riga airport, jet-lagged and culturally disoriented, as a Peace Corps volunteer in June of 1999. Latvia was only eight years independent from the Soviet Union and had not yet, as it would in 2004, joined the European Union. That summer, as the northern sun set later and later, I encountered a Latvia that defied the stereotypes of the former Soviet Union I had imbibed during the cold war 1980s of my childhood in the States. Yes, there were Soviet bloc apartments, and no doubt, there was poverty. But there were also shimmering lakes, open fields, crumbling medieval castles, and the pinnacle of that summer, a pagan solstice festival in which my host family and I linked arms and sang folk songs in a minor key, our heads topped with wreaths we braided from small white wild flowers. In Latvia, I experienced a connection to land, language, and traditions that acted in peaceful defiance to the aftershocks of the country's recent political changes and the rumbling of changes to come.

In my first few months in Latvia, I applied myself to the Latvian language with fervor—it took me a good week to learn to say "Nice to meet you" (*Priecājos iepazīties,* in case you're wondering, accent on the first syllable). Three months into my stay in Latvia, I was moved from a small ethnic Latvian town to the site of this study, Daugavpils. In Daugavpils, Latvia's second-biggest city, close to the Belarussian, Lithuanian, and Russian border, I soon realized I would need to learn another language: Russian.

Under the Soviet Union, citizens from Russia, Belarus, Ukraine, and other republics had been sent to Daugavpils for work. After independence, having raised families in Latvia, about half stayed.[12] Unlike in other parts of Latvia, the common language was not Indo-European, Roman-alphabeted Latvian, but Slavic Cyrillic Russian. Eager to integrate into the community in which I would be living and teaching for two years, I soon learned Russian well enough to give toasts at birthday celebrations, haggle over vegetables at the market, and develop friendships with some of the most generous, joyful people I have ever had the privilege to encounter. Daugavpils became, for the two years I lived there, home—home enough that I returned there for a summer in 2005 on a fellowship to improve my Latvian, and then again to conduct research for this book (in

Russian) in 2014, where old friends welcomed me—and this time my five-year-old daughter, too—as if we were family.

As with Jaú, it didn't occur to me until well after I had first fallen in love with Daugavpils that it would be an apt site for researching migration-driven literacy learning—though for reasons precisely opposite to those motivating my scholarly work in Brazil. Unlike in Jaú, when I conducted research in Daugavpils in 2014, Daugavpils's schools, workplaces, and streets were emptying of working-age adults. Due to the 2009 global recession, Latvia, dependent on external markets and having overspent in the real estate boom of the early 2000s, experienced the highest unemployment rate in the EU, leaving many unable to pay their mortgages.[13] Spurred on by Latvia's inclusion in the EU in 2004, which allowed Latvians to travel and work in member states, many emigrated, leading to what Latvian economist Mihails Hazans has called a demographic disaster. During 2009–2010 alone, Latvia lost between forty thousand and eighty thousand inhabitants.[14] With a population of only 2 million, Latvia was weathering one of the highest rates of population loss due to migration in the world.[15] The popular press circulated accounts of grandparents raising children, schools closing, and the iconic tragedy of Latvian civil engineers picking strawberries in Ireland.[16]

Daugavpils in particular was hit hard by this trend. As Latvia's second biggest city, Daugavpils is located in Latvia's most economically depressed region, Latgale, whose unemployment rate since 2009 had been hovering around 22.8%.[17] As a result of high unemployment, in 2012 alone, over four thousand residents of the Latgale region left the country, contributing to an overall trend of demographic decline in Daugavpils.[18] In 2014 the city's website revealed a population that had shrunk by 14.5% over an eight-year period.[19] Like other high-volume sending communities, Daugavpils's population was growing sparse.

In the *dacha* (summer house) community in which my daughter and I stayed for part of my fieldwork, each house in a block radius had a child, grandchild, or niece or nephew abroad. Often there were special rooms or toys safeguarded for family members' return for brief vacations. To offer a composite snapshot from my fieldwork and interviews: high school students showed up to graduation with tickets to England in their pockets, cell phones buzzed with text messages from the United Kingdom, and wives lived on the remittances of husbands working construction abroad. When I asked community members why they or their relatives had migrated or planned to, they often looked at me as if there were something *wrong* with me, as the answer seemed self-evident: there was neither money nor employment in Latvia. As two different community members put it, "You just are not needed here."

Emigration was a fact of life in Daugavpils in more ways than one. Years and sometimes generations earlier, many Daugavpils residents had migrated *to* Daugavpils from other Soviet republics in the East. And now people were migrating *from* Daugavpils to the West. This shift in migration patterns played out in language and literacy use: if Russian was the prestige language during the Soviet Union, Latvia's independence in 1991 made Latvian king—required for public-sector jobs, including teaching, and for citizenship applications. In the 1990s, Daugavpils residents were scrambling to learn Latvian. By 2004, when Latvia became a member state of the European Union, and certainly by 2009 when the global recession hit, while Latvian and Russian were still necessary, other Western European languages were in high demand. As readers will see in chapter 4, in this rapidly shifting context, homeland family members were stockpiling languages and literacies, accruing documents, and learning literacy in Polish, Greek, Norwegian, German, French, English, and other languages, in part in the hopes of reunifying with family members abroad and in part to shore up their skills against uncertain economic futures. In the absence of money, and faced with the prospect of long-term family separation, Latvians turned to literacy to both sustain family ties and to project a prosperous future.

If the stories people shared with me in Brazil allowed a close up look at how emotion, technology, and social class inhered in individual transnational experiences, the stories people shared with me in Latvia provided a view of a community saturated with migration, revealing how migration-driven literacy learning was woven through communal pasts, current needs, and desires for the future, with people learning literacy not just to stay in touch with absent family members but to prepare for their own migrations.

But there was more to understand. A focus only on homelands would have omitted a crucial dimension of transnational families' literacy learning: that of migrants themselves.

## *Wisconsin, United States*

I remember seeing Wisconsin in 2003 through the window of a U-Haul containing my brother, my then husband, and our cat. I had left a job teaching fifth and sixth grade English as a Second Language in the Dallas Independent School District to go to graduate school in English, a dream I had nurtured throughout my Peace Corps years and that I couldn't quite believe was coming true. Wisconsin's lakes sparkled, and the 80-degree June day felt cool compared to the Dallas heat waves to which I had become accustomed. In Wisconsin, I found friendships through my family's involvement in Latino league soccer, through my work in local writing-assistance programs, and through my participation in a Russian-speaking group. In this way, I began to feel a part of communities that, though located in the Midwest, linked me elsewhere. After finishing my PhD and moving away for my first faculty job, I encountered these communities again—this time when I returned to the University of Wisconsin as a new professor asking for their members' generosity in helping me understand the transnational aspects of their lives.

In some ways, the city in Wisconsin where I conducted this research is educationally and technologically saturated. According to the 2012–2016 American Community Survey estimates, a full 95% have completed high school, and 66% between the ages of twenty-five and thirty-four have completed a BA or higher, including the 9% of the population that is foreign-born.[20] Despite such statistics, the state is profoundly educationally stratified along racial lines: the gap in academic achievement and overall well-being between African American and white children is so immense that Wisconsin was ranked 41 of 44 in a wide-scale national equity survey.[21] Such stratification also occurs in the city where I conducted research, where immigrant youth and youth of color consistently fall behind white children in otherwise highly ranked schools. While the American Community Survey estimated 58% of whites living there had completed a bachelor's degree, for African Americans the percentage was 22% and for Latinos/as it was 33%.[22] Such inequity, a recent study on Latinos/as across Wisconsin has shown, can be compounded for many immigrant families. Depending on legal and economic status, first-generation members of these families often find themselves locked out of English literacy education for themselves, as they invest their labor in the education and upward mobility of their children.[23]

My ongoing work on literacy remittances in Brazil and Latvia made me suspect that migrants in Wisconsin were exchanging literacies with homeland family members. But how might the context of inequitable access to literacy shape their participation in writing remittance circuits? And what might be the emotional, economic, and educational implications of such participation for experiences of family literacy learning both in the United States and in homelands?

To answer these questions, I wanted to understand migration-driven literacy learning not necessarily across social classes, as I did with the LHIs I conducted in Brazil, nor across a community and its history, as I did with my more extensive field research in Latvia, but in the more intimate experiences of members of the same family. I hoped a multigenerational view of migration-driven literacy learning would account for multiple perspectives and experiences with literacy both within migrants' United States lives and in relation to their homeland families. For that reason, between 2015 and 2016, I interviewed and observed the literacy practices of members of two multigenerational families in Wisconsin, one from Latin America and one from Eastern Europe.

As readers will see in chapter 5, when immigrants remitted literacy home, they imbued it with the emotional and economic values gleaned from their experiences acquiring (or being locked out of) literacy education stateside. In remitting literacy to those they loved, ordinary migrants reinforced their own beliefs in its promise of emotional connection and upward social mobility. This work with migrants provided an important conceptual link among the field sites that led to the book's ultimate conclusion: as literacy circulates globally among loved ones, its material and emotional value for transnational families often accrues.

To hear and understand the stories that texture and bolster this claim, in the chapters that follow readers will follow the same path my research (and my young adulthood) took: to Brazil, to Latvia, and to the United States.

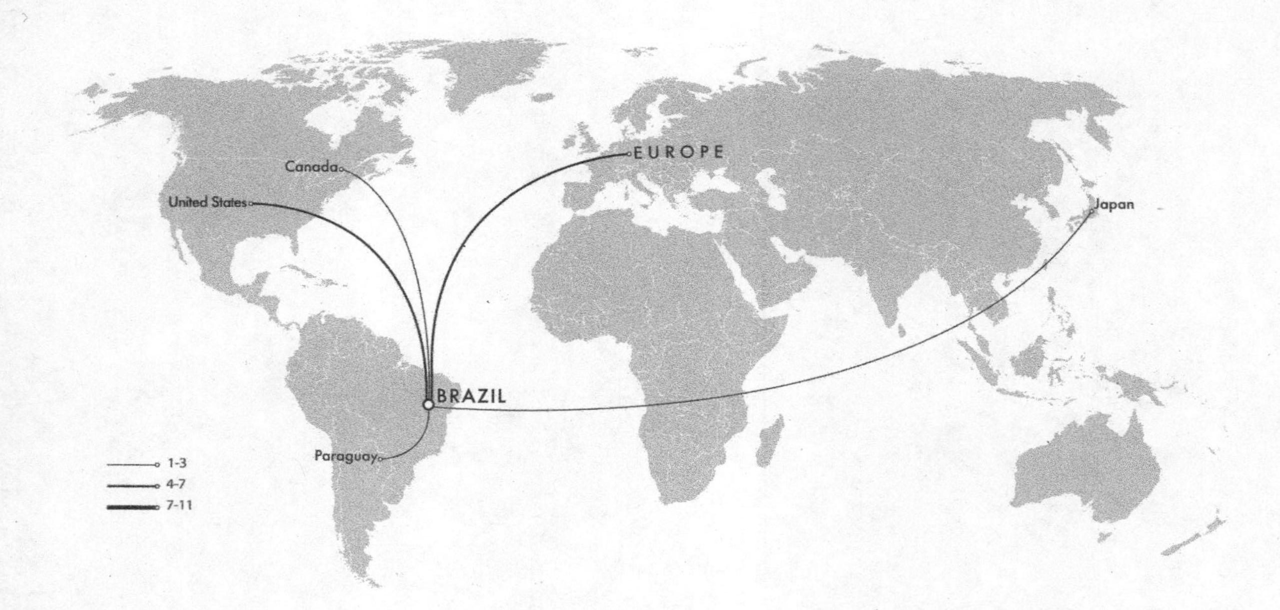


Map 3.1 Migration and literacy trajectories of participants and/or their family members in Brazil

Chapter 3

# Learning to Log On

## *From Post to Internet in Brazil*

"Ai, que saudades!" Eliana says of her brother, who has lived in the United States for twelve years. "How I miss him!" We are sitting in her spotless living room in Jaú, Brazil. It is 2011, and for the first time since I began to visit Brazil regularly in 2001, I am there not only to see family but also to conduct research. My sister-in-law has accompanied me to Eliana's house and nods sympathetically at the word *saudades,* that feeling of missing, nostalgia, and lack. *Saudades* is a signature sentiment of Portuguese-speaking cultures and characterizes the emotional cost of migration for many.

I sip the cold soda Eliana has offered me and proceed: How do you overcome these *saudades,* this intense missing? Do you talk on the phone? Write letters or emails? Use video chat? How, I want to know, do people remain close when they are far? With an embarrassed laugh, Eliana gestures to the laptop her brother sent her from the United States. It sits in a neat cabinet, topped with a doily, awaiting her children's help to turn it on. Eliana does not know how to use it. "I am becoming illiterate," she tells me. "But I want to learn." Eliana's brother's transnational migration, symbolized by the presence and communicative potential of the remitted laptop, demands what is for Eliana a new kind of literacy learning. As such, this middle-class homemaker has found herself at the forefront of some of the pressing technological and global changes that are shaping writing today.

The laptop represents what I am calling a "writing remittance." Writing remittances are the hardware (laptops and webcams), software (Skype, MSN chat, ICQ), communication (letters, emails, video chats), and literacy knowledge that family members laboring abroad often bring or send home to communicate with loved ones. They carry both emotional and economic value for transnational families and can sometimes be invested, locally and internationally, for gain. For those I spoke with in Brazil, the circulation of writing remittances formed part of a network of informal family-based transnational literacy learning, constituting a new chapter in writing's long-standing relationship to love and money.

This chapter draws from the stories of migrants' family members and return migrants in Brazil to elaborate writing remittances—a concept that underlies the exchanges described throughout this book. While the chapters to come provide a more community-wide (Latvia) and family-centered (United States) perspective on writing remittances, here we dive into variations on individual experiences of it across social classes and lifespans, revealing how writing's associations with love and money can be activated in literacy technologies, as they are passed among family members suffering from *saudades*.

## WRITING REMITTANCES

My first experience with writing remittances came in 2004, when I delivered laptops across the Brazilian border for my brother-in-law and a friend. I was a student at the time, and though the friend would pay me back, buying the laptops involved stretching an already overextended budget. But they were even more expensive for Brazilians. The high state taxes levied on imported technology continued to price many out of buying computers, which were becoming increasingly important tools of civic participation and upward mobility.[1] Plus, my brother-in-law needed one—both to ease communication with my family stateside and for his own purposes as a student, trying to study his way out of the punishing economic circumstances of Brazil's lower middle class to be the first in his family to graduate college. At customs my explanations for having multiple laptops were met with a suspicious stare and a hushed discussion among uniformed agents, but I was ultimately waved along, a bearer of transnational literacy technologies to be used for love and for money.

The work of transnational studies scholar Peggy Levitt helped me see this act as part of a transnational remittance circuit, what I began to call a writing remittance. Levitt coined the term *social remittances* in 1998 to describe exchanges of social and cultural knowledge, practices, and objects in families in Massachusetts and the Dominican Republic. Moving beyond purely monetary concepts of financial remittances, she found that elements of U.S. culture (certain kinds of T-shirts, for example) circulated in DR and that elements of Dominican culture (certain ways of decorating a house, for example) circulated in Boston.[2] Likewise, and among other exchanges, Boston Dominicanos took a stake in Dominican local politics, and Dominicans in DR remitted ideas to Boston about religious identity. Migration, Levitt argued, involved more than the transnational movement of people and money. It also involved the transnational movement of things, ideas, and ways of living. These social remittances can act on nonmigrants' identities, such that in some contexts they experience their lives, in the words of migration scholar Hilary Dick, "contrapuntally," that is, looking both back in time and forward in space to potential migration.[3] Such nonmigrant transnational looking, my experiences in Brazil suggested, involved literacy—and communication technologies specifically—leading me to the concept of "writing remittances."

To conceptualize how writing remittances simultaneously carried both financial and emotional value, as did the laptop I remitted to my brother-in-law, I drew from the work of economic sociologist Vivian Zelizer to envision the transaction as part of a transnational "circuit" of exchange.[4] Zelizer's studies of financial remittances among migrants show that remittance circuits can "convey powerful shared meanings," through which "participants are constantly negotiating, contesting, and reshaping their relationship to each other."[5] That is, the circulation of money in the form of remittances can express love. Sociological studies of Thai, Ghanaian, Filipino, Mexican, and other transnational families have shown the same: that financial remittances are tied up in emotions and culturally specific concepts of care.[6] I began to wonder, then, about how exchanging writing remittances, as social, material, and financial objects, might also shape people's relationships—with each other, with the shifting technologies of writing that allowed them to stay in touch, and with their understandings of literacy as a whole, as they incorporated migration-driven literacy learning into their past identities, current practices, and future plans.

## THE MATERIALITY OF LITERACY IN TRANSNATIONAL LIVES

As I began interviews and analyzed data, I realized that in addition to contributing an understanding of literacy to research about transnational social remittances, writing remittances could also help answer some persistent theoretical questions in literacy scholarship about writing.[7] Literacy has long been viewed on the one hand as an economic resource and on the other as an interpersonal practice. Exploring writing remittances helped me connect these two perspectives. In the cauldron of writing remittances, the social meanings of love and of money seeped into each other, and in fact interanimated each other, reconfiguring understandings of literacy and forming a rich motivational basis from which to learn new practices.

To understand this connection, I had to take seriously experiences of writing remittances' materiality. The issue of literacy's materiality may seem abstract, but close your eyes for a moment and think back to your earliest scenes of writing. If you learned to write in school, you may recall a chunky pencil or lined papers. If you wrote at home and didn't have money for paper, you may recall writing on the backs of the cardboard inserts your mother pulled out of old pantyhose packages. If you learned literacy in a religious community, you may recall a sense of righteous daring as you chalked your rebellion on the side of a church wall. Or consider, as literacy researcher Tisha Lewis does, the experiences of an African American mother who was visibly moved when touching her computer's motherboard—a material sign of the educational advantages she is providing for her son and the communicative digital practices the two of them use to stay in contact.[8] The materials we write with or on are anything but abstract. That literacy is instantiated in a *thing*—a laptop on a doily in the living room of a sister longing for her brother—means something.

But what?

In one sense, literacy's materiality means something for individual everyday writing practices. Material incarnations of writing—from scrapbooking[9] to instant messaging[10] to word processing[11] to mid-twentieth-century typing[12] to regimes of bureaucratic documents immigrants must negotiate to avoid deportation[13]—are "entangled" in sites of everyday literate production.[14] Glue, phone, computer screen, and immigration papers are part and parcel of how, what, and often to what ends people write.

But the meaning-making potential of particular literacy technologies also have implications beyond the everyday, in that they often act in concert with larger social systems. Lorimer Leonard, for example, has connected the materiality of the personal letter to bureaucratic structures;[15] Prendergast and Ličko have demonstrated how paper use in institutions of higher education hinges on funding structures;[16] and I have previously linked immigrants' literacy practices with immigration papers to the state structures that regulate their use.[17] Likewise, work on the materiality of writing systems themselves—from the Cherokee syllabary[18] to *khipu*[19] to the alphabet[20] to Mesoamerican codex books[21]—has shown how the intricacies and uses of such systems respond to the political circumstances, such as colonization, that inform their invention and use.

Finally, literacy's materiality allows meaning to travel, lending it its unique potential for transnational families. The kinds of mobility that literacy's materiality can facilitate has gone by various labels, such as "transliteracies," "new mobilities," and "deterritorialization"—all terms that describe different aspects of a similar phenomenon: the communication of meanings via material technologies among people differently positioned in time and space.[22] As Brandt and Clinton have postulated, in its potential to release meanings across these dimensions—via carrier pigeon, post, or Internet—literacy's materiality contributes to its sensitivity to social and political currents.[23]

Literacy's materiality, then, is both tied up in literacy's meaning-making potential in everyday cross-border practices (think WhatsApping on a phone) and shaped by larger socioeconomic and geographic situations (think how well you can or can't afford the payment for the phone you use to WhatsApp). But how precisely are the economic and emotional exigencies that shape literacy practices in transnational families activated in the materials necessary for their use—and with what implications for experiences of migration-driven literacy learning?

A partial answer to this question can be found in Brandt's 1998 concept of sponsorship.[24] "Literacy sponsorship" helps explain how capitalist production imperatives can result in the unequal distribution of literacy technologies, with those who are better positioned accessing the technologies that help pave the way for better-remunerated careers. This concept connects economic inequality and literacy's materiality. It does not, however, fully account for the stories people shared with me during my research, in which people saw both literacy technologies and the economic forces shaping their use as constitutive of some of their most intimate literate interactions. That is, sponsorship leaves out the possibility of *saudades* as fueling literacy learning. Sponsorship leaves out love.[25] The economic and material aspects of literacy did act on participants' life prospects as Brandt's model emphasizes, but these aspects of literacy also seeped into their relational and emotional lives via the literacy-infused practice of cross-border communication—in particular in relation to writing remittances.[26]

As I continued to investigate writing remittances, I came to see them as acting as the text-hearts in my chalkboard illustration in the previous chapter, ferrying meaning between readers and writers and engaging family members in an emotional and economic exchange. Via writing remittances, literacy's link to the inequitable world of labor and money was experienced in the heat of interpersonal relationships, revealing how literacy's status as a material and economic resource can contribute to producing or muffling feelings of love. As such, writing remittances acted as one current instantiation of literacy's historic role in love and money: they embodied economic inequity, literacy's materiality, and familial intimacy. Charged with these potentials, laden with these meanings, Eliana's remitted laptop was perched, expectant, in her living room.

What follows offers snapshots of experiences of writing remittances in Jaú taken from various angles: an aerial view of writing remittances across social class; a narrative view of writing remittances across one man's life; historically oriented views across the changing technologies of print and digital writing remittances; and future-oriented views as women and men described the potential payoffs of migration-driven literacy learning. (For readers interested in the details of methods for this chapter, please see appendix A.) Through this prismatic method of representation, I hope to provide a robust picture of writing remittances on which the rest of this book can build.

## WRITING REMITTANCES ACROSS SOCIAL CLASS: AN AERIAL VIEW

First an aerial view of how writing remittances were experienced across social class. Even in the relatively prosperous year of 2011, evidence of Brazil's entrenched class system abounded. One day during fieldwork I found myself in a spacious tiled three-story home interviewing a mother whose son had studied in Canada and had stayed on for an advanced degree. A wall-length portrait of her daughter in formal wear shone down from an alcove, and a uniformed maid brought us tiny cups of sweet strong coffee on a pewter platter. The next day, I was in a house's crowded concrete backyard that doubled as the family's kitchen and laundry room, interviewing a man whose son had left for the United States and planned to stay there. He too offered coffee, serving it himself.

As my fieldwork progressed, I began to organize participants' social class standing into three categories: those from the lower middle class, whose family members often left Brazil for work; those from the middle class, whose family members often left

Brazil to receive advanced degrees; and those from the upper classes, whose children often studied abroad in high school. This organization allowed me to see how writing remittances worked differently for those in Brazil who served the coffee and for those to whom it was served: the woman who owned the mansion had learned some new literacy skills from communicating with her son abroad but hadn't received any communication technology from him because she already had the means to buy the hardware she wanted. The man, on the other hand, had been gifted a laptop from his son that he shared with his immediate family and that he hoped to learn to use.

Such qualitative insights reflected larger trends in Brazil's digital divide: in the highest social classes, 98% of individuals had a computer in their homes, and 97% had accessed the Internet, compared with 9% and 6%, respectively, of individuals in the lowest social classes.[27] Since my data collection in Brazil, the use of Internet and communication technologies has become more widespread. Nonetheless, a 2017 study showed that racial, educational, and economic privilege still correlate not only with each other but also with access to the Internet.[28] My research likewise revealed that writing remittances were sent and received, and ultimately contributed to learning, in ways that were linked to the social classes in which people found themselves, as well as to the ones to which they aspired. Such findings jibe with what digital divide scholars have asserted: access to information and communication technologies is "not a matter only of education, but also of power."[29] Table 3.1, organized by how social class corresponded to types of migration (to work or to study), reveals that for migrant families from lower social classes, writing remittances involved the remittance of hardware (usually laptops) as a crucial element in maintaining transnational relationships—a pattern that held for all but one lower-middle-class homeland resident.[30]

Table 3.1 WRITING REMITTANCES IN BRAZIL BY SOCIAL CLASS

| *Social Class* | *Name* | *Relationship and Destination* | *Primary Mode of Transnational Communication with Loved One* | *Writing Remittance* | *Use of Writing Remittance* | *Education Level* |
|---|---|---|---|---|---|---|
| **Labor Migrants' Family Members and Returned Migrants** | **Felipe** | Brother migrated to Europe and United States | ICQ, Skype | *Hardware:* laptop *Practice:* learned ICQ from brother | Used migration-driven ICQ knowledge for access to English classes; used laptop for research | Undergraduate |
| | **Joao (J.L.)** | Son migrated to Europe, then United States | Phone | *Hardware:* laptop | — | High school |
| | **Maya** | Aunt migrated to United States | Phone, Skype | — | — | Undergrad student |

| | | | | | |
|---|---|---|---|---|---|
| **Eduardo** | Migrated for work in Japan as soccer coach (returned migrant) | Phone, Skype, emails | *Hardware:* laptop | Uses laptop from Japan to improve his analysis of goalies in his local work as a coach | High school |
| **Carla** | Migrated to work in United States as nanny (returned migrant) | Cards on special occasions, Skype, phone | *Hardware*: laptop | Uses U.S.-bought laptop for lesson planning in work as a teacher | Master's student |
| **Eliana** | Brother migrated to United States | Phone, Skype when children are present | *Hardware*: laptop | — | Undergraduate |

(*continued*)

Table 3.1 CONTINUED

| *Social Class* | *Name* | *Relationship and Destination* | *Primary Mode of Transnational Communication with Loved One* | *Writing Remittance* | *Use of Writing Remittance* | *Education Level* |
|---|---|---|---|---|---|---|
| | **Maria** | Son migrated to Japan | Letters dictated to husband, Skype | *Hardware*: laptop<br>*Practice*: learned to Skype | Provides access to computer and Internet for local grandchildren | Elementary school |
| | **Hugo** | Migrated to France; sister lives in France still (returned migrant and relative of migrant) | Letters, Skype, digital telephone | *Hardware*: webcam from sister; suitcase storing friends' letters (self)<br>*Practice*: learned about Internet from Minitel system in France | Uses technology knowledge for social status and in work as help desk | Undergraduate |

| | | | | | | |
|---|---|---|---|---|---|---|
| | **Gilberto** | Migrated to Italy, then to United States (returned migrant) | Letters, emails | *Hardware*: computer, books | Used books to further job as chef | Technical school |
| **Higher-Ed Family Members and Returned Migrants** | **Leonido** | Son studies in Germany | Emails, chat, Skype | *Practice*: used email and MSN like "never before" | Uses knowledge gleaned from emails about Germany to improve organization in the school he directs | Undergraduate |
| | **Loirinho** | Brother studies in Paraguay | Skype | *Practice:* learned Skype to communicate with brother | Used migration-driven Skype knowledge to take a distance course | Undergraduate |

(*continued*)

Table 3.1 CONTINUED

| *Social Class* | *Name* | *Relationship and Destination* | *Primary Mode of Transnational Communication with Loved One* | *Writing Remittance* | *Use of Writing Remittance* | *Education Level* |
|---|---|---|---|---|---|---|
| | **Antonio** | Studied in Europe (returned migrant) | Emails, chat, Skype | *Practice*: increased Skype and MSN | — | Some college |
| **High School Study Abroad Family Members and Returned Study Abroad Participants** | **Sylvia** | Son studied in Canada | Letters, emails, Skype | *Practice:* learned to "mess with the computer" to use Skype and send emails to communicate with son | Uses to communicate with family | Technical degree |
| | **Isabella** | Studied in United States | Skype | — | — | Completing high school |

| | | | | | | |
|---|---|---|---|---|---|---|
| **Emerson**<br>**Katia** | **Emerson** | Studied in United States | Skype | — | — | Completing high school |
| | **Katia** | Son studied in United States | Nextel telephone, Skype | *Practice*: son left computer loaded with Skype for communication, but she already knew how to use it. | — | Undergraduate |

Such hardware, remitted out of love, was also circulated locally by homeland residents to further professional gains: a soccer coach used a remitted laptop to improve his analysis of goalies' saves; a teacher used a remitted laptop in lesson planning; an engineering student used one in his research; and as readers will see in the next section, one homeland resident used a remitted webcam to build local status, eventually starting a technology business. Writing remittances in the form of hardware did not on their own reverse the economic luck of transnational families from the lower middle classes. But they participated in the hopes, dreams, and work of upward social mobility in a moment when such mobility was difficult to achieve.

In contrast, none of the wealthier, study-abroad families received hardware. Still, nearly all described receiving technological knowledge and support. In response to their family members' migrations, wealthy participants reported learning to "mess" with computers and generally increasing their use of email, chat, and Skype like "never before." So while migration did appear to drive some literacy learning for members of wealthier classes, their experiences were not as visibly enmeshed in global economic injustice as were those of labor migrants' family members.

This difference does not mean that economic forces were absent from the migration-driven literacy practices of the wealthy. Rather, the social class privilege of not having to rely on expensive hardware sent from abroad simply rendered economic inequity—so apparent in labor migrant families—more or less invisible in the families of the more comfortable. Many could and did buy laptops themselves. Some, such as the woman I interviewed in her palatial house, also had the means to visit their study-abroad family members in the United States or Canada, alleviating some of the *saudades* that writing remittances worked to resolve. Unlike labor migrants, who were attempting to earn more money to improve the conditions of their lives, study-abroad participants knew that materially comfortable environments were awaiting them at home in Brazil. For example, one returned study-abroad student described the difficulty of doing without her domestic maid (who washed, ironed, and cooked for her in Brazil) during her year abroad. Unlike many labor migrants, her main goal was not to help support her family but to have an educational life experience. For all these reasons, writing remittance circuits involving hardware were not as heavily trafficked among the wealthy.

While migration drove digital literacy use and learning across classes, then, economic inequality shaped the terms of such learning. What this aerial view of participants has suggested is that the form particular acts of writing for love took, and the potential of using writing remittances for professional gain, depended in part on the access people had to money.

## WRITING REMITTANCES ACROSS A LIFE: A NARRATIVE VIEW

While the above analysis of social class allowed me to compare writing remittances across the sixteen transnational families with whom I worked, I also wanted a more intimate understanding of individuals' experiences with writing remittances and how such experiences might promote learning. By literacy learning, I don't mean improving punctuation and spelling—though one study of a community in Brazil has linked the use of social media on mobile apps to improved technical skills in reading and writing.[31] I mean instead the sense that people had of their continuing development as literacy agents, able to learn new practices and use them for personal and communal ends.[32]

To this end, I also tracked how people experienced intimacy in relation to changing modes of transnational communication across their lifespans. In the life history interviews I conducted, people described their feelings as they wrote letters, used phone cards, discovered the nascent Internet, received emails, chatted, and logged on to synchronous video chat, revealing that experiences of intimacy across borders were tied up in the labor they perceived particular literacy technologies required to use, to learn to use, and to buy. Both writing to sustain transnational relationships and *buying* the writing technologies to do so were seen as work—work whose emotional and financial value was appraised and reappraised as the technological landscape changed.

## *Hugo: "It Was Worth More than Any Card I'd Gotten"*

To understand this change, consider Hugo, a musician in his forties. Used to communicating with foreigners, Hugo did not seem to think it unusual that one would want to speak with him, and he invited me into his studio with a generous sweep of his arm. My three-year-old was happily watching cartoons across town at her grandfather's house (*Dora the Explorer* in Portuguese, for detail-oriented readers), so I settled in for a long conversation. Hugo told me how he made the decision to move to France in the 1990s for higher education, putting him in a social class category between the upper middle class and the lower middle class. He decided on France because his sister, a labor migrant, was already living there.

Not a prolific writer before migration, Hugo nonetheless described an uptick in literacy use when he arrived in France. "When you are there, you get very emotional. Far from everything, far from your father, far from your mother." He first relied on phone cards to make international calls, recalling their foreboding "tic tic tic" as they emptied of credit in the middle of conversations. Both resourceful and lonely, he responded to his dissatisfaction with the telephone by writing ten to twelve letters a day to his friends and receiving ten to twelve letters a day in return. "When I was there," he said, "I liked to write." He wrote of the chocolates and yogurts he ate ("Their yogurt was so good!") and French cultural practices that seemed to border on rude ("You can't just bring an extra friend to their parties—they set the exact number of places of invitees!").

For Hugo, this increase in written communication highlighted writing's materiality—letters' physical volume, the work required to pen them, and the intimate meanings that their materiality conveyed. His story complicates economic understandings of literacy's materiality by showing how the particular material incarnation of transnational literacy that he received or sent acted on his emotions. For example, he described keeping all the letters he received from friends and returning home to Brazil "with an enormous suitcase of letters." In the work of writing and of carrying so much paper, literacy's materiality contributed to the emotional and physical labor of its production and circulation, as if these aspects of literacy were colluding to make meaning across borders.

This association between labor and love, inhering in paper, resonated in another account he shared with me, of a moving letter he received from his grandfather:

> HUGO: There was a card from my grandfather that he sent. He didn't know how to write correctly. And . . . it's that . . . when I received this card, I cried so much.
>
> KATE: Really?
>
> HUGO: *Nossa!* [Emphatic yes, literally "Our Lady!"] And he wrote on a dirty paper, you know?
>
> KATE: Yeah.
>
> HUGO: It was on such a totally dirty paper. He wrote with that kind of trembling handwriting, and *nossa* [wow]. His letter was the most beautiful that I've ever received. It had like three lines, you know? But it was worth more than any card I've gotten.

The materiality of trembling hands and dirty paper, suggestive of the rich, red farmland of Brazil's interior, emphasized for Hugo the work of writing. Hugo's grandfather was working his, in Hugo's view, limited literacy skills to send word via post in an effort to communicate with his grandson. As such, his grandfather's perceived cognitive and physical labor of literate production heightened the letter's emotional resonance. In fact, Hugo remembered the evidence of work etched onto the letter's surface—the paper, the handwriting—more than its content, which I had to prompt him to describe. ("It just said, I don't know, I miss you?" was Hugo's response.) Hugo judged the emotional worth of the letter not so much on its content but more on its surface, not solely on the meaning made from the symbol system of the alphabet but more on the meaning made from its having been written at all. Put another way, almost regardless of what the words said, the letter itself operated semiotically. The effort Hugo inferred that such writing demanded appeared to deepen its emotional value—value made material in "dirty paper" and in an "enormous suitcase of letters."

The materiality of paper, and its association for Hugo with effort and intimacy, intensified with the arrival of digitality—which entered Hugo's home as a writing remittance from his sister. Hugo, at home in Brazil at the time of our interview, communicated with his sister, still living in France, via video chat. Similar to the way he described his grandfather's letter, he spoke of his communication with her in relation to labor. He pointed out to me that they did not communicate via letter, explaining, "My sister, she likes to talk. She can talk for an hour and a half. Can you imagine if I had to read all that?" For Hugo, reading, like writing, required a kind of work that his sister's voluminous communication did not merit. His tone in relation to his sister and grandfather differed perhaps in part due to age and gender. (My feminist hackles were raised at his invocation of the trope of the talkative woman.) Still, Hugo's connection of labor to print remained consistent. With the arrival of the digital, writing seemed like work. Words on paper appeared rare and precious, whereas digital talk seemed cheap.

Undergirding these shifts in his experiences with migration-driven print and digital literacy was an economic logic by which particular literacies were worth more than others in relation to cost, to labor, and to love.

To be clear, the economic value of migration-driven literacy was more than a metaphor or an emotional state for Hugo. He also invested his migration-driven literacy knowledge, gleaned across his transnational experiences, for social and financial gain. During Hugo's stay in France, he became familiar with the Minitel shopping system, a national telephone-based Web service, accessed through terminals with keyboards and screens, which he described as laying the groundwork for his later facility with Internet-mediated technology. When he returned to Brazil, he became one of the first in his neighborhood to buy a computer. Shortly thereafter, his sister, who had remained in France, remitted him a laptop and the first webcam he had seen, leading him to adopt video chat. Neighbors and friends soon visited, asking him for technological advice and logging on. He circulated his technology knowledge locally, teaching his friends and family. As he put it, "I don't like to keep all the knowledge to myself." His descriptions of his house as a local center of communication technology resonate with historians' descriptions of the early post office, whose outward-directed literacy infrastructures could also foster intensely social in-person local interactions. As Hugo spoke, I could see it: him directing a group of people crowded around a computer and webcam, gesturing, offering sodas, leaning in to type, laughing at a joke.

Hugo invested this migration-driven literacy knowledge not only locally, for social status and community building, but also internationally. He described how an American woman studying abroad in Jaú had learned that he knew how to access an Internet-connected phone line and would come "hang" on the phone in his office to speak with family and friends stateside for "hours." To his irritation, she broke the phone three times. Still, he took pride in his ability to circulate writing remittances internationally: "I said, 'Whoa, you live there [the United States] and I'm the one giving you technology lessons?' She even worked in telecommunications!" Through such everyday practices of circulating migration-driven literacy knowledge, Hugo came to question and indeed resist notions of the supposedly advanced technological knowledge of the United States. He was an international digital literacy maestro, with valuable knowledge to share.

In fact, he was able to leverage this status for financial gain. To supplement his income from his career as a musician, he began working independently at a help desk call center he set up from home, often offering technological advice to people in the United States. He found it ironic and also empowering that he assisted those living and working in Los Angeles, for him a supposed hub of technological sophistication. Importantly, Hugo's experience emphasizes that advanced literacy knowledge emphatically does not stem from the Global North. Tracing the influence of migration on Hugo's remunerable literacy learning reveals that for him such flows were bi-directional, resonating with local and international social and professional pressures, desires, and opportunities.

During the technologically and economically tumultuous period of the 1990s to 2011, Hugo's commitment to killing transnational *saudades* fostered an economically buttressed, materially resonant, and financially auspicious relationship with print and digital literacy technologies. Literacy's material face changed across Hugo's transnational experiences, as his grandfather, a farmer, reached across the Atlantic in a trembling hand, as Hugo returned to Brazil with knowledge of the pre-Internet Minitel system, and as his sister sent hardware, skills with which he developed and circulated both locally and internationally. Hugo valued letter writing for the labor it entailed, used video chat to avoid what he saw as the drudgery of print literacy, and invested his knowledge of and work with digital communication technologies both in Brazil and abroad. In Hugo's migration-driven experiences of literacy, literacy's materiality resonated with both the economics of transnational migration and the family relationships dear to his heart.

For Hugo, these resonances shifted with changing literacy technologies, as they did, albeit in different ways, for others, as readers will now see.

## WRITING REMITTANCES ACROSS SHIFTING TECHNOLOGIES: A HISTORICAL VIEW

### *Pre-Internet: Letters, Love, and Money among Returned Migrants and Nonmigrants*

For those participants who migrated or whose family members migrated before use of the Internet, textual communication via letters was crucial for upholding family relationships. As one mother put it, "You think you can stay far away from your family and not feel one *saudade*? You will! In one way or another, you will!" Distance gave rise to *saudades,* and participants accessed what technology was within their means to resolve them.

For most, as with Hugo, phone calls in the early aughts and late 1990s were too expensive to rely on as a primary means of communication, though some exceptions did exist. One upper-middle-class participant described buying a Nextel radio-connected telephone from a client of her husband's, with which she could make phone calls to her son studying in Canada at no cost each morning to wake him up. And another middle-class participant described weekly [illegible] her brother, an expensive—though emotionally [illegible]l that allowed her to imagine he was back in Jaú, close [illegible] used to regularly speak on the phone. For most, how- [illegible]nal phone calls before the availability of the Internet were prohibitively expensive. Like Hugo, many negotiated the cost of communication by writing letters, in which money, love, and literacy's materiality, in the form of paper folded into an envelope, interanimated each other.[33]

Like Hugo, many other returned migrants described letters as an emotional—and even physical—necessity while abroad. Some compared communication with loved ones to sustenance. Such was the case with Gilberto. In his forties, Gilberto ran a successful Italian restaurant in Jaú, known for its outsized calzones filled with prosciutto and mozzarella. I spoke with him the first time just before his busy evening shift, in the old train station he and his friends had refurbished to create the restaurant, where he sat smoking in his chef's apron, a warm breeze wafting through the wide-open doors. Of Italian descent, Gilberto used his Italian passport to live in Italy from 1992 to 1994, returned to Brazil for two years (where he described himself as being "without money and without possibilities"), and then left again for the United States, where he lived in New York for six months, frying chicken in a fast-food restaurant, and then in Florida for four years, where he worked in Italian restaurants and sold cigars. In the United States, he communicated occasionally with his family in Brazil by phone, despite the crushing expense. While the phone allowed for nearly synchronous interaction, Gilberto longed for the letters that he complained were few and far between. "When you are alone," he told me, "you hope for letters much more, understand?" "Morria de saudades," he said. "I was dying of missing them." His invocation of death in relation to *saudades* is a common idiom in Portuguese, but it nonetheless speaks to what for Gilberto was the physical necessity of communication, made scarce by want of money for phone calls and few letters from family.

Likewise, many who remained home appreciated that transnational communication could be a matter of migrants' survival. In his thirties, Felipe was from a lower-middle-class family. His brother had migrated to Europe in 1999, returned to Brazil briefly in 2000, and then left for the United States in 2002. Felipe recalled that his brother wrote him a letter stating that he didn't have enough food to eat—an admission that made Felipe see his own situation differently: "I read that letter, my brother hungry, and then I looked at all the food we had. A big pile of rice and beans." While Felipe's family often relied on government subsidies of oil, rice, and beans for the month, he perceived his own family's modest supply of food as one of plenty in comparison to his brother's.[34] As a result, Felipe and his family started sending a letter—often with money—to his brother every ten days.

On one hand, there were financial reasons to send the letter: "We put money in an envelope, such that the money wouldn't be seen, because it could get 'lost' [i.e., stolen] along the way." And there were psychological reasons. Felipe was concerned that, in his words, his brother would "go out of his mind, because no one understood his language." The letters acted as material and psychological support, as Felipe's family attempted to care for his brother from a distance through a textually mediated proxy.

In cases when one family member's literacy was insufficient for solo writing, the labor of such textual care was often shared among family members. Consider Maria, who had a second-grade education and described her literacy in this way: "I know how to read and write, but not to 'write,' you know?" Her son had worked as a soccer coach in Japan since 1997, having migrated due to a lack of job opportunities in Brazil. He eventually married a Japanese woman and had a child, Maria's distant grandson. During our interview in Maria's cozy living room, her granddaughter (her daughter's daughter, who lived locally) napped in an adjoining room. She woke mid-interview with a cough and a cry, offering a warm bodily example of the difference between local and transnational family. While local family members could be held, the transnational family was represented by Japanese remittance objects in the room—a painting, a clock, a laptop, and an album of her son's life in Japan that displayed photos, cards, and the inky baby footprints of her newborn grandson. To overcome such *saudades* pre-Internet, given her self-reported limited literacy, Maria described how she engaged in collaborative letter writing. She dictated personal letters to her husband, who would transcribe her words. She was writing—whether or not she could "write." For Maria and for others, as families attempted to include absent loved ones in daily life, and as those abroad worked to maintain relationships and identities across borders, they communicated through letters in ways that offered sustenance, familiarity, participation.[35]

Letters' sociomateriality facilitated their widespread uptake in matters of love and money. First, letters' technical affordances meant they could be carried (Hugo), kept (Gilberto), supplemented with cash (Felipe), and returned to in moments of longing (Maria). Second, that the transnational postal system is a literacy institution subsidized by governments made letters cheaper than phone calls. And finally, letters operated affectively. That is, the work they were perceived to require underlay their value as a medium of intimate communication: For Hugo, his grandfather's card was of worth partly because he thought his grandfather struggled to write it. For Gilberto, the fact that his family only rarely made the effort to write a letter left him feeling unmoored, alone, and resentful. For Maria, the labor of writing was so difficult and yet so necessary that it had to be shared. And Felipe concretized the relationship between literacy's materiality and its economic purchase by enclosing money along with words in his brother's own language. Letters, as writing remittances, circulated in a financially stratified and emotionally charged transnational realm.

## *Post-Internet: Labor, Learning, and Laptops across Educational Experiences*

What, then, changed about the relationship of writing to love and money with the use of the Internet in Brazil for transnational communication? If print letters mattered emotionally and economically in part because of the very *matter* of letters (the paper, the envelopes, the handwriting), then how did the heart and the pocketbook inflect Brazilians' experiences of digital literacy—of keyboards, of microphones, of webcams?

In other contexts, such as the Philippines, scholars have documented an array of media choices for families separated by borders, calling this communicative abundance "polymedia."[36] In contexts of polymedia, family members choose particular media (computer, cell phone, letter, cassette tapes even!) to mediate emotions. For example, cassette tapes can be played over and over again in Walkmans, so migrant women can listen to the voices of their children or partners as they work. While Brazilians with access to multiple modes of communication described making similar rhetorical choices, what struck me most in our conversations was not only how particular types of communication were used for different emotional purposes but also how the remittance of writing technologies, sent with money earned from labor migration, made pedagogical demands on their recipients.

Such was the case with Maria, described in the previous section, whose son lived in Japan. Pre-Internet, she had shared the literacy labor of writing letters with her husband. Later, when her son remitted a new laptop to them from Japan—where, in Maria's words, technology was more "advanced"—Maria was obligated in an economic and interpersonal exchange to use it. With the help of her local children, she learned how to log on, sign in, and use Skype to communicate. Maria interfaced with print-mediated log-ins and cutting-edge software via a computer keyboard, at the same time as she made use of the visual and aural modalities of video chat to listen to her son's troubles at work, offer advice, and see her grandson. Learning this particular literacy practice was Maria's role in her family's transnational remittance circuit. To learn it, she engaged with print and digital literacy and drew from her experience as a mother, doing what she described doing for her son throughout his life: listening and conversing. As such, her migration-driven print and digital literacy learning grew from practices she had cultivated in family relationships and then digitally extended across borders.

Her son's role in the exchange was to buy the computer, a Japanese laptop beyond Maria's means, which cost him both in money and in time—an outlay that Maria emphasized in our interview. She said her son worked twelve hours a day and had paltry vacations. She wished she could see him more often. Seen this way, the price of the laptop was quite high. It was evidence of her son's greater earning power, the reason he migrated in the first place, and thus symbolized a kind of payoff for his absence from his family. Hence its value. This valuable remittance heightened Maria's obligation to communicate through the technology. Bolstered by this delicate and mutual exchange of materials, communication, and learning, they maintained an intimate mother-son relationship across time (fourteen years at the time of our interview) and distance (11,400 miles).

Such circuits of economic, emotional, and educational exchange did not always work, leaving some homeland residents feeling left behind not only physically but also technologically. Such was the case with Eliana, whose story opened this chapter. Eliana had had a career as an accountant, which she left in order to raise her children, who, at the time of the interview, were in their late teens and twenties. Her brother, as readers will recall, worked in the United States as a labor migrant and remitted a laptop to the family to communicate. This laptop was crucial to maintaining their relationship: Because of his undocumented legal status in the United States, his visits home had been few. The expectation that was delivered along with the laptop to Eliana's gated front door step was that she would learn to use the laptop and that brother and sister (and the brother's new daughter!) would be united over cyberspace, fulfilling if not the embodied experience of togetherness, then at least the visual and aural aspects of it.

Yet at the time of our interview Eliana was not able to fulfill her part of the exchange by learning how to use the computer, compromising, in ways inflected by social class, her ability to "kill" her *saudades*. As I mentioned in the opening to this chapter, Eliana interpreted her inability to use the computer as a sign she was becoming "illiterate." I first understood her nervous laughter when she pronounced this word as discomfort being around a researcher, or perhaps shame at not being able to use digital technology in the way that she assumed I, as a younger woman and a foreigner, presumably could. Still, her use of the word struck me.

It was only when I listened to the recordings again that I realized why: instead of saying *analfabeto*, the standard way to say "illiterate" in Portuguese, she laughed that she was becoming *anarfa*. *Anarfa* operates on a couple of levels. On one level, it's slang, a shortened version of the more formal *analfabeto*. On another level, her pronunciation, substituting the *r* for the *l*, represents a mockery of a country Brazilian accent. This common cultural trope of the person who instead of *l* pronounces an *r* in the middle of words is one of someone uneducated, who works the land, who isn't privy to the cosmopolitan ways of the rest of the country. Why would Eliana invoke this classist figure?

The rest of her interview gave me another clue. I was struck by how, unable to participate in the remittance exchange, she said she touched the computer "only to clean it." This former accountant seemed to be metaphorically aligning herself with a common occupation for uneducated Brazilian women, that of a domestic, at the same time as her joking invocation of *anarfa* emphasized her own middle-class status. The need to bolster this position when faced with questions about her digital literacy seemed to arise precisely because the laptop called this status into question. She felt unable to bring her history of privileged print literacy to bear on this literacy technology. Instead of learning to use the expensive remittance object, Eliana cleaned it, labor that did not fully pay the interpersonal debt incurred with the expensive gift. While labor migrants across the board sent home writing remittances as material and economic investments in transnational relationships, that investment, in this case, had not yet born fruit.

As a result, Eliana felt powerless to ameliorate the absence of her brother. The *saudades* could not be killed. Of the occasions when her children helped her turn on the computer, she said, "I find that when we see each other [over video chat], girl, I get so upset. I end up with increased *saudades* . . . the sadness of seeing each other, but not being able to be close." Such mediated communication, while perhaps better than nothing and certainly better in this case than the post ("No letters; not one . . . just writing on the back of photos," she told me of the written dimension of their postal correspondence), nonetheless emphasized the bodily absence of a close relative, the absence that is one of the defining features of transnational migration. By highlighting this absence, video chat seemed to strip her of the cultural capital she had acquired as an educated, middle-class homemaker, who might otherwise be enjoying a place physically in the middle of an extended family. For Eliana, this loss was symbolized by the frequently dusted laptop remitted by her brother with money he earned working in a bakery in Boston.

Experiences of migration-driven literacy learning across changing print and digital technologies were uneven. On one hand, Eliana's and Maria's stories seem to suggest that digital writing remittances have the potential to upend the associations between literacy and social class that prevailed during the reign of print. In this reading, as a result of their interactions with writing remittances Maria, with a second-grade education, became more literate, and Eliana, with a college degree, became less literate, reversing seemingly fixed social orders. But print and digital literacy, as ideological and contextual constructs, do not have a priori effects on social positions.[37] That is, literacy and social class do not determine each other. Rather, as Eliana's and Maria's stories have illustrated, class-based ideologies of literacy and the material realities of stratified access to literacy often interact, texturing people's experiences of learning (or not) to write in new ways to negotiate transnational family life. In this sense, Eliana's self-description as *anarfa* speaks not to the effects of writing remittances in themselves, but more poignantly to the anxieties they can symbolize—anxieties about how to maintain social standing, how to secure one's footing, in a world spinning with the movement of people and technologies.

At their core, what these accounts of transitions among print and digitality reveal is how migration-driven literacy learning operated within the larger capitalist logic of scarcity that undergirds global labor migration: what seemed distant and unattainable for some appeared close and easily attainable for others; what was difficult for some was seemingly effortless for others. Writing remittances' emotional value for those who spoke with me lay precisely in these shifting terms of which literacy resources were scarce, which were abundant, and for whom. One returned migrant, a frequent video chatter, agreed with Hugo that personal letters required more effort to write, "like the person is really thinking of you," making them seem "more intimate." But letters did not actually objectively require more effort than synchronous video chat (just ask Eliana), nor did they objectively signal more care. Rather, the emotional resonance of writing remittances, as objects born of labor migration, resided in people's perception of the labor that they entailed—whether that labor was expended in the buying of a writing remittance or in the act of writing itself.

In the stories people shared with me, literacy's changing materialities, the stratified economic circumstances of its circulation, and passionate interpersonal longing all flooded moments of migration-driven literacy learning, sometimes keeping writing remittance circuits coursing across borders, and at other times shorting them out.

## INVESTING WRITING REMITTANCES: AN ASPIRATIONAL VIEW AMONG WOMEN AND MEN

While the receipt of a writing remittance did not autonomously transform people's educational trajectories, writing remittances also did not remain hermeneutically sealed within family circles. Literacy, after all, is a social and human resource that travels. People adapt it, appropriate it, riff on it, build from it, compose with it to meet their goals. Against the backdrop of the rapidly digitizing and newly prosperous Brazil of the early 2000s, then, some people took up writing remittances as one resource, among many literacy resources, that could help them reach their professional aims—albeit in ways that reflected gender and class stratification. In the hands of some savvy homeland family members, such as readers saw with Hugo, transnational literacy remittances could be transformed into local resources. In addition to sustaining love, writing remittances appeared to also be able to help people make money.

To understand in more detail how the local investment of writing remittances can work, consider Felipe, the man who readers will recall sent cash to his brother enfolded in letters. Felipe was from a lower-middle-class family. While he aspired to become an engineer and the first in his family to complete a bachelor's degree, he faced some significant financial challenges to attending university. In Brazil, public universities are both free and also prestigious, which would seem to an outsider to bode well for Felipe's chances of attaining his dream, despite his family's modest circumstances. Unfortunately, admission to these free and highly regarded public universities is class-biased: the highly competitive entrance exams favor the well-off, who often pay for years of private preparation to ensure their success. Felipe knew early on that he would need to have, in his words, "um outro caminho," another path to becoming an engineer.

Felipe's migration-driven literacy learning did not single-handedly catapult him into a dream job or a large house. His brother's migration played a more subtle—but still important—role in his class mobility, helping him establish social status, augment his technological know-how, and move forward. When his brother migrated to Europe, and then later to the United States in the late 1990s, as readers will recall, their early communication was via letters. Soon, however, partly as a result of his own career ambitions, he was able to communicate with his brother via the Internet. Focused on his goal of finding *um outro caminho* to becoming an engineer, Felipe, neither desperately poor nor well off, had managed to save money to buy a used computer for what he described as research purposes. He took the hard drive apart. Then he put it back together. But there were things about computers he didn't know—things that his brother's migration put directly into his line of vision.

It was this desire to communicate, motivated by love for his elder brother—the one who stepped in front of him when a sandal flew out of his father's hands in punishment, the one who he worried was going hungry abroad, the one who was always a step ahead, forging new paths for himself, this time through leaving home—that indirectly contributed to Felipe's upward social mobility.

Consider the following chain of migration-driven literacy events. In the late 1990s, Felipe's brother suggested that they communicate through ICQ chat. A dial-up Internet connection was still expensive for Felipe then, so he chatted only with his brother, and generally only for urgent matters. As his used laptop became insufficient for the project of communication, his brother sent him a remitted laptop. At the same time, Felipe enrolled in an English-language school, in part to more fully understand the cultural context in which his brother was enmeshed in the United States. Though he continued to speak to his brother in their native Portuguese, he also wanted to read greeting cards sent from the United States and understand song lyrics his brother shared with him and that played on Brazilian radio stations. There was also another reason for Felipe to learn English: the scientific reports he was beginning to read for his engineering degree were published in English, and he wanted to keep up with new developments, to be in the know. His brother's migration to the United States, then, coincided with a larger globalizing reality in which Felipe saw English as linked to upward mobility.

As it turns out, Felipe used the remitted knowledge of ICQ chat to contribute to his goals. One day at the English school in Jaú, he noticed that one of the school's directors was having trouble using ICQ, a new technology at the time. He peeked over her shoulder and asked if she'd like some help. She did. In return, she gave him private classes in English. As he put it, "It was a way of us helping each other." The private English classes, gifted in exchange for the remitted knowledge of ICQ chat, and learned in part on a remitted laptop, did not make Felipe fluent in English. But they served their purpose: he used English to play music, to understand the culture in which his brother was enmeshed (his sentences in our interview often started knowledgably with, *Over there in the United States . . .*), and to access the knowledge about engineering that, along with a punishing schedule of full-time work and late night studying, helped him complete his degree and eventually earned him a job teaching at a technical college. In a follow-up interview, in which I visited his modest home where he lived with his wife and two dogs, it became clear to me that his standard of living had risen above that of his parents, and perhaps of his brother, whom he described as still struggling to make ends meet in the United States.

In sum, ICQ chat and the U.S.-purchased laptop, as writing remittances, helped open wider a door Felipe had already cracked. His growing familiarity with English, in turn, facilitated his engineering-oriented computer research, an activity that he reported engaging in daily throughout his later years as a college student and, at the time of our last interview, as a teacher at a technical school responsible for staying up-to-date with innovations in his field. In a local professional context, in which understanding English and conducting Internet-based research were increasingly important skills, Felipe took up writing remittances as one literacy resource among the many he used to shape his future. For Felipe (like for Hugo), investing writing remittances advantaged him in competitive professional realms that, more and more, demanded digital fluency. The remitted laptop now sat on his desk, webcam atop, used for both work-related research and transnational communication with his brother, for both love and money.

To be clear, I am not suggesting that technology from supposedly more developed destination countries "saved" Hugo, Felipe, or others from poverty or stalled mobility. For Hugo, readers will recall, while technological knowledge flowed from the Global North to the Global South (from France to Brazil, via his own experiences and his sister's remittances), it also flowed from the Global South to the Global North (from Brazil to the United States, via his help desk call center), likely attendant with more complex circuits of exchange than my fieldwork captured. And for Felipe, writing remittances were part of the larger wave of technological and scientific advances experienced by many professional Brazilians and that he actively pursued as part of his project of social class mobility. Writing remittance practices acted on homeland residents' local material circumstances, but they did not autonomously transform them. They were one kind of literacy resource in a larger field of sometimes abundant and sometimes scarce local literacy resources. They could supplement the time, money, and energy participants had already invested in their literacy educations, sometimes offering an outside advantage that provided a leg up.

Like other kinds of investments, however, writing remittances perhaps most benefited those in favorable social positions, namely those ascribed by gender. It was no accident that Hugo and Felipe, both young middle-class men, were able to profitably invest them. For some women, remittances worked differently. Some women pointed out that the writing remittance of video chat highlighted their inability to speak with younger relatives born abroad who had limited Portuguese skills, thus eating away at their literacy-infused status as competent (female) members of their extended families who were often expected to fulfill the gendered labor of caring and communication. Writing remittances from abroad interacted with local professional and social pressures to learn new and often foreign literacies, bringing into relief what some women perceived as their own literacy shortcomings. They described feeling left behind, not only by their family members but also by global technological and linguistic trends.

In the stories people shared with me, writing remittances coincided with pressures to accumulate new literacy skills. When invested well, by people in favorable social positions, writing remittances could provide some advantages in local and international economies. At the same time, their very presence in the lives and living rooms of those in less favorable social positions could emphasize global literacy inequality and could work to devalue existing literacy skills. In the midst of the rapid global movement of other people and their writing, literate technologies of connection could also be reminders of separation.

## STAYING CLOSE WHILE TRAVELING FAR: SOME ANSWERS AND SOME QUESTIONS

This prismatic view of writing remittances has offered variations—gendered and classed, print and digital—on how writing remittances were (and were not) taken up among the Brazilian family members and returned migrants with whom I spoke. For many, writing remittances formed a crucial piece of how families remained close despite distance, demanding literacy learning as a tacit condition of their exchange. For those who could participate in migration-driven literacy learning circuits, and for those who were appropriately socially positioned, these literacy resources could be reinvested to meet local goals. As people fused the labor they perceived writing remittances required with the feelings of intimacy such remittances afforded, they continued to write, emphasizing how love and money can interanimate each other in material sites of real-world communication. What, after all, could be more motivating than money and love?

While the concerns of love and money may appear to be only personal or only familial, the kinds of critical awareness of inequality required to engage in a writing remittance circuit is not. In this sense, writing remittances can be seen as one piece of the larger context of composition-oriented, forward-looking media literacy education in Brazil. Such education, as shown by a nationwide survey of 240 out-of-school digital literacy programs, by and large emphasizes content production—in other words, writing.[38] This content production, the survey shows, is aimed at a kind of social empowerment that involves both creative and critical capacities, in which one learns, in the words of digital literacy scholar Fantin, "através *das mídias,* com *ou* sobre *elas,*" that is, *through* media (think Felipe), *with* media (think Hugo), and *about* media (think Maria).[39] These efforts at critical digital literacy may also include *creating* media via coding.[40] And here I think of Felipe again, taking apart a laptop. Putting it back together. In other words, what is being learned in the seemingly private sphere of transnational family literacy resonates with, and can perhaps serve, the broader social and educational aims of developing a digitally empowered populace.

At the same time, the transnational literacy learning site of the family has its own unique social potential. Developed in family networks that stretch across borders, writing remittances involve a set of practices, materials, and relationships that flow underneath the eyes of the state. Given recent Brazilian history, namely the military dictatorship that suppressed speech, transnational writing can be seen as a site of resistance—if not to the (now defunct) dictatorship, then perhaps to the terms of global labor inequality that, in a moment of neoliberal economic policies, promote migration in the first place.[41] As the military-era protest song "Cotidiano," "The Everyday," intones, "All day I think of being able to stop / at mid-day I only think of saying no / and then I think of the life I am leading / and I shut my mouth full of beans." Beans, that staple of the Brazilian diet that sustains families as they gather at midday for lunch, recalls the moment of transnational awareness when Felipe decided to send money along with letters to his brother.[42] Viewed as a response to the digital and economic stratification that often strips opportunity from the Brazilian lower classes, writing remittances symbolize the critical and creative power that can be activated in transnational family literacy.[43]

Seeing this glimpse of writing remittances' social and educational potential in Jaú raises more, as yet unanswered questions: First, how might writing remittances function for children? It is perhaps significant that the youngest person with whom I spoke in Brazil, Maya (age twenty), was the only participant whose migrant relative was a generation older, and also the only person *not* to have reported learning a new communication practice associated with migration. Second, this chapter examined a largely middle-class community with moderate emigration. How might writing remittances be experienced in communities more profoundly marked by mass emigration? And finally, Brazil in 2011 was a fairly stable, if class-stratified democracy. What might migration-driven literacy learning look like in communities where political change is more recent, more present, more widely felt?

I address these questions in the next chapter, set in Europe, in a community hard hit by outmigration. There, two and a half years after my work in Brazil, I reconnected with the community I lived with as a young woman in the Peace Corps to examine how transnational families wrote for love and money in a quite different context.

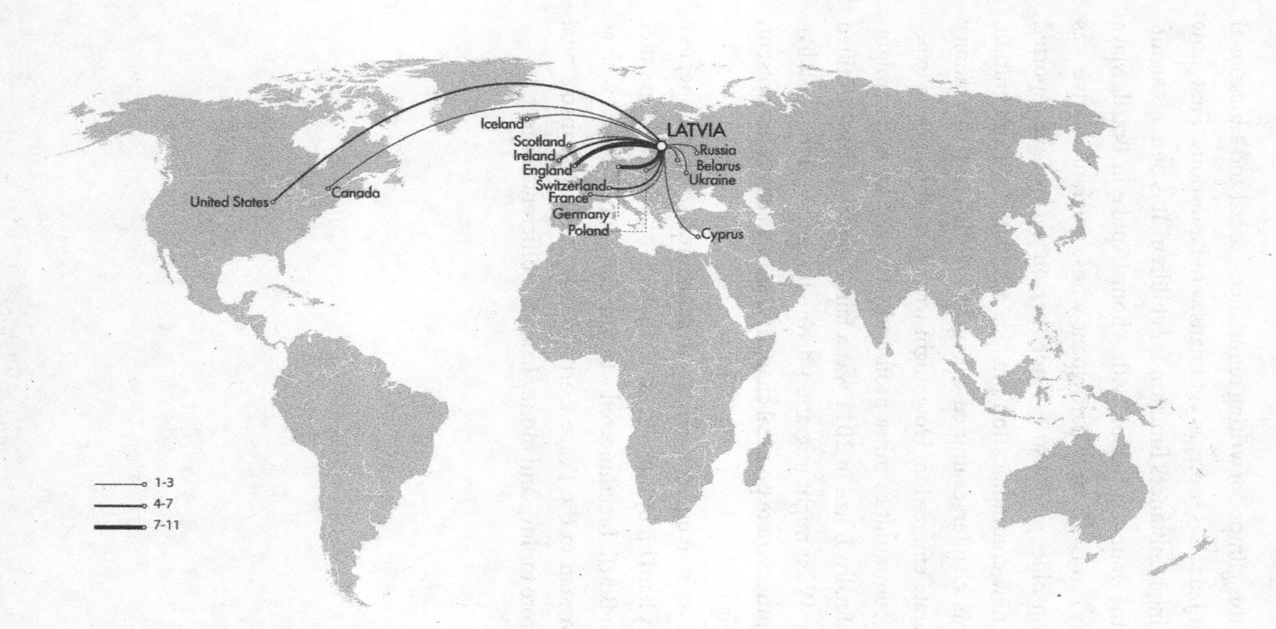


Map 4.1 Migration and literacy trajectories of participants and/or their family members in Latvia

Chapter 4

# Learning Languages

## *From Soviet Union to European Union in Latvia*

"Kate, wow!" Katrina says in the English she must have learned in the fifteen years since I have last seen her. My daughter, five, and I have just arrived in Latvia's capital city of Riga, where we are staying with a friend to shake off our jet lag before the journey by train to Daugavpils, the next field site for this study of migration-driven literacy learning. My daughter has spent the morning vomiting, and amid my panic at the fact that I neglected to purchase international health insurance, I remembered that during the years I was back in the States Katrina, my former Russian tutor's daughter, has become a doctor and moved to Riga. She picked up her phone after one ring and arrived within the hour.

"Wow," I say back.

I remember Katrina as an adolescent from my Peace Corps days, when she often accompanied her mother on outings with the foreigners: a family of missionaries from Texas who gave free "English camps" using the New Testament as a text and whose red-white-and-blue sprinkled cupcakes, shipped direct from Houston, I ate one Fourth of July; an NGO worker from Denmark, who rented a large apartment downtown with a bathtub in the middle of the living room and who claimed a superior knowledge of wine; and a radical journalist from the United Kingdom who told of having been illiterate until the age of eighteen and who knew twenty different ways to fry bread. Katrina's mother taught this motley crew the Russian names for local trees and corrected our case declensions, while Katrina, bright eyes and cheerful disposition, remained observant. I often wondered what, if anything, Katrina was gleaning from these early experiences with foreign language learners. It was only after she spoke with me about her literacy history and shared her practices with me that I identified my misplaced Western egotism. We were but a blip on Katrina's larger transnational screen.

For Katrina, transnational literacy stretched back to well before the Peace Corps arrived in Latvia. Migration-driven literacy learning began for her in early childhood, when she moved from Russia to Latvia as a preschooler under the Soviet Union, joining the many other families from Belarus, Ukraine, and Russia who were relocated there for work in its railroad industry, its educational institutions, and the military. Separated for the first time from her grandparents, who remained in a village outside of Moscow, she learned to write letters to them in Russian. Migration-driven literacy learning continued for Katrina during her adolescence, which coincided with the financially punishing years of postindependence, when she learned to write emails to her closest aunt, who had migrated to Italy and had sent her a writing remittance—her first laptop. Finally, migration-driven literacy learning also stretched ahead, into her future, as by the end of my fieldwork in Latvia, disgusted with the working conditions for doctors and demoralized by the fallout of the 2009 global recession, she decided to leave, taking advantage of Latvia's 2004 accession to the European Union to seek work as an anesthesiologist in Germany. In preparing to migrate, she joined many other Latvians in learning the language of the country that would become her new home. Spanning Latvia's transition from Soviet to independent to EU member state, Katrina's migration-driven literacy learning represents how many ordinary Latvians wrote for love and for money both across geographical space and also across time, in relation to the changing borders that characterized their historical moment.

In the early summer of 2014, though, Katrina has not yet migrated. And I am grateful. She washes her hands and moves to my daughter, who is glassy-eyed on the couch clutching a stuffed bunny. As she examines tongue, ears, eyes, skin, Katrina speaks to her in low, soft tones, then calls in a colleague who specializes in pediatrics. When my daughter can finally keep down liquids, Katrina and her colleague say goodbye, gifting her a stethoscope.

## DEMOGRAPHIC DISASTER IN DAUGAVPILS

Despite the many gifts Katrina had to give Latvia, it was no surprise that she, along with so many others, was preparing to migrate. At the time of my fieldwork in 2014, Latvia was politically whiplashed and economically devastated. In 1991 the country had gone from a Soviet republic to a struggling independent country plagued by corruption. In 2004, its citizens voted in favor of European Union membership, and Latvia found itself in a short-lived period of prosperity: people renovated bathrooms on credit and traded in their Soviet-era Ladas for, in some cases, BMWs. But soon the 2009 global economic crisis thundered in, leaving Latvians facing large-scale unemployment and bringing the brief honeymoon to a halt.

In response, many people migrated. As members of the EU, Latvians could legally work in more prosperous European countries. So, among other destinations, many left for England, Ireland, and Germany. Once abroad, they often temporarily gave up their previous professions, such as interpreter, teacher, engineer, or journalist, for the factory work, house cleaning, and construction jobs that made use of a different skill set, and that allowed them to send remittances home.[1] According to Latvian economists, during this period a full 14.5% of the population left Latvia. It was a "demographic disaster."[2]

This rapid increase in outmigration represented a stark change from the Daugavpils I knew and loved when I lived there as a Peace Corps volunteer. In 1999 Daugavpils was poor and troubled, yet the city thrummed with the hope that things could be better: There was always a crush of people in the markets and on the streets, and many residents, including my colleagues and friends in the schools and NGOs, were innovating—writing grants, seeking out local and international collaborations, developing educational programs, and generally working, with appetite and heart and resourcefulness, for change.

In 2014, when I returned for fieldwork, the city was, indeed, changed—though in ways different than we had envisioned fifteen years earlier. Infused with EU money, the streets were cleaner and sleeker. The Geiger counter that once sat atop the concrete gray Hotel Latvia in the city's center had been removed, and the hotel had been redone in curving sparkling glass. It gleamed. But it was unclear whom the changes served. The streets felt empty, apartments stood vacant, and, unlike in 2001, I did not have to elbow my way off or onto the city's trams. The population had visibly thinned.

## BRAIN DRAIN?

The loss of skilled workers caused—*is causing*—problems: separated families, the devaluation of Latvian educational degrees, the gap in Latvian civil society of working-age adults whose ingenuity is needed for the country to, yet again, rebuild. Such loss cannot be understated. Emigration has entailed undeniably negative social consequences, leading many to worry over the educational fallout.[3] Unlike in Brazil, where outmigration was low, brain drain in Latvia, with its high emigration rates, was of widespread concern. While some hoped for return migration, and the potentially increased human capital that migrants might bring home, the community had yet to reap such benefits. Sparsely populated classrooms, unemployed teachers, and quiet streets were causing despair. Many labeled this despair "brain drain."

Brain drain can be a useful, macro-level concept, which, despite the problematic conceptual separation of migrants' "brains" from their "bodies" that I discussed in this book's introduction, nonetheless speaks to how certain kinds of intellectual resources are often inequitably distributed across the globe.[4] But this concept, along with its more optimistic cousins, "brain gain" and "brain circulation," is steeped in the discourse of formal educational attainment, with the result that other kinds of learning are often hidden from view.[5] Ironically, it is often precisely this other, less institutionally visible, more informal "educational work" that globalizing processes such as migration can foster.[6] As educational ethnographer Karen Valentin has put it, the "social and geographical space of migration" can itself be a learning environment.[7]

Such learning environments, shot through with the potential (if not the lived experience) of mobility, lend themselves in particular to the learning of literacy. Far from locally circumscribed, as it was once theorized, literacy is now often understood as a material and embodied semiotic resource that travels with and without people.[8] While literacy's mobility did not make up for Daugavpils's profound communal loss, its potential to move and be adapted did contribute to a transnational sense of community that in some cases facilitated creative solutions to persistent problems. Latvians made use of literacy's mobility in ways that were profoundly integrative—of here and there, of family and individual, of past and present, of body and mind. Which is to say, they did not offer their or their family members' brains wholesale to the West. Rather, to meet the widespread challenges of familial separation and economic inequity—challenges that dogged Latvians in different ways under the country's various political formations—Latvians worked to enhance their literacy and language capacities in ways they hoped would serve them and their families both at home and abroad.

## WRITING ACROSS CHANGING BORDERS

In part because of the way migration infused the Daugavpils community as a whole, and in part because of Latvians' histories with politically driven migration, writing remittances looked different in Latvia than they looked in Brazil—which called my attention to new dimensions of the phenomenon of migration-driven literacy learning. Specifically, Latvians' migration-driven writing, Katrina and others helped me to see, could not be understood in a static context through which people and literacy moved. It had to also be understood in a context that was itself mobile—even for those who stayed (spatially speaking) put.

To conceptualize the shifting temporal dimensions of transnational literacy learning, I was helped by the work of linguistic anthropologists Maria Clara Keating and Olga Solovova, who have shown how language-learning changes in relation to "particular meetings of histories" in situations of unstable national borders.[9] Their key insight, grounded in the work of Dorothy Holland and Jean Lave, is that the history of institutions and the history of individual people "come together, again and again . . . not only in the face of changing material and social circumstances, but also in the changing terms of culturally produced forms," such as, I would add, *literacy*.[10] That is, people and their literacies were moving not only *across* time and space, but also *with* time and space, as people adapted past practices to accommodate present change.[11] As borders were re-drawn, writing practices were revised.[12]

This interplay between the movement of people and the movement of larger social processes is a hallmark of globalization, forming part of what globalization scholar Anna Tsing names "friction," a "force that produces movement, action, effect," such as, I would add (again), *learning*.[13] Across a shifting Latvian terrain, transnational families engaged in literacy retraining, seeking to supplement the languages and literacies they acquired in former regimes with those of new ones, and leveraging such practices to fulfill their aspirations. In this process, they drew from intergenerational experiences of past migrations and worked to imagine migratory futures.

My analysis of Latvians' experiences—experiences marked by recent historical changes that touched the community as a whole—builds on the more materialist understandings of migration-driven literacy Brazilian community members helped me develop. To the argument made in the previous chapter that writing remittances can unite transnational families in an economic and emotional exchange, I add that the pedagogical experiences promoted by such exchanges often gain force, meaning, and urgency from the historical and contemporary political challenges that people use literacy to meet.

In what follows, readers will see more of how Latvia's political transitions over time shape experiences of migration-driven literacy learning. Based on twenty-seven literacy history interviews and in-depth fieldwork, this chapter documents three kinds of migration-driven literacy learning in Latvia, all linked to the political shifts of the country's recent past. (I invite interested readers to see appendix B for more detailed methods and for tables that offer an aerial snapshot of findings across participants.) Specifically, under the Soviet regime, community members wrote letters eastward to maintain contact with family members dispersed to faraway republics, engaging in *print literacy learning*. When Latvia gained membership in the European Union, which opened borders to labor migration in Western member states, these literacy networks, rooted in the East, shifted westward. Here, Latvians took up *digital literacy practices* to sustain transnational family relationships across shifting borders. Further, the dire employment outlook of the post-2009 recession fostered *anticipatory literacy learning*, as potential migrants stockpiled languages and literacies to prepare for what seemed to be their inevitable eventual migration westward. That is, they learned literacy in new languages to reunite with loved ones already abroad and/or in the hopes of making better lives. These three kinds of community-based literacy practices both resulted from and allowed community members to respond to a social context that was itself mobile.

I proceed here chronologically, using participants' memories (and some of my own) to show how migration-driven literacy learning shifted from the Soviet Union to Latvian independence to the EU.

## LETTERS FROM LATVIA: MIGRATION-DRIVEN PRINT LITERACY IN SOVIET TIMES

Under the job-placement programs of the Soviet Union, many engaged with a transnational literacy institution that predates the Internet: the postal system. The post office was where people waited in line to make special birthday phone calls to those in distant republics and to write telegrams. But just as important to participants, it was also where they sent letters. In fact, letter writing during Soviet times was mentioned as a central way to keep in touch with loved ones by twenty-five out of the twenty-seven people with whom I spoke. Like for the letter writers in Thomas and Znaniecki's *The Polish Peasant*, and like for the Brazilians in the previous chapter, for Soviet-era Latvians, letters mediated the emotions that accompany transnational movement.[14] Motivated by *toska*—the Russian word meaning "longing" or "missing," a rough equivalent of the Portuguese *saudades*—people wrote to maintain connections with family separated by distance, practices that they later adapted to the digital, capitalist environment of the European Union.

## *Letters from Katrina*

Consider, first, Katrina's narrative of Soviet-era, migration-driven print literacy learning. I interviewed Katrina when she was in Daugavpils visiting her mother. We sat in a hip café directly across from the newly renovated Hotel Latvia. As Katrina walked me through her literacy education in Soviet Russia and then Latvia, I couldn't help but think of the hotel's location just at the end of what used to be called (and by some still was) Lenin Street. At the end of that street, I had been told, once stood the statue of "Uncle Lenin," whose encouragement to "study, study, and study once more!" was repeated by schoolchildren in both Russian and Latvian throughout the republic. It was that past regime, largely erased from the landscape, that informed some of Katrina's earliest literacy memories.

Born in 1986 in a small town in Soviet Russia, Katrina's first home was with her grandparents, who cared for her as her mother finished her degree in Moscow. At the age of six, Katrina was reunited with her mother, who had completed her studies in Russian literature and was being relocated to Daugavpils, Latvia, where she would teach in the local pedagogical institute. This move marked Katrina's first experience with migration—and also with migration-driven literacy learning.

Katrina described writing letters to compensate for bodily separation—one of migration's central problems for transnational families.[15]

> I wrote to my grandparents a lot, because when I moved, it was really a major trauma for me, because imagine, I spent six years with them. And I loved them so much and they loved me so much. . . . We were always together. And then just one day, they just picked me up and placed me in a completely foreign country for me at that time. Everything was so different here [in Latvia]. In Russia it was okay for me to, I don't know, kiss my grandparents, to cuddle with them all the time. And here it was different. . . . I felt kind of lonely maybe. . . . And so I wrote letters—not daily, but very, very often.

She missed her previous guardians' physical warmth, their cuddles and kisses, and attempted to reconstitute this sense of familial intimacy by describing day-to-day activities in letters. Letters became a material location where distant family members could not cuddle but could, at least, commune. While bodies could not travel easily, letters could, leading Katrina to write "very, very often."

An imperfect replacement for everyday familial interactions, writing was nonetheless the only frequently accessible communication option, which for Katrina and her grandparents elevated the importance of correctness in written expression, leading to Katrina's home-based Russian literacy instruction. While her Latvian kindergarten emphasized Latvian, an Indo-European language that uses the Roman alphabet, her family network depended on her learning Slavic Cyrillic Russian. Her grandfather, she said, was "very, very sad that [she] couldn't write in Russian properly." He asked that before posting her letters, she give them to her mother to correct, "because he was very sad . . . because he loved the Russian language very much."

As part of a family effort to sustain relationships across borders, Katrina was taught to scratch out grammatically appropriate letters in Cyrillic. Even as she was learning Latvian formally, she was also engaged in informal learning, the knowledge and resources of which circulated throughout a family-based literacy network that stretched from her Russian-based grandparents to her Latvian-based mother, and of which she was a crucial connective, and productive, node.

## *Letters, Families, and the State*

Across the stories people shared with me in Daugavpils, these informal print-literacy-producing networks took different forms, though at their core, all aimed at linking family dispersed by the demands of the Soviet Union. One Ukrainian-born Latvian woman recalled the community literacy event of reading letters from her aunt in Russia:

> We would all get together, it was interesting, and it wasn't even only our family. For example, there were neighbors, because this aunt came to us in the summer for a rest. She knew everyone. And in that letter there was some kind of message or hello for everyone.

In contrast to the sociality of such community letter reading, letter writing could be solitary. In an interview with three cousins, two of whom had husbands working in construction in Ireland, one woman recalled composing poems to include in letters to distant family. Living in a communal apartment at the time, she appreciated the moments alone that writing provided. While she and many others read and wrote with pleasure, still others found writing laborious. Her cousin disliked writing to such an extent that she copied the same letter (with different names) to her three different boyfriends, all in faraway republics. (She ended up marrying one of them—talk about writing for love!)

Whether writing was considered laborious or entertaining, solitary or communal, most agreed on the importance of letter writing for communication during Soviet times. "Yes," said the third interviewee in the group of cousins, munching on a pork filled *pirogi* that the two women had laid out in advance of our interview, "I kept all the letters written to me while I served in the army. I don't know why. There's just something. Something special there." As he spoke, as if in response, their house pet, a small blue bird that had previously been perched on a branch suspended from the ceiling, alighted on my daughter's head. *People are not birds,* I thought, mimicking the syntax and rhythm of the Russian aphorisms I had come to love. (Here's a good one from my hairdresser: *Hair is not a tooth. It grows back.*) *People are not birds. They cannot fly.* But letters do, and from their flight, people experienced connection.

Despite these contrasts in individual experiences in letter writing, for those with whom I spoke, the process of reading and writing letters brought together communities, families, lovers. As such, letter writing served as a literacy-laden cultural and material response to the pressures of state-driven familial separation. While correspondence was taught in schools, and while schools even organized pen-pal partnerships across the varying republics, letter writing remained centrally located in families, who undergirded school-based literacy learning with writing for love.

In such scenes of family letter writing, the state was, with varying visibility, always present. In fact, often letter writers were acutely aware that their letters were simultaneously responding to the top-down demands of the government and to the human desire to connect with people separated by that government. Such a negotiation was evident in the account of one woman, an engineer, who described her mother writing a letter to Soviet officials to free her uncle, who had been jailed in Siberia as an enemy of the state. In her case, the letter worked its magic. Her uncle was freed. A similar articulation among letters, the state, and separated family appeared in the account of a teacher, an ethnic Latvian whose aunt had fled the

Soviet Union after World War II and had made a home in New York. During the Soviet regime, this participant received letters from her aunt in New York that were heavily censored. Envelopes had been opened. Words were blacked out. If the materiality of letters on one hand afforded connection, their censorship also spoke to the communicative limitations of literacy materials that had to traverse a state apparatus to reach their intended recipients. In short, for these letter writers, using literacy to negotiate family separation also meant using literacy to contend with state sponsored repression—especially in the realm of speech.

In letters, state politics and family relationships bled into each other, with writers addressing both the infrastructural and interpersonal exigencies of their socio-historical moments. In this way, migration drove print literacy use and learning, lending shape and meaning to the written correspondence—from granddaughter to grandfather, from lovers to one another, from niece to aunt, from citizen to state—that circulated through the dispersed family networks of the Soviet Union.

## DIGITAL LITERACY LEARNING: FROM INDEPENDENCE TO THE EUROPEAN UNION

When Latvia was liberated in 1991, people continued to communicate with family in the former Soviet republics, but migration, and the literacy practices that accompanied it, shifted both geographically and technologically. Geographically, the borders of Latvia were redrawn. It was now an independent nation that would later join the EU, creating new political alliances and migration trajectories that would urge migration-driven literacy learning in new directions. Technologically, literacy was also changing. As one community member, an education professor at a local university whose son had migrated to Canada, told me, "When the Soviet Union ended, we stopped writing letters." Letter writing did not halt completely, of course. Like in Brazil, it simply came to be valued differently as new digital technologies became more prevalent. Still, others echoed this sentiment, speaking to how Latvian independence, the crumbling of the Soviet Union, and increased migration to the West under the EU were experienced as synchronous with changing communication technologies that necessitated new kinds of learning.

Just as the directives of the centralized Soviet government structured community members' print literacy use and learning, this new capitalist reorientation westward structured migration-driven *digital* literacy learning.[16] Like in the Brazilian context, here migrants laboring abroad invested in writing technologies and sent them home, in an economic and emotional exchange of literacy, love, and learning. Such literacy remittance objects crossed geographical and temporal contexts, becoming "recontextualized," to use the language of sociolinguist Catherine Kell, in new spaces and moments.[17] As transnational family members put finger to touch screen and hand to mouse, Latvians described adapting migration-driven literacy practices initiated under Soviet state-mandated migration programs to the new kinds of family separation brought on, this time, by Western capitalism.

### *Writing Remittances during the "Awful Years": Katrina Learns to Write an Email*

Participants were full of stories of the difficulties of independence, what they called the *zhutki godi,* the awful years. Boots were stolen from inside people's apartments. Hoodlums showed up on doorsteps asking for money and threatening children. And one participant recalled her shock at seeing a "bum" for the first time postindependence. "In the Soviet Union," she said, "you couldn't not work." And then she repeated the phrase—*you couldn't not work*—the double negative being the only way, it seemed, to come to terms with the unemployment and homelessness many faced during early independence. Latvians had a joke to describe these awful years: "During the Soviet Union, we had money but no goods. After it ended, we had goods, but no money."

The difficulties during this period were compounded for many in Daugavpils by new language and citizenship laws, which forced many of the city's Russian-speakers out of public-sector jobs and into a new minority status. Between 1940 and independence, 1.5 million people had come to Latvia from other Soviet republics. At independence, about half returned, leaving the other half to attempt to integrate into a Latvia where citizenship was not defined by birth within the country's borders but instead by bloodline and language and civics tests—a kind of governance that some have called an "ethnic democracy."[18] As linguist Aneta Pavlenko has put it, Russian-speakers "woke up one morning to a political and linguistic reality not of their doing and found themselves involuntary—and at times unwelcome—migrants in what they had previously considered their own country."[19]

To be clear, my point here is not to critique the liberatory and necessary practice of Latvian language reclamation after decades of Russification and repression.[20] Rather, it is to observe that for many Russian speakers, the language laws that accompanied their new minoritized status after Latvian independence intensified what was for many an already difficult moment. I recall the side hustles of my Peace Corps host mother during the months I lived with her in 1999. An ethnic Russian home-economics teacher who was faced with learning Latvian, a language she struggled with, or losing her job, she bred exotic kittens in her one-bedroom apartment to sell Saturdays at the bazaar, and one evening modeled for me the clever multipocketed vest she had invented to cart beauty products for sale across the Russian border. According to Latvian economists, this kind of ethnically inflected economic desperation since independence has promoted the migration of Latvian Russian speakers at a higher rate than that of others, in part explaining Daugavpils's high emigration rate.[21]

Such economic desperation, political instability, and technological change acted across the former Soviet republics during this moment of transition, all contributing to how Katrina, whom readers will recall learned to write letters in Russian via her grandparents, learned to write an email—this time to an aunt. Katrina's "favorite" aunt was working in a chemical scientific laboratory in Moscow, living in, in Katrina's words, "devastating" poverty. She accepted a contract to work as a pharmacist in Switzerland in 1994 and soon thereafter moved to Italy. At first, Katrina exchanged letters with her aunt, receiving postcards of "beautiful places, like the Swiss Alps."

Soon, though, they came to write emails. Katrina sent her first email to her aunt, which said, "I'm officially stating this is my first email." And soon thereafter, her aunt sent Katrina her first computer, a Macintosh, which she used to prepare school reports, though she did not initially have an Internet connection at home. The impulse to write an email and the possibility of using a computer for homework were underwritten, both financially and emotionally, by a transnational familial connection that, in part as a result of post-Soviet poverty, now extended toward the West.

In contrast with the Soviet-era letter writing mediated by a socialist state, such digital literacy practices were shaped by the demands of free market labor. Katrina's aunt was offered more money abroad and then left, allowing her the financial heft to purchase a computer to send to Katrina. This writing remittance solidified and helped to maintain an interpersonal connection, both through the act of giving and through the potential of the technology itself to facilitate communication. At the same time, it evidenced the economic inequality that necessitated migration. The hardware and infrastructure required to communicate digitally, after all, was not cheap, especially for those living in the former Soviet republics during the *zhutki godi* of the early 1990s.

To be clear, Katrina's aunt's migration was not solely responsible for Katrina's uptake of digital literacy. In Latvia, her mother's university received Internet-connected computers in the 1990s. Likewise, Katrina recalled computers becoming common among some friends. Still, such technologies were still relatively rare even in 1999. I recall one afternoon that year, when after having mounted the steps to Daugavpils's Internet café and settled in amid the scores of sweaty adolescent boys (four heads to a video game to save money) to bang out some emails home, that the room suddenly became quiet. I was immersed in my words when I heard from somewhere behind me, "It's like she's playing the piano!" Having been shuttled into typing class in my suburban Texas public high school stateside and having used computers throughout college in the 1990s, I was touch-typing. My foreign educational background was on display.

This confluence of increasing local digital access and digital literacy's association with migration westward helped Katrina's migration-driven digital literacy take. It resonated with Katrina's longer history of transnational communication with her grandfather, forming what literacy scholars have called a "laminated" literacy activity.[22] Through this mechanism, Katrina's writing an email to a distant aunt reverberated with both the past activity of writing a letter to a distant grandfather and the present buzz of Internet communication that was already connecting many Latvians to a different political reality than that into which they had been born.

### *Reorienting Westward under the EU: Pensioners Learn to Log On*

Katrina was not the only one for whom migration promoted digital literacy learning. Especially as migration increased under the EU, migrants' remitting of communication technologies and practices across changing borders necessitated an expansion of literacy repertoires at home. During my fieldwork in 2014, out of twenty-three family members of migrants I interviewed, eighteen described receiving laptops, webcams, mobile phones, and/or new knowledge about digital communication practices from loved ones living abroad. Internet connections for many were considered a modern necessity, like electricity. To pay for this extra bill, some relied on financial remittances from migrant family members, highlighting the simultaneously interpersonal and economic nature of such exchanges. As in Brazil, for the Latvians with whom I spoke both love and money were on the line in migration-driven digital literacy learning.

Such learning was especially evident among pensioners (of whom I spoke with six and regularly observed the practices of one) whose adult children's and grandchildren's migration was connected to Latvia's accession to the EU. All formally educated within the Soviet system, they described how, during independence, they engaged in a period of retraining to learn the Latvian language and often to learn a new profession (from chemist to entrepreneur, for example). Now retired under the EU, they were adapting their literacies yet again, this time not so much for employment but instead for another purpose: to communicate with faraway children. Their stories revealed their engagement in an EU-era intergenerational literacy learning circuit—a circuit I describe here from the perspectives of one parent, one grandparent, and one adult returned migrant who taught his father to type.

In what geographers Kaiser and Nikiforova have called "enacting place" in changing political environments, many Latvians seemed to have reoriented at least part of their spatial imaginations westward, a process that was on display at one gathering I attended of several pensioners, all of whom had been born outside of Latvia in other former Soviet republics.[23] Even in 2014, a full twenty-three years after independence, they pined for aspects of the Soviet Union. Two of the attendees were accustomed to making a yearly trip to Ukraine to see family, but because of the ongoing war, they were opting for the first time to instead visit their son, who lived and worked in Belgium. A third guest lamented that he could no longer drive across the border to Belarus and come back with some of that country's famous sausages—sausages that did not have the chemicals he said were added under the new EU regime. "By the way," he added (at this point in the party his arm was looped around the shoulder of one of the other guests), "anyone know where I can get a good price for my Lada?"

Shifting borders had worked to redirect the trajectories of this group of retired Latvian residents: while they still held ties to the former Soviet republics of their birth, the possible courses of movement laid out to them forced an often begrudging reappraisal of their spatial and historical location—a reappraisal that rendered the former staple of Belarussian sausages a newly rare ethnic food, a reappraisal that de-exoticized formerly unattainable Belgian chocolates, a reappraisal that required the host couple's son to Skype in from Canada earlier that morning rather than to raise a glass in person that afternoon. *Where are we?* was the question humming underneath the birthday celebration (a question perhaps highlighted by the presence of an American researcher and her daughter). Such questioning of where they were located, how they identified, and where they could and could not go shaped migration-driven literacy learning for many retirees with whom I spoke.

Consider the digital literacy learning of Lida, a retired chemist and small business owner in Latvia, and an old friend, who was part of the *dacha* (summer house) community in which I conducted part of my participant observation. Lida received a computer from her adult son, who had been working in Belgium for seven years. He brought it to her on a visit home and taught her how to turn on the Internet and log on to Skype. He wrote all the instructions in a notebook she showed me, which she kept near the computer and webcam she used to video-chat with him. After the brief lesson, her son told her she had to learn on her own. She complied: she read a book on computer basics and took a computer course for pensioners. Fluent in Internet-based social networking and communication by the time of my fieldwork, she showed me her *flashka,* a device she plugged into her computer at her otherwise digitally unequipped dacha to access the Internet, which her son paid for monthly, so that they could chat. During my observations, she viewed photos of the apartments he was considering buying and shared the options with me and with her neighbors. She stayed logged on and was able to offer advice ("That seems expensive"), in between watering the lettuce and attempting (and alas failing) to feed my daughter homemade *borscht.*

As we spoke with her son over the laptop sitting on the wood table in the *dacha* she and her husband had constructed by hand during Soviet times, I couldn't help but remember a moment in 1999 at that same table, looking out over the same rose bushes, when Lida, her son, her husband, and I sat around the table, face to face, eating *plov,* a filling dish of rice and meat. At that time, postindependence and pre-EU, Lida had been studying for her citizenship exam in Latvian and had been trying to make a go of her new bookstore after having been fired from her position as a city accountant when the local government let go of nonethnic Latvians. And I also couldn't help but imagine a time before that, during the Soviet Union, when according to Lida's literacy history interview, she wrote copious letters in her native Ukrainian to family back home in Ukraine until, finally, her mother joined her in Daugavpils. The wooden table, the rose bushes, the iron pot in which *plov* was baked, the solid construction of the dachá remained constant. Similarly, just down the dirt path, the Daugava River, the river that connected Daugavpils to the capital of Riga and outward to the Baltic Sea and then further westward, continued to flow. But the country's borders, and the literacies required to navigate them, had shifted, as her family had separated, reunited, and then separated again, maintaining connections with the changing technologies of literacy, presently incarnated in the remitted laptop and webcam that she used to speak with her son.

Similar to Lida, Tatyana, an elderly retired street cleaner with a high school education in her late seventies, received a writing remittance from one of her granddaughters living abroad in Ireland—a shiny iPad through which they could video-chat, a writing remittance which, again, highlighted how not only space but also time shaped migration-driven literacy learning. While many Latvians had been able to modernize their apartments following EU accession, Tatyana's apartment remained organized in the Soviet style, with a washer-bathtub combination in the bathroom and red concrete flooring throughout. In this environment, Tatyana's iPad at first seemed to me incongruous. But it wasn't for Tatyana. She had incorporated it into her daily practice as a post-Soviet grandmother active in her transnational family's life. The tablet sat plugged in on a coffee table, next to a notebook listing her password and login name. A local woman who checked in on Tatyana in the absence of her grandchildren told me that Tatyana often called her if she had technological trouble (but that she couldn't convince Tatyana to unplug the device, ever). Driven by her grandchildren's migration (one in Ireland, two in Germany), Tatyana—the oldest of the Latvian research participants at seventy-six and the one with the least amount of formal education—sought out and learned from informal digital literacy tutoring.

As young people laboring abroad taught parents and grandparents how to log on, their tutoring bridged not only generational gaps in literacy learning but also political and historical ones. This point became especially clear in my interview with Vasily, a returned migrant born in 1985. In 2014, he and his wife had just returned from the United Kingdom to Latvia, where they hoped to find more appropriate medical care for their ill infant son.

Vasily began our interview describing how he had prepped his father for international communication before he left for the United Kingdom. The story started out as what I had come to expect as a rather typical premigration, adult-child-to-parent digital-literacy tutorial:

> VASILY: We set up everything and we just simply said to him, right, you press that button, and then you go over there. You see this green button? That's the name. When this light comes up, then you can see that she's online or whatever. You can press that green button, and you can call. That's where you can switch on the camera. Basically, all like that. Then I said any problems, just restart the computer, and it's gonna pick up like that again. [*Laughter*]
>
> KATE: Just restart the computer, that's what you told him?
>
> VASILY: Yeah.
>
> KATE: Did he call you for help with it?
>
> VASILY: Sometimes. Yeah. [*Laughter*] Sometimes he called on the phone. He's quite right with them, but he couldn't type or whatever that kind of thing, right?

This method of teaching his father to use Skype on the laptop jibed with the process of migration-driven literacy learning that Lida and

Tatyana had described—and also with what many had shared with me in the interviews I had conducted three years before in Brazil.

It was his answer to a follow-up question, however, that made me see how this process of intergenerational literacy learning, what Rebecca Lorimer Leonard calls a "literacy relay," not only responded to family members' migration across space but was also experienced as intimately connected to Latvia's shifting political borders.[24]

"He couldn't type or whatever," Vasily had said during the above exchange. So I followed up:

> KATE: Why is the typing difficult but the Skyping isn't? It's just he's not used to it?
>
> VASILY: He's not used to it, yeah. Because all his life he never kinda was working with a computer or whatever. . . . It was USSR but then when the USSR fell down, there was like, we became separate, like Belarus and Latvia. So that became a border. He used to be there, and it was like a village where—because it was just after the war. It was even, as he sometimes told me the story, there was sometimes even hardly electricity and stuff like that . . . like in the villages.

Vasily's answer at first appeared to me to be a non sequitur: I asked about typing, and he responded with a history lesson that started back before Latvia's occupation by the Soviet Union. I soon realized I had simply failed at first to grasp his more nuanced historical logic: his father's typing practices could not be explained without reference to the changing borders that shaped his access to and exigency for particular writing technologies. Having grown up in an electricity-less Belarussian village, Vasily's father had lived through post–World War II impoverishment, migration to Latvia, and the fall of the Soviet Union. These events flooded scenes of contemporary intergenerational migration-driven literacy learning: electricity, war, borders, migration, computers, typing, Skype, a father, a son. That changing times demanded the flexible use of literacy was not lost on Vasily. In light of the recession and EU membership, Vasily had gone to pick strawberries in England, later gaining enough biliteracy to be promoted, and still later, as I describe in the conclusion, working to leverage his experiences abroad to make a new life for his family in Daugavpils. History was alive in these literacy-learning encounters, for both father and son.

As Vasily came to a pause in his discussion, and I moved to turn off the recorder, I looked at my daughter. We were sitting in a café, and she was occupied with a game on my iPhone. I wondered which lessons about writing the moving tide of history, economics, and politics might bring her to teach me in the future.

## *Love, Money, and Digital Literacy across Time and Space*

Readers have seen thus far how the transition from independence to the EU brought new economic and political formations that animated Latvians' migration-driven digital literacy learning. Migrant children and grandchildren, earning more money in the West than they could in Latvia, remitted expensive laptops and tablets to parents and grandparents who were subsisting on Latvia's paltry pensions. For Lida and Tatyana, these objects also exacted a price, the labor of learning how to use them to communicate. Lida went so far as to take an informal computer course to more effectively interface with the new hardware sent by her absent son. And Tatyana sought out frequent refreshers.

Like for the Brazilian women who spoke with me in the previous chapter, in Latvia the price of digital literacy learning was one paid to uphold relationships stretched across distance. Lida would have preferred her son to remain in Daugavpils ("All he has time for is work, no family," she said), and Tatyana longed for her grandchildren, showing me photos of one of her granddaughter's local wedding, carefully arranged in a pink photo book. ("They are moving back here," she told me excitedly of her granddaughter and her new husband toward the end of my fieldwork. She added with pride: "They miss home!"). Their use of such "objects of nostalgia" actualized their loved ones' presence in a context of absence.[25]

The stories Latvians shared with me also highlighted how people integrated contemporary migration-driven literacy learning into their existing literacy identities.[26] For example, Tatyana's interactions with the remitted iPad extended her otherwise print-focused family literacy activities, such as flipping through photo albums to entertain guests. In fact, during my visit she shared with me another album, this one sent to her by her other granddaughter in Germany. Across both remittance objects, the iPad and album, she practiced the identity of *babushka*, grandmother, reconfiguring that central figure in Russian childrearing to negotiate conditions of transnational separation. And Lida, who had once devotedly written letters to family in Ukraine, now routinely Skyped with them, anxiously monitoring the effect of the war with Russia on her family's neighborhood. In this way, older print-based family literacy legacies laminated newer, digital ones, offering transnational family members a rich array of practices with which to innovate in order to address their families' contemporary challenges.

At the same time, just as such practices were a continuation of some existing literacy practices, they also represented change. Historically, geographically, and culturally at the crossroads of the EU and former Soviet republics, Lida, Tatyana, and Katrina adapted their literacy practices to meet the demands of the globalizing present. As such, what activated informal digital literacy learning was not western destination countries—in fact, the inventor of the Russian social networking site Odnoklassniki (Classmates) is Latvian, and the inventor of Skype is Estonian!—but was instead the exigencies of migration itself, as a recurring historical fact whose contours changed with Latvia's borders, attendant with emotional, political, and economic turbulence.

I believe that this confluence of factors contributed to the digital fluency I witnessed in Katrina, with whom I'll end this section: in multiple encounters with Katrina, I never once saw her without her iPad, for which she checked diagnoses and medications for my daughter's vomiting, video-recorded Latvian folk dancers at a show we attended together, posted updates on Facebook, checked tram schedules, took photos, updated her blog. While her digital literacy had multiple sources and uses, migration played a crucial role in activating it across a tumultuous economic and interpersonal reality. In fact, so tightly linked were migration and literacy learning for Katrina across her lifespan that, as readers will see in the next section, she turned to writing again to help prepare her for her own migration elsewhere.

## ANTICIPATORY LITERACY LEARNING: WRITING WESTWARD IN THE EU

Shaken by the global recession and high unemployment and spurred on by increasingly mobile peer networks, many community members planned to migrate, reimagining their futures not to the East but instead to the West.[27] People prepared for their potential migration in part by amassing literacy in as many languages as possible. Some learned languages "just in case" they might migrate. One woman, who was pursuing a medical degree in Latvia and whose husband lived in Germany, preferred to stay in Daugavpils but was learning German online, on the chance her husband could not find work on his return. For some parents of migrants, a wide range of language abilities was a source of pride, speaking to their children's ability to make homes wherever necessary. One mother boasted her migrant son could speak Norwegian, Polish, English, Russian, and Latvian. And others described knowing a foreign language as the very reason for choosing particular countries. One woman said of her husband, "He took English in school, so he went to Ireland," where he worked in construction. Finally, others studied to take tests to go abroad. Such was the case with one young man, whose English literacy skills earned the top score on a competitive exam, winning him a scholarship to study in the United States. To learn these languages, people cobbled together an array of pedagogical opportunities, studying off the clock, in families, in language camps, online, with books and newspapers, and in schools.

Planned emigration, whether migrants actually migrated or not, lit a language and literacy fire in Daugavpils—a practice I came to call *anticipatory literacy learning* and that was adopted by all the self-reported potential migrants with whom I spoke (see appendix B, Table 4.2). Against the backdrop of economic instability, residents turned to the promise of language and literacy, shoring up literacy resources when other resources were in short supply. In this sense, the stories people shared with me of anticipatory literacy learning help expand on linguist Bonnie Norton's concept of "language investment," which locates motivations for language learning in learners' identities, social status, and desires for possible future affiliations.[28] For the people with whom I spoke, such investment entailed hopes that language learning would help them address widespread economic distress. They were learning new literacies, at least in part, for money.

To be clear, there was not necessarily a clear-cut immediate or long-term financial payoff to language learning—an uncertainty which jibes with the findings of sociolinguists and economists who have attempted to understand how multilingualism may benefit migrants. These scholars have shown that in some cases, knowing multiple languages, including home languages, can provide a leg up in a destination country—but that language-related advantages often depend on ethnicity and class, in which economic sector migrants work, and which scale of analysis one uses to define a "leg up."[29] In other words, the value of multilingualism depends on multiple contextual factors. Still, whether or not anticipatory language learning ultimately bore fruit (and in some cases it seemed to), what seemed to matter most for community members' learning experiences was that they *believed* it did. These beliefs are important in and of themselves: when people imbue literacy with particular ideologies, those ideologies are often enacted in literacy practices and thus come to have implications for people's real-world experiences.[30] In the context of a mobile peer network that many imagined might, one day, include them, Daugavpils community members invested literacy with beliefs about its transnational financial value, giving it, receiving it, and learning it with determination and heart.

## *Why Stockpile? The Polish Plumber and Other Stories*

Stockpiling language and literacy practices to prepare for migration occurred against a backdrop of frequent communication between those abroad and those at home. The message was consistent: having the right language and literacy promised better work abroad.

Consider the warning of Dimitry, a former student of mine who had emigrated to the United Kingdom and agreed to speak with me over Skype: "It's much harder without the language," he warned. I had run into his mother at the central market adjoining the new Hotel Latvia and recognized her curly brown hair and determined gait. In 1999 she had worked in an administrative position at Daugavpils School Number Four, where I had taught high school English, and had kept a stern eye on the halls and keys to the building's classrooms. We were also friends. After having Dmitry in my class for two years,

I was invited for a lunch at her house, during which we all went swimming in the nearby lake. I have a picture from that day of us smiling, arms around eachother, our bodies streaming water. "Dimitry lives in the U.K.," she told me now, "but he's here visiting now and is going to leave tomorrow. He's upstairs at the restaurant having a farewell lunch. Come say hello." I paused to take in the fact that the market now had restaurants and obediently followed her up the stairs to greet him.

Dmitry looked the same to me but sounded different. He spoke to me not in Russian, but in a British clip, quick and slangy. Ethnically Polish, Dimitry could not attend college in Latvia as he did not do well on his Latvian language exam. Still, after EU accession, he managed to find work in Daugavpils as a part-time English-Russian-Latvian interpreter. But he struggled to make ends meet. So he did what others had done: migrated to the United Kingdom.

"I tried to write to you," he told me. "You wrote your address on that book about Texas you gave me, but I got water on it, and the ink ran." Dimitry shrugged. He was grateful, he said, for the English instruction. He credited his knowledge of English with his ability to work his way up from manual labor in a salmon factory in the United Kingdom to his current pursuit as an apprentice electrician, from what many called "dirty work" to clean. The language, he said, was key.

But for many, which particular kind of English would open the doors to which particular kind of employment was unclear: as one returned migrant, a teacher who had left Latvia to work in a factory, explained to me, "I could read in English. But the way they speak. I still don't understand." Another returned migrant, an announcer at a local radio station who had left Daugavpils to earn enough money to put her daughter through college, concurred. "The language there. It's not the same." Though both had studied English, their school-based English did not suffice for the kind of life they desired abroad.

For many Eastern Europeans, the bar for English in the West seemed perennially out of reach, a function of both Eastern Europe's economic status and prejudice.[31] Such prejudice was on display in 2014, represented by the widely circulated trope of the "Polish plumber"—the symbol of the Eastern European labor that was supposedly inundating Western European markets. (In response, Poles created their own poster of a dashing plumber, whose muscles rippled underneath a tight white T-shirt and who held a thick pipe in a suggestive position. The caption read: "I'm staying in Poland. Come over en masse.") Which is to say that while migrants such as Dimitry and returned migrants such as the teacher and radio announcer I spoke with above put their faith in having the right language and literacy, communication with locals in Western Europe was challenging not just for linguistic but also for sociolinguistic reasons tied up in biases against Eastern Europeans. The radio announcer with whom I spoke described her seven years in the United Kingdom as ones of intense loneliness, during which, once she finally earned enough money to buy herself a computer (after remitting one to her daughter), she "lived on Skype." While she blamed inadequate English in part for her isolation, it seemed to me that despite the white privilege that Europeans no doubt benefited from in the United Kingdom, there was also discrimination at play.

These stories, about the simultaneous inscrutability of Western European linguistic conventions and the necessity of mastering them, circulated throughout Daugavpils, themselves a kind of literacy remittance in the form of a warning: Your turn to migrate will come. Shore up your languages, learn what you can, you will need it. Would-be migrants could not control prejudice or the lackluster labor market in Latvia. What they could—and *did*—control, with extraordinary discipline, sacrifice, and resourcefulness, was their language and literacy acquisition.

## *Katrina: Writing Westward*

Katrina's experiences of anticipatory literacy learning are a case in point. A loyal Latvian, Katrina long resisted the pull to leave the country. ("I just loved this country very much. . . . The country is a little bit sick sometimes . . . but you just like Latvia, in spite of everything.") But she soon became embittered with the corruption in state hospitals and her low salary. Of her friends that had left, she said, "All the people I have studied together with, they all go around the world. They have cars. They have kids, which I cannot support." The emigration surrounding Katrina put into relief higher standards of living abroad, creating an atmosphere in which migration was not just one possible imagined future but instead a probable one. Still, she waited until the end of one of our conversations, at the end of my fieldwork, to share the news: "I'm meeting with a German healthcare recruiter in Riga next week." Then she looked down at her hands. "I haven't told my mother yet."

As a doctor, Katrina already had an elite level of literacy—but in light of her plans to migrate, she doggedly (and discretely) sought more. First, she had to track down and translate the appropriate documents, a literate feat in itself, what anthropologist Julie Chu, writing about the very different context of China, has called a premigration "file self."[32] Katrina's file self included a diploma, B2-level language certificate, a CV, papers that stated she had no criminal record, a document proving her health, and an "approbation," a paper obtained in Germany recognizing her diploma. Katrina described the process this way: "So, now I am trying to collect all the papers, to translate all the documents, which is kinda tricky and very expensive and trying to learn *die Sprache,* of course."

Already literate in English, Russian, and Latvian and conversant in French and Italian, her plans for migration also promoted the rapid acquisition of a high level of literacy in a foreign language that Katrina told me she disliked, German. She activated this learning across a network of pedagogical sites. She arranged her work schedule to take expensive classes at a local language school. (As an anesthesiologist, she sometimes missed classes due to operations.) She asked friends abroad to bring or send her German newspapers. (She preferred hard copies so she could annotate them more freely.) And finally, she used workbooks to develop the medical literacy in German she needed to pass her boards. Self-directed, Katrina collected literacy resources in German where she could, gaining fluency via private instruction, transnational friend networks, self-sponsored popular reading, and subject-area specialized study. She amassed her literacies against both the known and unknown demands of a foreign future.

Curiously, part of her preparation also included a flurry of sophisticated—though again, informal—literate activity that developed her skills in another foreign language: English. She created an English-language blog, devoted to the day-to-day travails of the premigration process, for an audience of those preparing to migrate. Throughout the potentially destabilizing migration process, writing the blog in English became a touchstone: "I have so much going on in my life right now," Katrina told me, "it helps me gather my thoughts." At the same time, she believed it helped her improve her writing. "If you write a blog," she said, "someone can come up and read. It makes you consider more what you're writing." The specter of a reader provided, in Katrina's words, "discipline." Just as the community members I described above learned as many languages as possible in face of potential emigration, Katrina developed her rhetorical skills in a blog in an "extra" foreign language to prepare for her move, participating in an online community of present and future migrants that she hoped could emotionally support her throughout this learning-intensive period.

Katrina's Soviet-era letter writing to her grandfather in Russia, her EU-era emailing to her aunt in Italy, her anticipatory blogging—these informal migration-driven literacy learning events animated one another across Katrina's life, which spanned stunning economic and political changes. Once oriented eastward, she now wrote herself westward.

### *Natasha: Earning One's Piece of Bread*

Such anticipatory literacy learning also occurred with ferocity within families, as parents attempted to prepare their children for the eventuality of migration. Consider the efforts that Olga, a small business owner in her early fifties, made to prepare her daughter, Natasha, eleven, to leave the country. During my interview with her and participant observation in her family, Olga told me that all of her family was abroad: sisters, nieces, nephews, and her older daughter lived in Switzerland, Sweden, Norway, the United States, and Cyprus. Olga herself had moved from Georgia to Latvia as a young girl, and her husband had moved to Latvia from Russia. These experiences made migration seem possible and potentially positive.[33] "We want," Olga said, "for Natasha to leave Latvia. We are her parents, you know, and we are already orienting ourselves [for this future]. . . . We are already preparing her to leave."

Even as they saw migration as one answer to the dearth of prospects in Latvia, their experiences also made them cognizant of the precarity of transnational educational trajectories in times of political change. Olga's husband's education as a historian at Moscow State University was cut short with the demise of the Soviet Union, which led him to leave Russia for Latvia before the border closed. In my interview with him over sausage and dill sandwiches in the hunting shop he and Olga owned, he pulled open his top drawer to show me his report card from that last semester before independence—all excellent marks above 8 on a 10-point scale, sealed with the official hammer and sickle of the now defunct USSR. Natasha's parents were familiar with the educational fallout of shifting borders. They knew how credentials valued in one system could mean nothing in another, how home could look one way when one went to bed and look quite different when one woke up. As Olga told me, "It's that nobody knows for whom or how things will turn out in this life."

In light of this uncertainty, they were determined to give their daughter the best possible vantage point from which to succeed. This preparation involved intensive language and literacy training. "This is why," she told me, "we want her to deeply study English and German. This is our goal right now." Olga enrolled Natasha in German language camps in Latvia and an English language camp in Cyprus, where Olga's older daughter lived. She was also enrolled in an elite semipublic high school in Daugavpils, known for its excellence in languages, where Natasha took French, Latvian, English, and Russian. In addition, Olga sought out English-language books for Natasha from acquaintances in the United Kingdom, the study of which she oversaw, despite not knowing English herself. This conglomeration of literacy resources, accumulated through private camps, schools, and friendship networks, was activated in the informal literacy-learning hive of the family. Olga neatly summed up the economic logics underlying literacy learning within this relationship-based network: "Families need to push their children to study," she told me with certainty, "because studying is such a huge labor."

As an English speaker, I too became part of her plan to prepare her daughter for a globalized literacy landscape when she invited my daughter and me over for a private English lesson/play date. Their apartment was Euro-sleek, almost bare, with a bright green teakettle accenting the sharp white kitchen walls, a large television dominating the living room, and the toys in Natasha's room neatly arranged in a compartment underneath her bed. To my eyes, the careful organization seemed consistent with Olga's disciplined attention to the "labor" of training her daughter to leave.

As part of this labor, Olga consulted with me about the English books she had acquired for Natasha. The books ranged from the academic (one on the history of Egypt) to the popular (one about Disney princesses). All of them revealed evidence of Natasha's work. She had penciled in translations in Russian above hard-to-decipher English words (such as "plumage" in the book on Egypt). There was something simultaneously heartbreaking and admirable about the careful Cyrillic notes and the choice of books. In one way, the likelihood that Natasha would need to know a word like "plumage" to succeed in any context seemed as slim as her needing to know about Disney princesses. That she pored over both with equal determination, however, evidenced her confidence in her ability to learn—a confidence bolstered by the faith her family put in foreign-language literacy to prepare her for a future elsewhere.

When her mother asked Natasha to read to me from a book so I could assess her pronunciation, Natasha refused, eyes wide and pleading. I sympathized with Natasha and explained that I wasn't sure what such an assessment would accomplish, but Olga waved me off. "Cyprus is very beautiful," Natasha reluctantly offered, describing a visit undertaken months ago to her sister laboring abroad. I nodded my head in approval, which seemed to satisfy Olga. I began to understand that, as with the word "plumage," the ultimate validity of my assessment was not really the point. What mattered was the *labor,* the practice, of offering one's child the best and the most language and literacy possible—a labor of maternal love that sought to clear a shining open path for Natasha to succeed in a world made uncertain by the whims of politicians and markets. "It breaks my heart," Olga said of the prospect of Natasha leaving the country, as she fed our daughters cream-filled pastries and small wrapped chocolates. "But there is nothing for her here."

In response to the "nothing" Latvia offered, residents did what makes sense in moments of change: reached for what they could and leveraged it for what they hoped was better. Anticipatory literacy learning appeared to offer a modicum of control over otherwise uncertain futures, as homeland residents activated informal networks of literacy and language learning to prepare themselves and their children for what seemed like inevitable diaspora. With such learning, they hoped to pave the way for a better life for their children, even if that meant letting them go.

In their often harried premigration accumulation of literacy in languages from Greek to German to English, families were responding to an economic and educational fact documented with depressing consistency across Latin America, Africa, Asia, and Eastern Europe: the literacy resources of those from economically struggling countries are often valued less than those of citizens from more prosperous ones.[34] Potential migrants in Daugavpils registered some indignation at this injustice, but not surprise. As they had experienced, linguistic, economic, and political regimes came and went, with outcomes that were rarely fair. Which is not to say people were resigned. Quite the contrary. To prepare for migration under these circumstances, people hustled, proceeding with the belief that by engaging in better and more literacy work, they could up their chances to meet their goals. Community members thus packed their bags with more certificates, more languages, and more literacies to compete in a globalizing context that was, as they and their families were, in flux.

## FROM EUROPEAN UNION TO SOVIET UNION: REVISITING BRAIN DRAIN

This flux characterized how Latvians wrote for love and money. They wrote across space, as print letters were transported to and digital communication was zapped to former Soviet republics, EU member states, and other destinations to which family members dispersed. They wrote across generations, as photo books and iPads were gifted to grandparents, as mothers tutored daughters, and as sons tutored fathers. They also invested in their children's literacy educations—investments made with the full knowledge that those educations could very well work to take their children away. They invested, as well, in their own educations, folding as many languages and literacies as possible into their carry-ons along with their hopes for a more prosperous future. By composing on screens and notepads, by learning by books or in classes or under the warm wing of a parent, they worked to orient and reorient themselves in both space and time.

This emphasis on both space and time in Latvians' migration-driven literacy learning enriches the concept of writing remittances established in the chapter on Brazil: because many Latvians with whom I spoke were sent far and wide in the Soviet republic, their migration-driven literacy learning stretched back in intergenerational memories, making the current instantiation of the phenomenon, and their plans for future migration, both familiar and new.[35] Their stories revealed how the changing political borders that often attend peak moments of migration can shape transnational literacy learning, activating people's muscle memories of the migration-driven literacy practices that have come before. If Brazilians' accounts of migration-driven literacy learning emphasized their experiences of writing's changing materialities, Latvians' accounts widened this lens, revealing how writing for love and money can operate not only across literacy technologies but also across generations, political regimes, and languages.

As a flexible grassroots practice, migration-driven literacy learning in Latvia formed a creative, relational, and hopeful response to the seemingly intractable and layered injustices of the country's recent history. It did not, of course, solve problems of global inequality.[36] In the Latvia of 2014, family separation seemed an inevitable fact of life. As Olga put it, "It breaks one's heart." Moreover, as migrants took expertise in engineering, teaching, medicine, and other professions elsewhere, Latvia lost important social contributions.[37] Daugavpils, for example, found itself in a medical crisis, in part because medical resources were in Latvian, and Russian speakers struggled to ask for and understand crucial information. In this sense, Katrina's multilingual gifts would have been put to good use in Latvia, if she hadn't chosen to migrate to Berlin. In this sense, brain drain was a real national problem. But brain drain only tells part of the story. For within this troubled context, migration-driven literacy learning offered transnational families an alternative set of navigational practices, helping people locate themselves, their loved ones, and Latvia itself in more expansive perspectives, perspectives that were temporally and spatially *trans*national.[38]

The transnational circulation of writing remittances, then, can be viewed as one grassroots answer to unjust economic policies, perhaps as what sociolinguists have identified as one of the "new sites of discursive production outside of state control" that can grow underneath, and despite, neoliberalism.[39] As such, migration-driven literacy can also serve as a learning ground for "creative communicative competence," a concept developed by Latvian education scholars that describes the ability to sensitively and flexibly mediate the demands of international communication in the face of changing circumstances—a kind of competence that might well serve those from a small country that cannot afford to ignore its geographic and sociohistorical position at the crossroads of East and West.[40] For those who engaged in migration-driven literacy learning in Daugavpils, such competence was practiced with every international letter they posted, every Skype chat they logged into, every foreign verb they saw fit to conjugate in preparation for an imagined future.

Seen this way, as transnational families sent and received writing remittances across space, time, and languages, their learning flowed underneath, around, and beyond the otherwise sharp edges of brain drain, creating spaces of literacy practice that were simultaneously global and intimate and that were capacious enough to hold and nurture people's hopes and dreams.

Map 5.1 Migration and literacy trajectories of participants in the United States

*Chapter 5*

# Teaching Homeland Family

## *Love and Money in the United States*

I stop in the restaurant in central Wisconsin with my daughter for our usual Sunday meal. A chicken taco with cheese for her, huevos rancheros for me. Carolina, her smile wide, asks us, in English, how we are and puts in our order in Spanish before we sit down at the counter.[1] I ask about her daughter, eight, around the same age as mine. I am Carolina's younger brother's college professor, and she knows I teach writing. As she works, she tells me about a writing contest her daughter wants to enter at school and asks for my help.

Her daughter, she explains, wants to write Carolina's immigration story—a story that would recount the details of her childhood migration from Mexico into the United States. Carolina has only recently shared this story with her daughter, inspired to do so in part due to renewed contact with family in her hometown. She tells me she wants her daughter to understand her roots, to give voice to her story in writing, and to use that writing for success. Her busy hands still for a moment, and her eyes meet mine.

"I want my daughter to win," she says.

For Carolina, using literacy to "win" stateside would require her daughter's engagement with both the injustices her family has faced in their transnational lives and the bravery and ingenuity with which they have persisted. It would mean writing words that would simultaneously honor a proud legacy of migration and facilitate educational advancement within the United States. "Winning," I would later understand, would involve the literate integration of past, present, and future; of here and there; of self and family. I am honored to play a small role in this complex literary process and agree to participate in whatever way Carolina thinks might be useful.

In supporting her daughter's transnational writing, Carolina was participating in a long-established and complex writing remittance circuit that, to differing degrees, involved her mother and brother in the United States and her grandmother, sister, and cousins in Mexico—a circuit that reveals how migration-driven literacy learning can be experienced not only among those who stay in and return to homeland communities, but also among those who make their livings in host countries.

## MIGRATION AS A FUND OF KNOWLEDGE IN DANGEROUS TIMES

In previous chapters, readers have seen how migration can drive experiences of literacy learning for homeland families. But thus far, this book has omitted an important piece of the transnational writing remittance puzzle: a focused analysis of the literacy experiences of immigrants themselves. It may seem that immigrants' lives carry on independently of the family members who remain in homelands. After all, immigrants are often the ones facing new challenges, new languages, and new ways of being in new contexts. Decades of research have shown, however, that across sites from Asia to the Caribbean to Africa to Latin America, the practice of maintaining contact with homeland families shapes immigrants' host country experiences—socially, politically, and financially.[2] Migrants are not discrete labor-producing units, as anthropologist Renato Rosaldo has emphasized of Latinx communities in the United States, but are members of complex binational family formulations.[3] For the migrant families with whom I spoke, such binational ways of being a family member extended to their participation in writing remittance circuits. Their stories revealed that writing remittances did not flow in only one direction, from supposedly "developed" countries to supposedly "underdeveloped" ones, from migrant-receiving communities to migrant-sending communities. Rather, participating in writing remittance circuits amounted to a bidirectional, binational educational exchange that enriched the literacy lives of migrant families themselves. This chapter explains how.

It does so by building on—and extending—the concept of funds of knowledge. Cultivated in out-of-school spaces, funds of knowledge are the "historically accumulated and culturally developed bodies of knowledge and skills" people use to live their lives.[4] In other words, funds of knowledge are the learning that is developed in homes, families, and communities. At its heart, a funds-of-knowledge approach to education involves "grasping the social relationships in which children are ensconced and the broad features of learning generated in the home."[5] "Grasping" funds of knowledge, however, does not mean developing static representations of migrants' cultures.[6] It means understanding how such knowledge is dynamically activated across, for example, community and family practices,[7] processes of cultural change,[8] digital literacy,[9] intersectional identities,[10] and written genres and generations,[11] as well as how it is historically assembled across the political and social conditions that necessarily animate family and community life.[12] Migration-driven literacy learning, as a dynamic spatial, temporal, and material process activated in families and communities, is one such fund.

Migration-driven literacy learning's unique potential for migrant families—and here is where I hope to widen the scope of observations about funds of knowledge—lies in its development in processes of communication that cross the borders of what is too often an oppressive state apparatus.[13] Let me explain in broad strokes what I mean by oppressive: in 2010 there were 11 million undocumented migrants in the United States, making up one-fourth of the total immigrant population, often living lives characterized by anxiety and fear of familial separation.[14] Such fears, while certainly not new, seem to have increased in the Trump era, when some gains in progressive immigration policies have been reversed, human rights abuses targeting immigrants have proliferated, and anti-immigrant rhetoric and policies have contributed to the criminalization of migrant communities and communities of color, regardless of legal status.[15] In this repressive context, despite the fact that Latin American immigrants make up the second largest group of so called skilled workers in the United States, Latinx migrants' funds of knowledge are widely devalued, with Mexican educational achievement in particular lagging behind that of peers.[16] Of course, not all individual migrants, refugees, or communities experience this context the same. Particular policies affect people from different countries and with different legal statuses (even within the same family) in different ways. The stakes vary. Still, it is clear that a cloud of hostility has settled over many migrant communities and has dampened many dreams. While I completed my data collection before the current presidency, the rhetoric of the "wall," legal difficulties, and anti-immigrant racism formed a bass line in my conversations with families. There was danger thrumming underneath their words.

In light of the political and educational violence done to migrant and refugee communities *within* the borders of the United States, grassroots practices that connected people to meaningful communities *across* borders were especially potent. After all, people were writing to family members not just across unmarked distance but more specifically across borders that were both political and politicized. These borders resonated with a host of restrictions and inequalities that transnational communication, in those privileged and fleeting dialogic moments of loving reader-writer exchange, mediated.[17] For the migrant families I spoke with for this book, migration-driven literacy learning, as a practice that operated within families, outside of formal institutions, and underneath state surveillance, formed an innovative site of potentially empowering literacy activity.[18] In practicing migration-driven literacy learning, migrant families created flexible funds of knowledge that they drew on to address contexts of injustice.

To describe this bidirectional, binational practice, here I share the experiences of members of two multigenerational families—Carolina's family, migrants from Mexico, and Nadia's family, refugees from Ukraine—who sent (and received) writing remittances in a context of political, economic, and educational struggle. (For readers who would like methodological details, please see appendix C).[19] For both families, the ties to home they concretized through writing remittances resonated in their literacy and language learning stateside, both as a path toward upward social mobility in unjust conditions and as an expression of familial love. As members of these families circulated literacy from host country to homeland and back, it appeared to accrue, amounting to a grassroots transnational family network of literacy "funds" that family members could call on in support of their aspirations in a hostile U.S. context.

To describe their transnational intellectual work, I first explore how, for two members of each family, the circumstances that conditioned their literacy acquisition stateside shaped their decisions about remitting literacy. I then put these families' experiences side by side in order to describe the "returns" on the transnational investments they made in both literacy and love.

## BUYING AND NOT BUYING LITERACY: CAROLINA'S FAMILY'S WRITING REMITTANCES

### *Carolina: Two Writing Remittances across a Changing Border*

Carolina migrated to the United States when she was thirteen with her older sister, Rosa, and her mother, Julia, from a rural village in Mexico. Her younger brother, José, then three, had gone to the United States by a different route and was waiting with family friends for his mother and sisters when they arrived. Carolina's younger sister stayed in Mexico to be cared for by her grandmother. Upon arrival in Wisconsin, the family moved into a two-bedroom apartment with a friend of Carolina's mother and made plans to pay off migration-related debt, reunite with Carolina's sister, and make lives for themselves in the United States.

The stories Carolina shared with me depicted a girl's, then a woman's, education in a zero-sum game with family finances in a context of what Carolina's brother described as labor exploitation. Soon after their arrival, Carolina, her older sister, and her mother worked shifts at a plastics factory lasting from 4:30 to midnight on school nights, and weekend shifts at a grocery store lasting from 9:00 a.m. to 9:00 p.m. While work at the grocery store required English, helping Carolina, she said, with her pronunciation, she also described difficulty completing homework: "I was so tired all the time. . . . I was exhausted." She hoped to study cosmetology, but the tuition of 6,000 dollars was beyond her means. Despite the fact that Carolina "paid for everything, food, rent, clothes," the family still owed a significant debt. They were strapped. Due to the exploitative conditions her family faced, work replaced homework, and tuition for technical college was too expensive. Literacy was not free. It had to be bought—a fact of Carolina's literacy life that infused her experiences of writing remittances.

In these circumstances, it might seem that Carolina would have little literacy to remit. But while diplomas are quantifiable, literacy, as a human and ideological activity, is not.[20] What mattered most for Carolina's practice of writing remittances was not how much literacy she had by institutional standards—but rather what and how literacy had come to *mean* for her and her family, meanings infused with both love and money.

Consider two strategic points in Carolina's writing remittance circuit. First, let's return in Carolina's memory to the 1990s, when as a teen pining for her sister back in Mexico, she despaired that she could not visit or even regularly call, as most people in her hometown did not have home phone lines. Her one option, her saving grace, was to write letters. In these letters, she shared her new English vocabulary. "I would write *gracias* means *thank you,* and *teacher* means *maestro*." At appointed times, she would follow up with a phone call to the town's local post office, where her sister would be waiting and would say, "Teach me some words!" and "What will we do when I arrive?" Their communication, via letter and phone, centered around their desire for a shared life together in the States. Just as the residents of Latvia stockpiled languages from family members abroad to prepare to migrate, Carolina, as a high school student, remitted English-language literacy through these letters to her sister to help prepare her for what she hoped would be their eventual reunification. Unable to travel to see her sister in person, Carolina promoted her sister's anticipatory literacy learning, sending the literacy remittances she could access and believed would be of value—linguistic knowledge—back home.

While such remittances were gifts between sisters, throughout this exchange Carolina also received literacy resources back, albeit in a roundabout way. Carolina was experiencing alienation at her new high school in the United States as she tried to "catch" the words, as she put it. "The pronunciation was so hard!" she said. But when she penned and spoke words to her sister, she wrote with linguistic authority, recalling her social position in Mexico as an elder sister and as part of a respected social group at her former school. Stateside, where learning was conducted in a foreign language, she felt such authority had been sapped. Within this linguistic remittance circuit, Carolina practiced modifying her relationship to English, at least temporarily shedding the role of inexperienced learner and adopting that of experienced teacher. In the shadow of a nearly impassable border, she infused her letters with nuggets of linguistic knowledge predicated on the hopes of reunification, forming a bidirectional practice of teaching (and learning) for love.

Fifteen years later, at twenty-eight, Carolina was able to return to Mexico to visit the family she had left behind as a girl. Back in her hometown for the first time in over a decade, Carolina was newly struck by its poverty: she told me that the children lacked toys, parks, and medical care. What's more, she said, her cousin's son couldn't read: "He has trouble with speech and they did an operation, but the place is too far away from the city for therapies." Stateside, in contrast, her five-year-old daughter was learning to read in a technologically equipped school. The difference was striking. "I still think about how they live over there, and how much stuff we have here. I told my family I don't want any presents [for Christmas]. If you want to give me presents, give me money." She collected 700 dollars with which she bought toys for the children and an iPad that she loaded with apps to teach her cousin's son to read. "The one problem was finding apps in Spanish, but now he can make the letters. My cousin said it's the best thing. That he's learning. He's making the letters." She gestured to the making of an "a" and an "e," gratified with her decision.

Carolina's beliefs around literacy—that it was dear in terms of both its value for human relationships and its financial cost—underlay both writing remittances. Her formal education was complicated in part by financial concerns, so she sought to teach her sister the English of school ("teacher," for example), preparing her for the hard academic work she imagined lay ahead. Likewise, her experience of education as expensive informed her decidedly financial take on helping her nephew learn to read, as she collected money and bought him a tablet. That is, it was by way of literacy practices undertaken in a context of economic injustice that Carolina developed the literacy ideologies that informed her participation in the writing remittance circuit. Carolina did not have access to great stores of the kinds of literacy credentials often deemed valuable in the United States. But the literacy that she had actively and strategically sought out, inflected with the political, economic, and interpersonal conditions of its accumulation, held transnational value, not only for her, but also for a web of immediate and extended family. Ultimately it appeared that Carolina remitted literacy to Mexico not *despite* the injustice she encountered stateside but rather as a way to mediate it and resist it. Writing remittances acted as a bridge across an unpredictable and punishing border.

## *José: Waiting to Remit*

I first met Carolina's brother, José, at the family's restaurant, where he worked as a waiter, two years before I began this part of my fieldwork. I had overheard him talking to an older man at the counter about his plans for entrance into college, the dorms in which he would live, and how he would pay for it all. I was delighted when on the first day of the first eighty-person lecture I was ever to teach (gulp), I saw his familiar face. José proceeded to be a star student. He often raised his hand and offered sharp insights in front of a classroom of predominantly white peers, all while, I later learned, holding down three jobs. Entrepreneurial and determined like his mother, who owned the restaurant, José doggedly followed an educational path that he hoped would land him in law school and that would eventually lead to a career that would allow him to reciprocate the support he had received from his family both in the United States and in Mexico. Literacy played a role in his plan, as a long term investment that would shape his approach to writing remittances.

In my conversations with José, I came to understand his experiences of literacy—and literacy remittances—as simultaneously linked to family obligation, financial solvency, and individual measures of educational success, in ways that differed from that of his sister. In his words, José was the most "cradled" of his siblings, having been too young on his arrival in the United States to labor in the factories after school alongside them. "We are all intelligent" was the consensus among Carolina and her older sister. The three of us were sitting around Carolina's kitchen table, talking education, migration, kids, and younger brothers. "We just didn't all have the chances José had." Later in my interview with José, he elaborated on these chances: "By the time I was thirteen," he told me, "there was a nice restaurant to work in. . . . My sister, at thirteen years old, was working in a factory." José was clear about the inequitable educational opportunities within his family, and as readers will see, was also clear that he would use his literacy resources to, in his words, "pay it back."

Jose's description of his biliteracy education stateside reflected this approach, in which he both built from and contributed to his family's existing resources from a young age, in part through his experiences with family-based businesses. For example, in third grade, he organized the selling of homemade tamales to his elementary school teachers, a process that involved making bilingual lists of who wanted pork and who wanted chicken. During high school, he continued to work as a bilingual server and administrator in his mother's restaurant, often translating complicated tax forms and negotiating licenses. "Sometimes I didn't know the words in Spanish or English," he said, but he learned as he went along. He continued this work through college. One busy Friday night I watched him negotiate a $107 takeout order, the requests of customers sitting at the counter, and payments from seated tables at the back as my daughter and her rambunctious friend made their own bilingual scene in front. The practices of working and learning infused each other in these entrepreneurial efforts throughout José's life, in which literacy came to be associated with doing one's share of collective family labor.

At the same time as José valued his literacy for its contribution to the family's well-being, he and his family also supported it as a means toward his individual educational success. "She [my mother] didn't understand my report card," José told me, "but there was an expectation that if she did understand it [and it was bad], I was going to get it handed to me." In light of such expectations, he successfully exited the ESL courses that helped him learn English in elementary school, showed up early to class in high school to print out assigned essays since his family didn't own a printer, and progressed to college on a full scholarship, where he arrived in my lecture course a confident leader with a detailed career plan. José viewed this process in light of his measured assessment of the challenges he and his family continued to face. When I interviewed him over the summer of 2016 in a café close to campus, he was recovering from a cold. Although it was summer break, he was worn out from working three jobs, one as a bartender, one as an intern in the law library, a position selected for its potential for his career aspirations, and another as a part-time manager at his family's restaurant. This schedule, he noted, differed from that of his predominantly white college peers, many of whom were relaxing in their families' cabins on midwestern lakes. As both a first-generation college student and, in his words, a "cradled" younger brother, José was aware that investing in literacy cost more in labor for some than for others.

Given José's access to literacy compared to that of Carolina, it would seem that he would have more literacy to remit than his sister. But as with Carolina, his remittance practices had less to do with formal educational attainment and more to do with lived experiences with literacy's economic cost and promise, which had come to form part of his beliefs about literacy and how it operated. For José, literacy demanded financial and familial sacrifice, entailed a long-term investment of labor and money, and thus amounted to both a personal privilege and a community obligation.

In this sense, his feelings about financial remittances mirrored how he felt about literacy remittances. For him to send cash to Mexico at the moment, he believed, was foolish.

> My sister tells me I should give fifty dollars to my dad, because he's in Mexico, but I honestly don't have money. . . . Fifty bucks is a lot given all the school I have . . . also how do I send it? Will I get charged ten dollars to send fifty? . . . Is that a good margin there?

Unlike Carolina, who prioritized pressing homeland needs, José took a longer view: for him, the cost of wiring money made financial remittances less wise in the short term, especially because it would detract from his long-term investment plan in school, regardless of the symbolic goodwill such an act might buy.

While this approach may seem like the detached perspective of a younger son who had to leave Mexico before he could memorize the faces and names of *tios* and cousins, José had not cut ties. Such a conclusion would occlude the more subtle ways money, love, and literacy were activated in his efforts to sustain relationships with homeland family. José was not writing off his contribution to his home community. Instead, he was following a family-based logic of investment in education by committing to work that would, years down the road, reap rewards: "In the future when I'm through with this stage in life . . . it will be exponentially greater. . . . It's a form of payback. . . . My father, my mother, I'll get them a house," he told me. Even if it had little immediate return for his transnational family, the labor of investing in his literacy education was also a labor of love.

This commitment extended beyond José's aspirations for a well-remunerated career that would allow him to buy his parents a house. He also hoped to remit literacy as a way of investing in his homeland community's store of knowledge: "What I'd like to do," he said, speaking of family in Mexico, "is help them understand the law. When my sisters and mother were working, they were exploited. They didn't know their rights. More than money, I'd like to teach my family there about that." Like Carolina had taught their sister English in preparation for migration, José had plans to use his law degree to participate in an anticipatory literacy learning circuit, empowering potential migrants from his hometown to demand fair treatment and pay.

In this sense, the collective transnational value of José's literacy stretched both back in time to the migration and labor that made his education possible and forward to potential future crossings of homeland family and community members, whom José hoped to equip for the journey.[21] Ensconced in this generational and geographic network, he planned to both "pay back" his family and to pay them, in his words, "forward." In light of the injustices that dogged his family's pursuit of educational goals, he felt obligated to those who had already sacrificed—in part through the very labor exploitation he hoped to remediate—for his aspirations. At the same time, he hoped his specialized education in law would provide a platform from which, if his family could just wait for their investment in him to grow for just a few more years, to pay his homeland family forward. In sum, if in the short term, formal literacy acquisition could drain collective resources, José held tight to the long view, that with patience and work, it could also produce them.

In one way, José was in a unique position to take this long view in relation to writing remittances. He did not have immediate family ties at risk. His mother, Julia, sat at the helm of a vast transnational family network of financial remittances revolving around livestock. She invested money in cattle and put family members in charge of overseeing their care and sale, securing her family's standing in their hometown. "If I were to go back there," José said, "I don't know anyone, but everyone would treat me special, because I'm her son." His hometown, he felt assured, would be there for him when he was prepared and willing to enter the remittance circuit.[22]

While José and his family continued to invest in his individual literacy, and indeed his individual success, literacy for him was never only an individual resource. Rather it was a collective and transnational one, meant to be shared among the family members on both sides of the border who directly and indirectly contributed to it. "I want to pay it back *and* pay it forward," José emphasized again toward the end of our discussion.

After our interview, as I was typing up my notes, I realized that though it had made sense at the time of our conversation, I wasn't sure what precisely "it" referred to. At that moment, I became newly aware of my gaps in understandings, of the social distance that too often chased away the construction of shared meanings. I thought back to the stories with which José and Carolina had entrusted me. In this reflection, "it" began to resonate for me with some longer-held meanings, with a border crossing, with long hours of work, with bilingual intelligence, with an entrepreneurial flowering of dreams, with a desire for justice, with bone-deep commitment to family and community both here and there. Though it's important to be transparent: I didn't have the opportunity to follow up with José on this particular point and so do not know if this is what he meant.

## "TIME IS MONEY": THE VALUE OF ENGLISH FOR NADIA'S FAMILY

I met Nadia (thirty-four), her mother, Oksana (sixty-four), her son, Dima (eight), and her daughter, Ira (two), at one of central

Wisconsin's small farmer's markets. Nadia and her mother were selling produce in what I recognized as a Russian accent, and Dima and my daughter appeared to be around the same age. As I bought eggs we struck up a conversation, and I got lost in the ebb and flow of Russian, such an unusual treat in my daily life. Our conversation was punctuated both by Nadia's interactions with customers, to whom she described in English methods of organic farming, and by her directives to her mother in Russian to bag more arugula. Soon my daughter and I were invited to pay a visit to their farm.

Unlike the majority of families whose stories I've shared in this book, Nadia's family were not migrants, but refugees. They had fled Ukraine just two years earlier, joining the nearly 1.5 million people who by 2016 were displaced in the war between Russia and Ukraine that began in 2014.[23] In Ukraine, they had been well off. Her husband, Pyotr, had managed a successful business; Nadia had been an architect for the well-heeled of Kiev; and Oksana had retired from a career as a pediatrician. At the onset of the war in 2014, however, their comfortable life changed. Nadia's boss was put in jail on specious charges, and she was told not to show up to work. When the new Putin-backed politicians asked Pyotr to sell his business for an absurdly low price and he refused, they took the business anyway, warning him they knew where his family lived and where his children went to school. The threat was clear. They packed their bags and fled.

When they arrived in the United States, via a contact Nadia had maintained with an American friend whom she had met as a teenager in Kiev, the family started from scratch as farmers. Like many immigrants and refugees, Nadia, Pyotr, and Oksana found their previous professional status and literacy skills downgraded.[24] Pyotr and Oksana felt their English was limited; the family lacked contacts to develop a business; and unaware that they were eligible for political asylum, their initial legal status meant they were unable to apply for jobs. Though Nadia found it gratifying to organize school group visits to the farm, "Selling eggs," she told me, "doesn't pay." In my conversations with Nadia, Oksana, and Pyotr, I saw a family navigating complex terrain: they were regaining emotional footing after the trauma of war and attempting to orient themselves professionally in light of the disorientation of their new economic and legal status. Unable to return to Ukraine for fear of violent retribution, they also found themselves structurally shut out of social and professional opportunities stateside—opportunities that they believed a better grasp of English might provide. When my daughter and I pulled up the gravel driveway in their farm on our first visit, they had been living in the United States for two years.

### *Nadia: "Time Is Money" and Other Valuable Expressions*

In light of these conditions, the writing remittances they gifted to family traded not so much on literacy's value as an educational and financial investment, as they did in Carolina's family, but instead on the international status of colloquial American English.

American English is not in itself valuable. Rather, its status is contingent on shifting political regimes (for example, in China and in Eastern Europe), U.S. economic dominance, assimilationist ideologies in the United States, and a history of British colonization. That is, the language gleans its global dominance from the institutions that have spread it and continue to reify its importance. That its value lies in its symbolic role within these larger systems of power, and not, say, on its grammar and syntax, however, does not make it any less meaningful for transnational families.[25] The stories Nadia shared with me associated colloquial American English with success, values that had been acquired throughout her years of studying and using the language and that she hoped to share, via writing remittances, with loved ones in Ukraine.

English, for Nadia, had almost always had a transnational, moneyed sheen. Nadia's first encounter with English was in school under the Soviet Union, though with the demise of the USSR, English soon came to be connected for her with Western opportunities. When an American photographer appeared in the newly independent 1990s and hired her as a model, one of her first jobs, she was able to converse with him and show him around town. After he returned to the United States, they kept up a friendly correspondence through letters, which she said helped teach her English, "real English," in her words, unlike what she had studied in Soviet-era textbooks. For her, "real English" meant understanding television shows and making trips to the United States—to Hawaii for an extended stay, to Wisconsin for a work stint to help take care of the photographer's aging mother, and then as a tourist. Beginning well before her eventual migration to the United States, her study of English linked her via friendship networks and pop culture to the international world of commerce, labor, and leisure. These were the domains through which her English experiences flowed.

When Nadia came to live in the United States, English's associations with professional international success thickened. But this time, in a context of legal and professional limbo, in which she shouldered much of the economic responsibility for her intergenerational family of five, the pressure to learn perfect English increased. As Nadia attempted to drum up business for her freelance architecture firm, she worried over her accent and difficulty with idioms. "We all learned English the same, in school," she explained, "but here there are these expressions that you only know if you were born here . . . slang." Not knowing the slang, she felt, made her sound uneducated to potential clients. "I can build a house," she said, "but I sound like an idiot." Now not just visiting but living in the belly of the Western capitalist beast, Nadia's career mobility seemed to rest on English fluency.

These associations were driven home by particular phrases in the language itself—phrases that reflected a specifically U.S. money culture. "Don't waste my time," she repeated to me as an example of a quintessential American English phrase. With what appeared to be partial admiration and partial criticism, she explained: "Here, time is valuable, more valuable than it is in Ukraine." For example, she described her surprise the first time she went to get her car fixed in the United States and found that the parts were cheaper than the labor. In Ukraine, she explained, it was the opposite. I thought of my four-dollar haircuts in Latvia that lasted hours and resulted in a veritable sculpture. In the logic of American English spoken in a U.S. context of relative prosperity, time was money and could be wasted or invested. From the perspective of Russian in post-Soviet Ukraine, *work was not a wolf,* as the aphorism went, *it did not run away into the forest.* In other words, work was ever present; one engaged in it or didn't. In the English idiom, work was a task whose value varied depending on how it expanded or contracted in relation to the otherwise empty container of hours. Her labor, conducted in what she identified as unidiomatic English, appeared not to be worth much at all.

This analysis is not meant to reify potential cultural and linguistic differences but instead to highlight how the financial meanings of American English inhered not only in its global economic hegemony, and not only in Nadia's personal history with it, but also in the meanings Nadia noticed in certain language practices themselves. For Nadia, this relationship between time, money, and language stateside was not abstract: as the family member with the most facility with the language, it was her responsibility to organize the family's health insurance, to coordinate communication with her son's school, to run the family business, to make phone calls. Fulfilling this linguistic responsibility meant she logged long hours as a mother and as a breadwinner. I often saw her yawning and rubbing her eyes. "Coffee?" she would offer as she made herself yet another cup. Time is money, after all, and Nadia, with a family of five to support, had been making the most of hers. The international context of English-language hegemony echoed through Nadia's experiences of it across decades. English resonated with a decidedly capitalist cultural outlook.

In the context of the ideologies of language acquisition Nadia had encountered in both her premigration and postmigration life, colloquial English was precisely the remittance she found most valuable to send back to her brother, the family member in Ukraine with whom she maintained most frequent contact. For Nadia, it didn't make sense to remit laptops or other writing technologies. In fact, she received software and other writing remittances from her brother, who, as a computer game designer, accessed them for free or at steep discounts. ("Ukraine," Nadia shared, "is much better off than the United States in relation to technology.") What she did send, then, was that precious global resource, colloquial American English, which she mined at the source.

While Nadia lamented her family's lack of English as the source of ongoing struggles, she also described how the English she could access, by virtue of living in the United States among native American English speakers, held transnational value, especially as a writing remittance. Since his video games were marketed to an international audience, Nadia's brother used English for scripts and voice-overs. As Nadia described: "He'll make a cartoon and the voice needs to say something, what it means, how it works." In this process, her brother wrote in Russian, and she translated it. Because video games involve not only written scripts but also audio, and because American English, as a prestige dialect, could provide her brother social capital in the video game market, she also offered him voice-overs from native English speakers, fellow farmworkers she recruited and whose speech she recorded. "I ask an American to pronounce it," Nadia explained to me, "so that there is an American pronunciation, because our pronunciation, it just doesn't do it"—*it,* as I understood the word, being giving her brother's games that American English glow to improve its chances of selling in an international market. In a way, similar to Carolina's letters to her sister, Nadia dispersed the very kind of literacy that she simultaneously valued and believed she was lacking.

Nadia's family faced a slew of challenges: legal status, lack of business contacts, the illegibility stateside of the adults' formal degrees, and the trauma of fleeing a war. In this context, and with little else to send to family members better off financially and technologically, it made sense that Nadia remitted English. American English, its value as an international resource seeming to hold steady in the midst of so much dizzying change, could be learned, borrowed, recorded, packaged, gifted, sold. So Nadia harvested it, offering up the fruits of her labor to family members she loved who remained in a country to which she could not return.

## *Oksana: Transnational English Olympiads*

A former pediatrician fluent in her native Ukrainian and Russian, as well as Hungarian, a Fino-Ugric language with little relation to Slavic Ukrainian and Russian, Oksana knew more English than she let on. She once asked me for help interpreting what an American farmworker was asking her, an interpretation which I flubbed, managing to mistake *weeds* for *watermelons,* before realizing that Oksana understood precisely what the worker was saying and was just (mistakenly) relying on me to double check. I soon came to realize that Oksana was not satisfied with knowing English only for instrumental purposes. And why would she be? She wanted the kind of linguistic facility that would allow her to be a respected member of a community, the kind of status she had before she left Ukraine. "When everyone is laughing," she said poignantly, "I want to know what is so funny." But English classes were expensive and difficult to get to without a driver's license and car. In this way, the different aspects of her isolation—physical, social, and linguistic—amplified one another, sharpened each other's knives, ultimately conspiring to leave Oksana meaningfully out.

In light of these circumstances, Oksana engaged in writing remittances in ways that pulled her more deeply into the beating heart of her immediate family. Via Skype, she orchestrated intergenerational transnational writing remittance events that united her grandson, Dima, stateside, and her granddaughter in Ukraine, placing her in a social role at the center of her grandchildren's learning.

The success of such transnational and intergenerational family-based pedagogical events depended on Dima's successful acquisition of English in the United States. Dima had originally tested as having "no English," despite having watched reruns of *Green Acres* over and over again while in Ukraine to the point of being able to recite whole episodes. (On a previous trip to the United States, Nadia had purchased a DVD player, only to find out once she hooked it up in Ukraine that it worked only for American DVDs, of which they had only the one.) Though Nadia was at first suspicious of ESL classes—*Why did Dima need special attention? And why would the school ask her permission? In Ukraine, teachers simply go ahead and do what their professional training says is best*—Dima attended them, socialized with friends, and though he described his first year in school to me as having been "hard," he soon expanded his repertoire beyond *Green Acres*. During my fieldwork, he and my daughter, who had retained only the sparest of phrases in Russian from our time in Latvia, alternated between playing outside on the family's tree swing and collaborating in English on computer games.

For Oksana, Dima's ease with the language on one hand shunted her out of his world (she could not, for example, help him with his homework). But on the other hand, it provided an opportunity for her to participate in English-language social events on her own terms, namely, by organizing transnational Skype English contests for her grandchildren. During these writing remittance events, she quizzed her granddaughter in English via her native informant, Dima, which she believed could provide her distant granddaughter a competitive advantage for the Ukrainian school-wide language Olympiads, high-stakes competitions for which children are encouraged to train and to win. In the process, she was able to commune with her grandchildren, one who lived far away, and one who, though physically close, was growing up in a social world to which she often felt she had little access.

In orchestrating these cross-border, Skype-mediated, family-based language training sessions, Oksana looped her grandson, Dima, into a literacy remittance circuit in which both his school-sponsored academic literacy and his colloquial American English united to promote the social status and community inclusion that Oksana, having gone from retired pediatrician to farmworker, from Ukrainian citizen to refugee, from multilingual professional to basic English speaker, so desired to regain.

## THE RETURN ON WRITING REMITTANCES

In sending literacy, members of Nadia's and Carolina's families weighted it with the ideologies around which they encountered it in the United States: entrepreneurial (think José selling tamales and the long-term investment of college); scarce (think Carolina working and sacrificing to earn it); capitalist (think Nadia and the concept of "wasted time"); and status and community-oriented (think Oksana wanting to be included in jokes). These remittance circuits functioned according to economic logics, albeit ones that were experienced differently across family members: José was holding out on remittances to increase their margin of return, Carolina sacrificed material goods to send literacy technologies home, Nadia traded on English's global financial value, and Oksana orchestrated writing remittance events to invest in her grandchildren's success. These logics, honed through multiple and repeated iterations of literacy practices, were folded into letters, technologies, and linguistic resources and sent by migrants to family members, constituting literate acts of transnational love.

But what does love matter? Put less philosophically, if from the perspective of migrants, the economic and emotional aspects of literacy interanimate each other in literacy remittance circuits, might the return on such remittances for migrants be not only the sustenance of relationships but also, perhaps, a transnationally enriched literacy repertoire that they might use to meet stateside goals? While in the literature on financial remittances, sending money to homeland family can result in fewer resources in host countries, with migrants sacrificing to support family abroad through generous financial gifts, literacy, for the families in this chapter, appeared to work differently.[26] For these families, when they gave literacy, *they also received it*, with implications for their stateside literacy lives.

Consider examples from the immigrants and refugees readers have met in this chapter. First, consider Oksana. Desperate to learn English, she had experimented with computer programs such as Rosetta Stone and Polyglot English, telling me that she would like to attend an English class in town but that "good classes are expensive." In remitting English to her granddaughter via her grandson, she didn't need to head to an English class. She *had* an English class, both in person and on the computer, in the mouths of her grandchildren, who were speaking in the language to each other across the globe. As she invested in her distant granddaughter's literacy education in English, she was also investing in her own.

Likewise for Nadia. Partly in return for the colloquial English she remitted her brother, her brother designed a website for her budding architectural design business stateside, forming a circuit of literate exchange that readers by now have likely come to recognize as characteristic of writing remittances.[27] The tagline her brother developed for this business was this: "Addicted for perfection." According to Nadia, "Americans don't say that. They say *to*. 'Addicted *to* perfection.'" So she asked her brother to revise the language, remitting him valuable knowledge (a tutorial in normative preposition use that follows no logic except custom) and simultaneously polishing the public face of her business. Participating in this bidirectional literacy circuit was mutually beneficial. It formed one way of advancing their entrepreneurial pursuits.

For Carolina, too, investment in the literacy learning of homeland family, via a writing remittance, was also an investment in the learning of her immediate family. She wanted to maintain strong contact with her homeland in part to inform her daughter's literacy education. She told me she wanted her daughter to appreciate the differences between her town in Mexico and her life in the midwestern United States to deepen what immigration scholars call "bifocality"—a kind of dual perspective on "here" and "there" that can benefit those who employ it in their daily lives.[28] She hoped to accomplish this bifocality in two ways: first, by sending her daughter to school in Mexico for a time so she could widen her appreciation of educational opportunities and familial connections in both countries, and second, by helping her daughter write her migration story for her school's annual book contest, as the introduction to this chapter described. "It's one thing to write, mami," she told her daughter. "It's another thing to win." In submitting a coauthored, intergenerational testimonio to a book contest in a U.S. public school, Carolina and her daughter were articulating transnational movement as a valuable educational asset, as a fund of knowledge that would allow them to "win" at the U.S. game of literacy. In this process, literacy appeared to act for Carolina as a kind of navigational technology, which she used both to situate herself and her immediate family in relation to those who were far and also to chart a path forward for those, such as her daughter, who were physically close.

With repatriation for members of both families unlikely, the literacy-learning experiences promoted by writing remittances provided both a connection home and useful resources stateside. Having succeeded at legalizing her family's status by the end of my fieldwork, Nadia registered a sense of defeat at being in the United States. Her family would have liked to go back but feared for their lives. In the meantime, they maintained mutually beneficial ties to homeland family, literacy accumulating across borders. English was given, technological advice received, and group digital projects to buttress businesses on two sides of the globe were developed. In this way, for Nadia's family, investing literacy in homeland communities was also investing it in their own immediate future.

Having firmly established roots in the United States, Carolina's family saw themselves using literacy to "pay it back and pay it forward," as José put it, both to those who invested in their success and to the next generation. And indeed, the family was reaping literacy rewards. Carolina's daughter was succeeding in school (second place in the book contest, first place in the science fair), José was nearing his senior year of college, and Julia's popular business continued to allow her to purchase cattle in Mexico.

Across borders that resonated with injustice after injustice, the families in this chapter sent and received writing remittances, deepening the grooves in these transnational and intergenerational literacy routes, holding each other up with their words. As literacy moved among loved ones in this way, it appeared to gain force, velocity, heft. That is, it accrued, forming a fund of knowledge from which families could draw to pursue their goals.[29] In this dynamic context, literacy acted more like love than like money. The more families gave, the more they got.

## WHEN LITERACY ACTS LIKE LOVE

In this bidirectional exchange of teaching and learning, the families with whom I spoke were lighting up cross-border writing remittance circuits with the electric buzz of both money and love. I have written elsewhere that literacy regulates immigrants' physical movement in the form of the documents migrants often must wield to cross borders.[30] I'd like to add here that from the perspective of writing remittance senders and receivers, literacy also appeared to regulate transnational life in the sense of regulating a nervous system. The act of sending literacy remittances seemed to order the otherwise potentially chaotic trauma of separation, especially separation undertaken under circumstances of economic injustice, persecution, and fear. Literacy remittances appeared to form a connective tissue to homelands, a kind of reparative suture that aided in constructing a viable U.S. existence under state repression—an existence that entailed both connection to homeland and to American-style success. Brain drain as a concept could not account for literacy's dynamism in this process, nor for the ingenuity and heart of the transnationals who remitted and received it. Migration did not split brains between here and there; rather, it set into motion transnational exchanges that generated collective literacy resources—resources which migrants used to ground themselves in relation to host country and homeland, past and future, self and family.

What of the future of such circulation of literacy for these families? So much depends not only on their movement across borders, but on borders' movement across them. For Nadia, Ukraine was Soviet and then independent, and then its borders were breached, resulting in her family's flight. For Carolina, the border between Mexico and the United States was difficult to cross when she was a child, but then opened for her as an adult. As of this writing in the United States in the second year of this chaotic regime, what constitutes a border for whom often feels up for grabs.

We often think of borders as incontrovertible facts. If you have an atlas (or an app with an atlas), you can trace with your finger the outline of a seemingly contained country. Here is a river. Here is a desert. Here is a bounded territory that can be measured in kilometers or in miles. But from the perspective of people who have moved, are moving, or are planning to move, the view is different. The lines keep getting redrawn. Depending on your papers, your phenotype, your last name, your religion, and on the whims and decisions of those in charge, the borders shift. As freshly cruel policies are written in the United States, the perimeter of what is a livable space for many has constricted.[31]

Such changes to borders can short-circuit, reroute, or create new paths and new exigencies for writing remittance exchanges, such as the ones I have documented here. Though the future is unclear, what is certain is that as the U.S. state continues to violate human rights laws with regard to migrants and refugees, it is more important than ever to examine, understand, and support transnational family-based funds of knowledge—funds that gain their critical potential from the very processes of cross-border exchange in which they are developed. Migration, migrants' stories have demonstrated in various ways, is an educational resource.

I end this chapter with a return to Carolina's daughter's prize-winning story, itself a writing remittance that appears to embody the relationship among changing borders, transnational movement, and literacy as experienced by host-country family members. In telling her family's story, she also protested political injustice, writing of her sadness that families are separated across a border that is not safe, she emphasized, for anybody. As a host-country actor in an intergenerational writing remittance circuit whose genesis preceded her birth, Carolina's daughter is using her words to help sustain this circuit across a politicized border. In doing so, she animates the family connections that state policies have sought to strangle. Her writing is their pulse. It brings them life and blood.

# Conclusion

## *Migration-Driven Literacy Learning in Uncertain Times*

When my daughter and I arrive at the café where I am to conduct my interview with Vasily, he is already there. Neat hair, button-down shirt, he stands up to shake my hand. After I settle my daughter with an outsized chocolate mousse and the Internet-optional if educationally questionable iPhone game of popping virtual bubbles, Vasily explains that he returned to Daugavpils from the United Kingdom because his infant son had been ill. He and his wife trusted the Daugavpils doctors more and wanted to be close to family. They had been in the United Kingdom for over five years, where Vasily traded on his knowledge of English and Russian and background in engineering to work his way from picking strawberries to managing private flights between the United Kingdom and Russia for wealthy Russian citizens. He had been doing well. There was pride in his voice.

How did he feel about returning? I ask.

He looks down at his smartphone. We are conducting the interview in English, his preference, his accent a kind of tight trot compared to my slow American vowels.

"Well," he finally says. "We needed to come back."

"And what is your plan?"

"Well, the more you talk about it, the less chance you'll yield it up."

In Latvia there had been so many disappointments, such damage and pain for so many generations that often one didn't dare voice hope. I remember Katrina's response to my daughter's vomiting. "I'm very worried," she had said, proceeding to paint nightmare scenarios of invasive treatments in Soviet-era clinics. The phrase "very worried" pronounced by a doctor in the United States, or at least in the Midwest, would likely mean a prognosis of death. In Latvia, it worked to lower expectations to cushion the disappointment to which many had become accustomed. But Vasily has hopes. As he talks, I glean that the plans he does not dare specify aloud involve opening some kind of business—a business that would make use of the language and literacy resources he has amassed from both his own international migration and from the shape-shifting borders around him.

"As you see," Vasily continues, "I picked up a lot of language. I picked up great experience in aviation. I picked up a lot of . . . the stuff that I wouldn't pick up if I probably stayed in Latvia and then didn't go abroad. As you see, that's my story. . . . We have a lot of plans to start some, let's say, businesses or whatever."

*As you see,* he keeps repeating.

And so, at his direction, I look. I see that he made contacts, learned how international businesses work, upped his technological game. "I did pick it up from there," he continues, "because I was involved in it, in quite all, the business process. It did help me to see how it works from the inside." As he speaks, I begin to see more. I see that in using spreadsheets to coordinate flights across languages, in tutoring his Belorussian-born father on how to Skype, in composing poems to his family on special occasions because he believes copy-and-paste Internet messages are impersonal, in jockeying between Russian elites and English business people, in reading books in Russian on a Kindle while abroad to retain some sense of his cultural roots, in charting a path from manual laborer into the heart of an international business—I see that if migration promoted his transnational literacy learning, and it is clear that it did, his love for his family sustained it.

I nod. I want him to continue talking while my daughter still has some dessert left, some virtual bubbles to pop.

He complies. "I would think that our experience now in Latvia much more appreciated, than any other experience, if I would pick it up in Latvia," he says.

Another word lodges itself in my mind and begins to run a loop. *Appreciated.* His literacy appreciated as it traveled, circulating from Daugavpils School Number Ten to England, where he built on it and expanded its uses, back to Latvia, where he taught it to his father and others on a remitted computer to mitigate the pain of his absence, and then back again, in a different form, as he plans to invest it in Daugavpils. His literacy also appreciated as it was shared, growing his father's and others' literacy repertoires. And perhaps it will appreciate into employment opportunities for Daugavpils citizens. As his literacy circulated, sometimes as a personal resource, sometimes as a remittance, sometimes with his body and sometimes by technological proxy, it spread and grew.

As literacy traveled transnationally for Vasily, and for the others who shared their stories with me in Brazil, Latvia, and the United States, it appeared to amass ideological, emotional, and financial values—values that amplified each other in material sites and practices of written communication. Such values were "picked up," to use Vasily's words, like so many postcards and souvenirs, reminding users where literacy had been, through whose hands it had passed, how it had been changed. As literacy coursed through the lives of families that were separated across borders, it both expanded and proliferated.

Seen this way, Vasily's brain was not drained. Rather, there was a more elastic process at work by which his migration—the ties of love it tested, the financial rewards it promised—distributed his learning, such that the transnational community network of which he was a node accumulated potentially remunerable and emotionally satisfying literacy resources. Such processes are possible to grasp only when Vasily is seen as more than a brain. He deserves to be seen as a father, husband, son, and community member—and more even than these roles, as a breathing, thinking, feeling human. When one takes migrants' desires, histories, and family and community relationships into account, it becomes possible to see migration not as a detriment to literacy learning, but instead as a powerful instigator of it.[1]

This is not to say that Vasily's migration did not amount to a loss of important knowledge. Who knows, after all, what this talented bilingual engineer and community member could have contributed to Latvia during those years abroad? Rather, it is to point out that Vasily did not leave in his wake a vacuum. His body left Latvia for six long years. But during that time, across the uncertainty of shifting political borders and economic disarray, his migration drove his own and his family's experiences of literacy learning, as they wrote and learned new ways of writing for those two ends that drive so many of our human actions: love and money.

## LOVE AND MONEY: IMPLICATIONS FOR RESEARCHERS

Let me return, then, to love and money, to make explicit why I believe they matter, both for researchers and for educators.

First, money. Transnational families in this book wrote for money because money attached itself to their writing practices at every turn. Global economic injustice reverberated through: the literacy technologies purchased, in class-stratified ways, with migrant labor (Brazil); the changing political regimes that devalued literacy in some languages and valued it in others (Latvia); the intergenerational financial sacrifices people made to acquire specialized literacies (United States); and the monetary value of privileged dialects (United States); and the ways, overall, that literacy at some moments and in some locations paid off for some and did not for others.

But in the stories people shared with me, they emphasized writing for more than money. They also wrote for love. As a communicative practice, writing connected grandparents and grandchildren, mothers and daughters, nieces and aunts, close and distant family, alternately stoking longing and relieving it. The text "Mama, everything is okay" tapped into a cell phone in Iceland and appearing on another one in Latvia brought a wave of relief and a return to life. For this reason, writing was also seen as a gift. Paper letters were kept in boxes, both virtual and physical, and remitted laptops were, if not used for Saturday morning family Skype chats, dusted with care. And finally, the practice of promoting children's literacy learning, by encouraging them to write family migration stories or to learn the languages that would let them write their own, made writing part of a transnational family pedagogy of care. For the families with whom I spoke, it was in this role as a lightening rod for both money and love that literacy played its unique transnational role.

Money and love, I hope to have shown, were not experienced as separate and distinct aspects of the social phenomenon we call literacy. Rather, the families featured in this book revealed how writing's emotional purchase and its economic meanings interanimated eachother in contexts of transnational labor migration. In the chapter on Brazil, readers saw how the social class inequality that spurs different kinds of migration seeped into the intimate emotional experiences of communication. I think here of Hugo and the letter on "dirty paper" from his grandfather that made him cry. In the chapter on Latvia, readers saw how homeland residents stockpiled languages for economic leverage, investing in language learning as a form of care. I think here of Natasha's mother, of the "labor" of studying, of her broken heart. And in the chapter on the United States, readers saw how economic circumstances informed how and why and with what emotional force literacy was remitted in the first place. I think here of Carolina's sacrifice to buy the tablet to send to Mexico, of her hard-won bifocal and bilingual logic, of her commitment to the literacy development of her family both in the United States and in Mexico.

These transnational families were using literacy to reach the two life goals that globalization consistently threatened: economic solvency and meaningful human relationships. Literacy was, in a way, a one-stop shop.

How money and love materialized in migration-driven literacy learning, this book has attempted to show, was a historically contingent process. That is, just as the movement of people and writing across space mattered for people's literacy, so too did movement across time. In Brazil, technologies changed across lifespans, necessitating new digital literacy learning. In Latvia, borders changed across lifespans, demanding new language learning. In the United States, politics changed across lifespans and generations, instigating writing remittance practices that migrants adapted according to circumstances, needs, and desires. While recent work on transnational literacies has tracked the movement of literacy objects and people across borders, the stories presented here ask us to take seriously the mobility of social, economic, and political contexts themselves, as they shift across people's lives.[2]

Examining love and money in light of these shifting contexts leads to a line of questions that could be productively taken up in further studies. Of the chapter on Brazil, data for which were collected in the now technologically distant year of 2011, we might ask: As Internet-mediated communication technologies become more commonplace, how might their economic and emotional value change? And what of the technologies that have become more widespread in Brazil since 2011, such as smartphones and apps that facilitate chatting across borders and are often cheaper than computers? More pressing, as Brazil's "boom decade" of 2004–2014 has ended amid corruption and recession, potentially driving the tens of millions of Brazilians who emerged from poverty back into newly punishing material conditions, will Brazil see a resurgence of emigration?[3] And if so, what role might writing remittances play—both for those trying their luck abroad and those who remain?

Likewise, there are further questions to ask of the chapter on Latvia: How has Brexit, for example, shaped the prospects of those Latvians who have pitched their dreams on the learning of English? What will happen to migration-driven literacy learning if other EU countries follow suit? And what other forms of transnational literacy learning might arise? Daugavpils, the city Western tourists were warned away from during independence because it was "too Soviet," has now reframed its Russianness as a marketing tool, attracting thousands of students from the United States and Western Europe to Daugavpils University's new "Learn Russian in the European Union" initiative. While Russian was demoted in Latvia postindependence, it now accounts for a robust business of high-paying educational clientele, who temporarily repopulate the small city as consumers of Latvian literacies. Literacy, it appears, is one of the resources Daugavpils trades in, with consequences for learning not only locally but also internationally.

And of the U.S. context, we might ask what will happen to literacy remittances—and financial remittances—if the state continues to double down on restrictions on immigrants and refugees. If a wall is indeed built between the United States and Mexico? If refugees and asylum seekers continue to be refused? If the children kidnapped from their parents (writing these words stops one's heart) are never returned? What forms—Testimonios? writing to heal? writing for peace?—might migration-driven literacy learning take?[4]

Answering such questions requires an analysis that simultaneously honors people's everyday literacy practices and critically appraises the larger historical trends that promote these activities. That is, as history takes its course—and as people of conscience do their part to change it for the better—the contours of literacy learning, its ideological heft, financial value, and interpersonal resonance are at stake. People likely will still write for love and for money. But precisely how remains to be seen.

## LOVE AND MONEY: IMPLICATIONS FOR EDUCATORS

This book has worked from two premises: first, that literacy is often encouraged, honed, and acquired in informal community-based practices,[5] and second, that such practices are often shared, developed, and adapted across national borders.[6] These premises allowed me to track how, for the communities featured here, global migration worked to propel sites of community learning beyond local, in-person contexts to those of transnational networks.[7] Hugo, in Brazil, widened his digital literacy repertoire in part via his sister in France. Katrina, in Latvia, honed her writing in Russian in part via her grandfather in Russia. Carolina's daughter, in the United States, won second place in a school writing contest in part via her family's migration from Mexico. In these mobile, family-based, pedagogical sites, people were practicing and learning literacy.

What would it look like to integrate such rich transnational experiences of writing for money and love into educational institutions? Education researchers have documented the pedagogical promise of bridging community-based literacy practices with classroom learning, an approach that in some cases has been to shown to be especially effective for working-class students with transnational backgrounds. Literacy researchers Moje et al., for example, have examined how students' home discourses surrounding their parents' farm work and their families' migration can support science-related literacy in a high school.[8] And literacy scholar Kris Gutiérrez has described a unique college learning community whose purpose is to activate a "third space" for students with migrant backgrounds, building from their histories, their intimate experiences of mobility, and their lived testimonios.[9] Likewise, love and money, as enduring aspects of transnational community-based literacy learning, have the potential to be productively taken up in educational programs, in ways that support a range of literacy practices, including multi-modal and/or digital composition.[10]

Social-justice-oriented educators, responding in part to the unjust "emotional regime" of the school and contexts of persistent racial injustice, have proposed love as a way of not just emotionally engaging youth but of honoring their identities and thereby contributing to the development of their political subjectivities, critical awareness, and dialogic practices of literacy.[11] Love, as bell hooks has proposed, is a powerful pedagogical and critical resource.[12] And love, as theorist Chela Sandoval has painstakingly envisioned, can serve as a heuristic to develop a more just world. In a moment of what she calls the "transnationalization of capitalism," love offers the potential for people to connect across a "new decolonizing global terrain," which can unite them both "within and across national borders."[13] That love already flows through many students' out-of-school writing practices provides a pedagogical in for further developing love-based critical literacy opportunities within classrooms.

Seen this way, I hope the stories I shared in this book encourage educators to continue to see the purposes for students' writing, transnational or not, as extending outside the academy and into the human muck of the shape-shifting world, with its tangle of complicated relationships, political injustices, and financial transactions.[14]

One example of a college writing class that takes this assumption as its starting point is that of Professor Catherine Prendergast at the University of Illinois, in which students write in order to be published for money. Following her lead, I have recently begun to teach a general education composition course at my university aimed at writing from the heart and for the pocketbook in times of technological and political change. Inspired by the communities featured in this book, I call the course "Fast Writing in Fast Times."

Fast times, as the transnationals in this book have shown, require fast writing—or at least fast learning—a kind of willingness to adapt literacy to new contexts and to do it quick. In their literacy activities, successful transnationals activated what scholar Evan Watkins has called "just-in-time" human capital.[15] According to Watkins, just-in-time human capital is not the reserve or store of skills that served workers of the past. It is using literacy "just in time"—to move, to act, and to adapt entrepreneurially across borders and media at a moment's notice and often in inequitable circumstances. Felipe, for example, used his knowledge of ICQ chat for English lessons, and Vasily used his biliterate digital repertoire to dream up a new business. Nadia used farmworkers' American accents for her brother's design business, and a young José used his biliterate knowledge to sell tamales and later to negotiate a liquor license for his family's business. What these instances of ingenuity reveal is this: if literacy is uniquely sensitive to larger shifts in political and economic circumstances, it is also uniquely flexible in the skilled hands of resourceful transnationals. They are not only keeping up. They are *stepping* up with a kind of literacy savvy that meets their changing circumstances head on.

For readers not previously familiar with the communities I have described in Brazil, Latvia, and the United States, these sites may seem a far cry from the concerns of everyday literacy classrooms. The transnational circumstances I have described here may seem, well, distant. But even students who do not think of themselves as especially transnational, like many of those who study in the predominantly white university in Wisconsin where I make my living, are affected by literacy's globalizing economic trends. To home in on my own locale for a moment, Wisconsin has been the site of: a large-scale research study showing how a college education is increasingly out of reach for many students in light of public defunding; a *Glamour* magazine article on college student homelessness; and a report of students selling body parts, such as eggs, to pay for tuition.[16] Students in my classroom, with or without transnational ties, are investing in and adapting literacy in the hope that literacy will pay.

A poem that a student in the class I offer on writing and money felt moved to write and share makes this point better than my prose. I include excerpts of it here:

"Means to End" by Dan Waitrovitch

You labor away today tonight
Tomorrow and the next
Push your endurance for me
For you for me for food for
Me to live to learn.

You labor for me to leave
To learn from them to
Live better than you and
Me and we have lived from
You until me until now.

. . . . . . . . . . . . . . . . . . . .

They demand more my
Soul more a kidney more
My first kid until less than

A dusty silent piggy bank
Remains to offer and still

......................

And so with a sore brain and
Soulless body I labor today
Tonight tomorrow and the
Next for me for food for
Me to earn to learn to live.

The relationship between love, money, and literacy learning, I have argued, is uniquely visible in transnational families. But this poem suggests it is also present for many others. I believe that all students deserve an understanding of how to make literacy work for them, as both a means of human connection and an economic resource. As this poet tells us, their futures, their brains, their families, their *kidneys* for God's sake, are all on the line.

For both transnational and nontransnational, monolingual and multilingual students, literacy is a global economic resource that happens to live in the people who use it and are used by it. It is mined by corporations for profit (as in workplace writers),[17] used by governments to control populations (as in immigration documents),[18] and sometimes taken up for political liberation (as seen in the work of abolitionists)[19] and upward social mobility (as in rags to riches stories that hinge on education).[20] Literacy is at once small and big. Both personal and political. Both intimate and economic. My research in Brazil, Latvia, and the United States has convinced me of the importance of helping students appreciate this power and this breadth. It has taught me to do my best to listen well to the poetry that results.

The writing of this conclusion is interrupted on a Saturday morning by a Skype call with family in Brazil. It is afternoon there, and we are still in our pajamas. My daughter, shy in her heritage language, remains silent, hovering around the edges of the screen, as I keep up a stream of inquiries about family, the weather, and how big my daughter's cousin has gotten. Our call is interrupted due to technical difficulties, once, then twice. It is my computer that is the problem, I think. They have long abandoned the laptop I once remitted to them. It is now outdated. We try the cell phone, but my apartment gets terrible reception. So we Facebook-message, my daughter's aunt and I. "Family is important," she writes in Portuguese, "and we would like to maintain contact." We agree to plan another date and time to Skype. "I hope it works, haha," she writes. And I think of the tenacity of human ties and also of their fragility. I think of the power we invest in literacy to sustain love in a world that often seems dead set on taking it away.

# Afterword

## *The Mothers*

In a context of the rapid movement of people and of writing, I have tried in these pages to momentarily bring into focus the blurred images that can result from going too fast. In this process, I have fished for a through line, a narrative, a story that would in some way bind together the meanings that are often rearranged by familial separation. I have written these pages as a hopeful gesture, as a way to participate in the possibility of wholeness. To guide me in this work, I have looked to the mothers.

Mothers, as ethnographer Gabrielle Oliveira has put it, are at the center of constellations of transnational care.[1] In the astronomy of migration, they are the sun. As a mother, accompanied by her daughter in this work since she was three (she is ten as I complete revisions), I was most pierced, most warmed, most burned by the stories of mothers. The bright force of their love, filtered through the crevices and imperfections of my own maternal heart and writer's mind, brought me—brought *us* (I hope we have traveled far enough together, reader, you and I, to now be an *us*)—here.

What I mean is I had an ear to the rumble of coming loss when a mother told me she was teaching her eleven-year-old English and German to prepare her to emigrate because Latvia offered them nothing. And I had an ear to the timbre of anger when another mother said her children had to leave the country to "earn their piece of bread." I flinched at the twinge of desperation when a mother confided that she just needed one small daily text from her son laboring abroad that said, "Mama, everything is okay." I felt the heat of despair crowding the professional voice of the teacher, who lamented that children showed up for their high school graduation with tickets to England in their pockets. And I warmed with the flush of hope and pride that one's child, with a different kind of literacy education, would live in a world where borders, racial, economic, political, did not shut fast against hopes and dreams.

*You think you won't feel saudades?* one mother warned, apropos of exactly what, I do not recall. Was it in this interview or another that my daughter's feet swung from her chair, that she kicked at my shins, that she blessed me with a gap-toothed grin, strawberries on her breath? *Oh, you will.*

Yes, these stories revealed, community ties often fray over space and time. But if we listen closely, we can hear the ever-present hum of the mothers, knitting them back together.

# APPENDIX A

## *Methods Used in Brazil*

In Brazil I conducted nineteen literacy history interviews with sixteen individuals who either had family members who had lived abroad or had returned from living abroad themselves—including labor migrants, those who traveled for higher education, and high school study abroad participants—from a variety of social classes. I did not seek out key or focal participants, as might have been appropriate in other forms of qualitative work, but instead gathered life histories that were consistently nuanced and detailed across participants. Because it is not readily apparent who in Jaú is a returned migrant and who has family abroad (i.e., I did not find any local community organizations or networks of these groups), I recruited participants through a snowball sample, starting with a family member and extending to a local English-language school, the proprietor of which knew many family members of migrants and returned migrants. Participants' ages ranged from eighteen to sixty-five and educational levels from elementary school to a master's degree. Immigration destinations included Paraguay, Japan, the United States, France, Canada, Germany, and other sites in Europe. I did not ask directly about income and instead ascertained how participants experienced their social class through their discussions of education and explanations for their or their family member's migration, and by observing living and communication environments in homes. Conducted in Brazilian Portuguese, these interviews (1) addressed how family members had communicated across national borders across their lifespans; (2) elicited memories about how they learned to write via particular technologies (including letters and computers); and (3) asked for descriptions of how they used writing and associated technologies in their work and personal lives and what benefits they had experienced from such uses. Interviews lasted between thirty minutes and two hours, and I interviewed three participants a second time, six months later, to ask follow-up questions. Additionally,

I took notes on informal talk about transnational communication, reflecting the intertextual nature of interviews, which often spill over into other communicative events.[1] While my position as a foreigner made me an outsider to the community, my regular visits to and communication with local residents for over a decade and the transnational nature of my own family provided a basis of identification. In many cases, I found common ground with participants by discussing my then-three-year-old daughter, who accompanied me to Brazil on the research trip to visit her grandfather, uncles and aunts, and cousins, whom she had previously seen only across a computer screen in video chats.

To analyze both interviews and field notes, I used a constructivist approach to grounded theory that takes into account researchers' active roles in interpreting data.[2] This approach allowed a rigorous examination of the data at the same time as it acknowledged the active nature of my interpretation in light of my long-standing community relationships. Analysis included four rounds of coding. First, I coded for motivations (psychological need, missing a family member), types (letter, email, video chat, telephone), and frequency (daily, weekly, monthly) of transnational communication. I noted that all participants reported that migration led to an uptick in the frequency of their use of literacy technologies, due to *saudades*. In a second round of coding, I identified how *saudades* were resolved (or not) in relation to how participants spoke of valuing particular media (whether they promoted closeness, seemed to require labor, made the participant feel alienated, etc.).

Third, to account for how the technological and economic aspects of literacy coalesced, I coded for how those differently positioned with regard to social class came to own or use particular communication technologies. Labor migrants often sent the technology back home as a gift to their family members. Moreover, the labor or effort involved in buying the technology, learning to use it, and using it helped establish an intimate connection via that medium. In other words, how people valued the labor of their family member—valuations connected to their social class standing—shaped how they experienced communication across distance.

To describe the relationship among *saudades*, materiality of communication, and labor, I turned to migration studies' theories about remittances and my own remittance experiences. Such theories address the educational impact of financial remittances that are invested in infrastructure and tuition for families back home, as well as social remittances, such as cultural practices, that circulate between host country and homeland.[3] Using a constant comparative method of theory building, I posited that literacy, as a sociomaterial resource tied to wider economic realities, could work similarly across transnational networks.[4] I coded this remittance circuit as *writing remittances*.

Much like economic remittances, writing remittances appeared to function as circuits involving what economic sociologist Zelizer has called "interchange, intercourse, and mutual shaping."[5] Such a description coalesced with what participants told me of receiving literacy-based remittances that then demanded an exchange of labor—in their case, the labor of using the remittance or learning to use it to emotionally support migrants abroad. In other words, writing remittances formed a bidirectional transactional circuit. To track the implications of such remittances for homeland residents, in a fourth round of coding, I examined (1) how the remittances functioned pre- and post–Internet access and (2) how participants invested (or did not invest) such remittances both locally and transnationally.

APPENDIX B

# *Methods Used in Latvia*

Having served in Daugavpils as a Peace Corps English education volunteer in 1999–2001, I have maintained contact with community members for sixteen years, speak Russian, and have basic conversational ability in Latvian. This background facilitated my participant observation, which I undertook over a concentrated period of five weeks in the summer of 2014. Specifically, I took ethnographic notes on informal literacy practices and talk about migration in three Daugavpils communities: a *dacha* (summer house) community (mostly retired people whose children have left for abroad), within a community of educated young adults preparing to migrate, and in a family preparing their children to migrate elsewhere. During my fieldwork, my daughter and I were living with one of the central families in the *dacha* community—a mother and father whose son had been working in Belgium as a lawyer for seven years and whom I met in 1999 as a Peace Corps volunteer. Introduced initially through a mutual acquaintance, between 1999 and 2001 I often stopped by the local bookstore that the mother ran for tea and conversation and soon became a friend and frequent visitor at her house. Likewise, I entered the community of young adults through contacts made from my Peace Corps years. I met one of my focal participants, Katrina, in 1999, when she was fourteen years old. The daughter of my former Russian tutor, with whom I maintained a warm relationship during the intervening years, Katrina was eager to speak with me and introduce me to her friends, many of whom were planning to migrate or who had already left. Finally, I encountered the family preparing their children to migrate elsewhere, thanks again to Katrina, who went to school with the family's eldest daughter, then living in Cyprus. The family was eager to meet with me, in part, I came to understand, because they believed I could provide English-language assistance. Working with these diverse communities gave me a sense of how family constellations shaped migration-driven literacy learning.

Because Latvia's social context is shaped not only by movement across space but also by historical movement across time—namely, the collapse of the Soviet Union, the impoverished years following independence, its new status as a member of the European Union, and the global economic crisis—I also used literacy history interviews to track individuals' literacy use across their lifespans. I conducted 27 LHIs (all but two in Russian, the native language of all but one interviewee, whose native tongue was Latvian), to understand how this larger history acted on the practices that I observed. In these interviews, lasting between thirty minutes and two hours (and in five cases including extensive follow-up interviews), community members detailed their literacy experiences in relation to these changes.

Table 4.1 below, co-developed in its initial form with Madina Djuraeva, attempts to capture key elements, by individual participant, of experiences with migration-driven print and digital literacy practices throughout Latvia's political transitions. This table seeks to complement both the composite story I tell in chapter 4 and the tight visual story told by that chapter's map by representing key experiences across all participants. Table 4.2 offers a snapshot of who reported receiving or sending writing remittances and who described experiencing anticipatory literacy learning.

Table 4.1 MIGRATION-DRIVEN PRINT AND DIGITAL LITERACY PRACTICES AMONG LATVIANS

| | *Andris* | *Helena* | *Vadim* | *Valera* | *Vanessa* | *Olga* | *Julia* | *Pavel* |
|---|---|---|---|---|---|---|---|---|
| **Year born** | 1960 | 1968 | 1963 | 1959 | 1948 | 1960 | 1974 | 1971 |
| **Primary relative abroad** | Daughter | Husband, Daughter | Stepson | Daughter | Son | Sister, daughter | Husband | Stepson |
| **Where, length of time, education/ occupation** | Cyprus, since 2009, BA, offshore business | Ireland, since 2005, husband in construction | Canada and England, since 2002, MA, psychology/ international development, project manager | England, five years, student | England, since 2002 vocational college, factory worker | Sister: Switzerland since 2002, manager Daughter: Cyprus, five years, international business | Ireland, since 2012 years, construction | Cyprus,? years, hospitality industry |
| **Education/ occupation of participant** | Incomplete MA in history, business owner | Nurse | MA, psychology, professor | Higher education/ security guard and construction worker | Higher education | Higher Education in nutrition, small business owner | Cook | Salesperson |

(*continued*)

Table 4.1 CONTINUED

| | *Andris* | *Helena* | *Vadim* | *Valera* | *Vanessa* | *Olga* | *Julia* | *Pavel* |
|---|---|---|---|---|---|---|---|---|
| **Letters** | Doesn't write letters ("they are time consuming") though occasionally receives postcards. During Soviet times, "everyone wrote letters." When served in the army in Turkmenistan corresponded with mom, and recalls mom writing to his sisters. | Receives postcards from husband on birthday and sometimes from friends. Exchanged letters with friends and family in Russia during Soviet Union. Received poems and letters from husband even while living in the same city. Finds letters more "emotional" than Skype. | Didn't exchange letters, only postcards with his son. Stopped writing letters in general after Perestroika. Used to write letters to his relatives in Riga once in 3 or 6 months. Feels nostalgic about writing letters and sending postcards. | In 1980s, often wrote letters and sometimes called family in Ukraine. | — | — | Received and wrote letters while husband was in Soviet army. Letters with friends and family in Russia. | Received and wrote letters while serving in army. Wrote letters to distant republics under school's pen pal program. |

| | | | | | | | | |
|---|---|---|---|---|---|---|---|---|
| **Digital communication** | Usually Skypes with daughter in the evenings for an hour or more. Skype is also used to gather as a family and have quality conversations. | Skypes every day with husband. Talks to daughter on Skype. | Prefers Skype over email, has been using since 2002. Skypes once a week or so, after stepson sends a text message setting up a time. | Prefers Skype, as can see their daughter and granddaughter. | Often uses Skype to chat with son at *dacha*. Uses Odnoklassniki, a Russian-language social media site, and writes emails to friends. | Skypes with daughter and to gather as a family for long conversations. Uses Skype to communicate with her sister in Switzerland, (first without a webcam, then with a webcam). | Rarely Skypes with husband because of time difference. | — |
| **Telephone** | Sometimes texts. When urgent, makes phone calls. | Texted after mobile phones appeared but before had access to Internet, because it was instant. Uses text messaging to make plans to Skype. | — | — | Before Skype used to call and text message more often. Uses text-messaging as a way to check in. | Occasionally texts, but calls for urgent demands. | — | — |

(*continued*)

Table 4.1 CONTINUED

| | *Andris* | *Helena* | *Vadim* | *Valera* | *Vanessa* | *Olga* | *Julia* | *Pavel* |
|---|---|---|---|---|---|---|---|---|
| **Context of computer use** | Got first personal computer around 1995–1997, when his children were students. Has used computer for work for 15 years. | — | First time used computer was in 1980s in school. Received university courses on different computer-based programs. Received computer from son in 2013. | Had computer before going to England, while his daughter was in school, because he wanted to "stay young." | Got computer around 2009 to Skype. Her grandson gave her his used laptop. Learned to use computer in 1990s for work. | Husband saved money to get a computer, mainly to play games. Now she gets his hand-me-down computers when he buys a new one. | — | — |

| | *Liga* | *Oleg* | *Marina* | *Ljudmila & daughter Nadia* | *Nadezhda and Michael* | *Dimitry* |
|---|---|---|---|---|---|---|
| **Year born** | 1959 | 1954 | 1946 | Tatyana: 1963<br>Nadia: 1992 | Nadezhda: 1959<br>Michael: 1959 | 1984 |
| **Primary relative abroad** | Son and aunt | Son | Son and daughter | Son/brother | Son | Self |
| **Where, length of time, education/ occupation of family member** | Son: Berlin since 2011, engineering student; aunt: New York for 70 years. | Chicago since 2002, vocational degree, runs a day care center. | Son: England, since 2010, student and factory worker; daughter: Russia, since 1989, higher education, human resources | Iceland since 2010, higher education, cook | Ireland and then Scotland, since 2001, higher education, taxi driver | England, since 2010, factory work |
| **Education/ Occupation of participant** | MA degree and second BA degree, real estate | Specialist in oil drilling | Vocational degrees, retired school office assistant | Higher education | Higher education, retired | High school, incomplete higher education, various skill-driven certificates in different areas, including translation; factory work |

(*continued*)

Table 4.1 CONTINUED

| | *Liga* | *Oleg* | *Marina* | *Ljudmila & daughter Nadia* | *Nadezhda and Michael* | *Dimitry* |
|---|---|---|---|---|---|---|
| **Letters** | Doesn't exchange letters with son. Used to exchange letters with aunt who fled to New York after World War II. | Didn't write letters to son. During 1970s when worked in Iraq, wrote letters to family in Russia. | During Soviet Union, when her daughter migrated to Russia, they exchanged letters twice a month. Also exchanged letters with husband when he was serving in army. Exchanged letters with relatives in Belorussia. | Ljudmila: No letters from son, only postcards and gifts; received letters from husband when he was serving in Belarus in 1980s; Nadia: received letters from grandparents while abroad in Germany. | Michael wrote some letters to his parents and siblings in the Caucasus before they moved to Latvia; Nadezhda exchanges letters with her friend in Poland; no letter exchange with son. | Wrote his last letter 2008 or 2009 to his friend, but now mostly uses Facebook or Skype. His dad used to write his brother in Ukraine once a month. |
| **Digital communication** | Uses Skype for messaging and daily synchronous video chat with son and aunt. Coordinates Skype with 81-year-old mother. | Got Skype in 2009 and uses it to talk to son once a week. Sends text messages to set up a time to Skype. | Uses Skype often to talk to her son. Was virtually present at his wedding in Cyprus. Uses text messaging to let her son know to log on to Skype. | Skype: "It's simpler and cheaper to talk on Skype." Tatyana learned to Skype to talk to Nadia when she was abroad in 2007. Uses Facebook messaging almost every day to coordinate Skype times, as time difference makes synchronous chatting difficult. Used email with friends before Facebook. | Use Internet to chat on Odnoklassniki with relatives and friends. Talk to grandson every day through messaging on Odnoklassniki. Prefer Skype over messaging or phone. The "livelier" the talk, the better. | Uses emails to write official letters, including to a landlord, government official, and college administrator. Uses Facebook mostly to communicate with people whose phone numbers he doesn't have. |

| | | | | | | |
|---|---|---|---|---|---|---|
| **Telephone** | Her son uses two phones, one specifically to call Latvia, as incoming calls are less expensive. Was told by her children to get a better phone to write longer messages. | Kept in touch with his son through phone calls in 2002. | Phone was used frequently during first years her son was abroad. She often uses text messages to keep in touch with her daughter. | Her son calls his grandparents since they don't know how to use computers. When Nadia was abroad, she called her mom every other day rather than Skype. Ljudmila often awaits "one little text," from her son that says, "Mama, everything is ok." | Talk to their son on the phone every other day, since he doesn't have access to the Internet at his job. | In 2004, used calling cards to call his mom. Now, uses mobile phone since his mom is not good with computers. |
| **Context of computer use** | First computer in 2005 | First computer around 1994 for work | Learned how to work on old computers at work from 1987 to 1993. Also, she and her husband helped to get computers for their children. Her son bought a laptop in 2003. | Had computer since 2002. Got Internet later. Used computers because it was a trend and handy for work. | Juris had a computer at his job in 1990s before his son left. Later they got their own computer to pay bills and to talk on Odnoklassniki. | Although his mom has a computer, she has little knowledge of how to use it. Bought his first computer in 2003 after working abroad and saving some money. |

(*continued*)

Table 4.1 CONTINUED

| | *Lida* | *Vasily* | *Katrina* | *Alexei* | *Julija* | *Natasha* |
|---|---|---|---|---|---|---|
| **Year born** | 1951 | 1985 | 1986 | 1964 | 1954 | ? |
| **Who is abroad** | Aunt and eldest son | Himself and sister | Grandparents, aunt, boyfriend, best friend | Daughter and son, sister-in-law | Son and his family, friend, relatives | Herself, daughter, extended family |
| **Where, length of time, education/ occupation of family member** | Aunt in Moscow for decades; son in USA and then Belgium, seven years; master's degree, works in European law | Both in United Kingdom, where he lived for five years before returning (initial trip was 2006 for summer work). | Grandparents in Moscow; aunt in Switzerland then Italy since 1994, scientist; boyfriend in France since 2012; best friend in Germany since 2011 | All in Germany for 2.5 years; vocational education | Son and family in Germany for five years, partial completion of higher ed., uses professional skills in fixing cars and massage; friend in United States; relatives in Poland | All in United Kingdom. She has been there since 2010 and has a master's degree in English education (previously taught at Daugavpils Polytechnical University); her daughter has been there since 2013 to study at the university. |
| **Education/ occupation of participant** | Higher education in chemistry; retired small business owner/ former chemist | Higher education in engineering; entrepreneur | Medical degree; doctor | Vocational college | Higher education; mechanical engineer | Master's degree in education; former teacher working in a factory then caring for elderly in United Kingdom. |

| | | | | | | |
|---|---|---|---|---|---|---|
| **Letters** | Her mom wrote to her aunt in Moscow; aunt used to write addressing everyone in neighborhood; wrote to brother during college years. When studying abroad, son wrote letters once a week in tiny handwriting. Last letter wrote to her son was 2007. | Postcards on holidays or birthdays; recalls mother writing letters to relatives in Ukraine and Belarus. | She wrote first letters to her Russian grandparents after she moved to Latvia. Received postcards from her aunt and wrote her letters. Still writes letters with poems, pictures to her best friend who is abroad as a way to cheer her up. | Doesn't have any memory of writing or receiving letters—only some gifts, like a camera, from his children. | Doesn't exchange letters due to lack of time. Before Skype, wrote letters to her friend in United States. In the past, exchanged letters with Polish relatives. | No letter or postcards were written during her work abroad. However, in her early years, she would exchange letters with girlfriends in Georgia, relatives in Poland, a suitor in France (in French). Finds letters more intimate than digital communication. |
| **Digital communication** | Email feels "concrete" and has written to son since 2007; emails to former classmates and relatives; also regularly Skypes | Used email during work in aviation industry and once purchased a laptop, used Skype for local and international communication | Communicated with relatives abroad through Facebook at Internet cafés. Emails aunt abroad and mom in Daugavpils (every day). Skypes/ Facebooks with godparents in Italy, boyfriend in France, and best friend in Germany. | Skype: "It's simpler and cheaper to talk on Skype." | Uses Skype twice a week, the other times talks on the phone. | Started using Skype as soon as she bought computer on her first good salary after half a year abroad to communicate with daughter, who taught her to use it. |

(*continued*)

Table 4.1 CONTINUED

| | *Lida* | *Vasily* | *Katrina* | *Alexei* | *Julija* | *Natasha* |
|---|---|---|---|---|---|---|
| | | | | | | To keep up with people's lives, uses Facebook; also Facebook messages when no other connection is available or to convey an emotional (not instrumental) message. (Her daughter would write "I love you, Mom.") |
| **Telephone** | Rare phone calls. First mobile phone was a gift from Norwegian host family of younger son. | First year abroad communicated through mobile phone/text messages once a week; bought a smartphone in 2010; uses WhatsApp for pictures and frequent communication. | N/A | When not at home near the computer, texts with children. Talks with his children every day on the phone at unscheduled times. | Uses phone along with Skype. | Used phone to call home daily during earlier stay abroad; uses WhatsApp often. |

| | | | | | | |
|---|---|---|---|---|---|---|
| **Context of computer use** | In 2010 (right before retirement), her son gave her his old computer bought in Belgium. He taught her how to use it and she took a computer literacy class to follow up. | In second year abroad got a laptop. Reads books through Kindle. Gave his old computer to parents and taught dad to use Skype. Parents bought him his first computer in high school, before he went abroad. | Used computers for the first time when she was 8 or 9 at school. Sent her first email during school years to her aunt in Italy. At the age of 20 got a Mac from her aunt. | Before his children went abroad, he had both computer and Internet. Son taught him to use the computer. | First purchased in 2002–2003, although Internet was connected later. Often uses computer to read news and translate texts from Latvian. Learned how to use a computer from husband. | First family computer was bought by ex-husband for their daughter, who was in eighth grade. Daughter used the computer to communicate with her while she was abroad. Uses computer and Internet for online/dating relationships. |

(*continued*)

Table 4.1 CONTINUED

| | *Galina* | *Mariana* | *Tatyana* | *Karina* | *Anastasiya* | *Ilona* |
|---|---|---|---|---|---|---|
| **Year born** | 1986 | 1983 | 1938 | 1968 | 1964 | N/A |
| **Who is abroad** | She was abroad for a summer (and returned); has friends in Germany and England; brother and father both abroad. | She was abroad (and returned); sister was abroad at time of interview. | Three grandchildren and her sister | She was abroad and returned, and her close friend and daughter are abroad. | Her sister | Sister and cousin |
| **Where, length of time, education/ occupation of family member** | Worked in Scotland for 4–5 months picking strawberries, is completing a Russian PhD, sells tea in the market, tutors in Russian; friends have been abroad since 2004 and 2010, respectively. | She was in Ireland for six years working as a maid, a nanny, and a cashier to support her sister in Latvia in the wake of her parents' death. The sister recently left for Ireland. | Granddaughter in Ireland since 2009 working as a maid and a cashier; other granddaughter in Germany since 2004 working as a nanny; grandson in Germany since 2012 working as a doctor; sister has lived life in Belarus. | She was in England for seven years working as a maid, then in a flower factory, and her friend has been there since 2009. Her daughter is a student. | Switzerland since 2004 working as an artist; daughter was in Ukraine for a year but returned. | Her sister was first in Germany and then Switzerland and has been abroad since 2001. Her cousin was in England and then Sweden since 1999. Sister runs a kindergarten. |
| **Education/ Occupation of participant** | MA in pedagogy | College degree in biology; seeking employment | High school; retired city employee | Higher ed. with a degree in early childhood education; radio disc jockey | Higher ed. with degree in English education; teacher | N/A |

| | | | | | | |
|---|---|---|---|---|---|---|
| **Letters** | During her time in Scotland, she wrote letters and sent postcards to a friend for fun, about once a month. Didn't have access to a personal computer or Internet. Exchanged letters with dad and brother. | Wrote letters and sent postcards on birthdays. Wrote letters in her childhood to her grandma, who lived in a different Latvian city. | Wrote letters and sent packages during the Soviet Union, as the system worked well and was free. Stopped writing letters when Soviet Union collapsed, as it's become too cumbersome. | Exchanged letters with a friend who went to England in 1995. They wrote long letters and sent pictures. As a child, exchanged letters with dad in Russia. Thinks of the letter as connected to an individual soul, while computer messages are generic. Still keeps love letters from her youth. | At the beginning of her sister's migration, they exchanged letters every other month. In her childhood, parents wrote letters to relatives in Lithuania, Moscow, St. Petersburg, and Belarus. | Hasn't written letters since Soviet Union collapsed, though remembers parents writing each other letters. |
| **Digital Communication** | While abroad, sometimes wrote emails using a shared computer. Uses Odnoklassniki, Skype to communicate with friends. Had Draugiem, a Latvian social networking site, but tired of too many social sites. Now has Facebook only. | Uses Skype a lot, although not being able to keep/save Skype conversations is a disadvantage in comparison to letters. | Doesn't write anything to her grandchildren; talks to them on Skype via the iPad they gave her. | While abroad for two years used Internet at the library to write emails. After getting her own laptop, used Skype every day. Says she "lived" on Skype. Used and uses Facebook messages often. Because she speaks for a living on the radio, prefers to write, not to speak, to family and friends abroad. | Prefers Skype to text messages. She used to text, Skype, and Facebook with her daughter while she was a student in Ukraine. | Got a webcam for her computer because she thought her sister needed to see her family, due to the longing she experienced abroad. |

(*continued*)

Table 4.1 CONTINUED

| | *Galina* | *Mariana* | *Tatyana* | *Karina* | *Anastasiya* | *Ilona* |
|---|---|---|---|---|---|---|
| **Telephone** | When was abroad, frequently phoned friends and spoke 1–2 hours, as it was cheap. Had own cell phone and used cards. | She bought and sent phone to her sister. Often called and sent messages to relatives and friends. | Used to make calls from post office during Soviet Union. Tends to call more often now from cell phone. | When she was abroad, talked to her mom on the phone, since she couldn't use Internet. She then bought her mother a laptop and taught her to use Skype. During Soviet times made calls from the post office to relatives in Siberia. | Sometimes talks on the phone with her sister and often with her husband's parents, who are in Ukraine. | Used to keep in touch with her relatives through phone. |
| **Context of computer use** | Opened her first email in high school. Bought her first computer with her own money for her studies in 2009 or 2010. | Bought her first laptop after 4 years in Ireland to use Skype to speak with friends. | Got iPad as a gift on her 70th birthday from her granddaughters. No computer. | Bought a computer for her daughter for school. After 2 years abroad bought a laptop for herself to communicate with her family and friends every night. | Had computer with Internet since 2003 for school, which was before her sister's migration. Sister bought a computer for their parents to communicate. | — |

Table 4.2 WRITING REMITTANCES AND ANTICIPATORY LITERACY LEARNING AMONG LATVIANS

| | *Andris* | *Helena* | *Vadim* | *Valera* | *Vanessa* | *Olga* | *Julia* | *Pavel* | *Liga* | *Oleg* | *Marina* | *Ljudmila and Nadia* | *Nadezhda and Michael* |
|---|---|---|---|---|---|---|---|---|---|---|---|---|---|
| **Writing Remittance** | | WR | WR | | WR | WR | | | | | WR | WR | WR |
| **Anticipatory Literacy Learning** | ALL | ALL | ALL | ALL | | | | | ALL | | ALL | ALL | |

| | *Lida* | *Vasily* | *Katrina* | *Alexei* | *Julia* | *Dimitry* | *Natasha* | *Galina* | *Mariana* | *Tatyana* | *Karina* | *Anastasija* | *Ilona* |
|---|---|---|---|---|---|---|---|---|---|---|---|---|---|
| **Writing Remittance** | WR | WR | WR | WR | | WR | WR | | WR | WR | WR | WR | WR |
| **Anticipatory Literacy Learning** | ALL | ALL | ALL | | ALL | ALL | ALL | ALL | | | | | ALL |

## APPENDIX C

# *Methods Used in the United States*

Having looked at variations in migration-driven literacy learning experiences in the previous chapters across a range of participants living in homelands, I aimed here to understand this process from the perspective of migrants, through portraits of two multigenerational families in the United States. As in the previous chapters, I recruited research participants beginning with relationships I had already established in the community. I recruited five participants from two families who had made homes in Wisconsin—Dima, Nadia, and Oksana who had recently emigrated from Ukraine, and Carolina and José, longtime Wisconsin residents who had migrated from Mexico as children. I did not specifically seek out families that I knew engaged in writing remittance circuits, reasoning that if they did not (as was the case with José), the conditions surrounding that choice would be important to explore. As in the previous chapters, I used literacy history interviews to understand how writing remittances formed (or did not) a part of their longer literacy histories.

Working with members of the same family allowed me to explore age- and experience-based variations in migration-driven literacy learning, having to do with (1) experiences in formal educational institutions in the United States; (2) opportunities (or lack of opportunities) for language learning; (3) literacy experiences in home countries; and (4) relationships with both home country and local family members.

Tracking these practices across generations offered two insights that helped explain how migrant families experienced writing remittances. First, it revealed how participants' beliefs about what literacy is and can do, developed in their practices, guided their approaches to writing remittances. Second, it revealed how writing remittance practices involving family in homelands moved bidirectionally, which I label "writing remittance resonances stateside" in Table 5.1, enriching the informal literacy learning occurring within families in host countries.

Table 5.1

| | *Literacy Beliefs and Associations* | *Writing Remittance Practices* | *Writing Remittance Resonances Stateside* |
|---|---|---|---|
| **Oksana** | English is necessary for community and family participation | Holds English contests with granddaughter in Ukraine and grandson in Wisconsin | Practices and mediates English learning within family |
| **Nadia** | Colloquial English promotes business success, social acceptance | Records English speech for brother's video game business; edits his English | Develops website for business |
| **Dima** | English was hard to learn at first | English practice contests with cousin in Ukraine | Learns some Ukrainian from grandmother |
| **Carolina** | Literacy can be difficult to acquire; it is costly | Teaches sister English words in letters; saves money to send tablet to cousin's son to help him learn to read | Supports daughter's entry into book contest with her migration story |
| **José** | Literacy is a long-term investment and an individual and community resource; biliteracy is part of literacy | Plans to wait to send writing remittances, in the form of legal knowledge, until attains law degree | Develops "pay it back and pay it forward" as a guiding educational philosophy |

# NOTES

*Preface*

All maps were developed by Casey Kalman of the University of Wisconsin Cartography Laboratory.

An early version of chapter 2 appears as "Writing Remittances: Migration-Driven Literacy Learning in a Brazilian Homeland," *Research in the Teaching of English* 50, no. 4 (2016): 422–449. An early version of chapter 3 appears as "Shifting Global Literacy Networks: How Emigration Promotes Literacy Learning in Latvia," *Anthropology and Education Quarterly* 49, no. 2 (2018): 165–182.

1. Burke and Mendoza, "At Least 3 Tender Age Shelters Set Up for Child Migrants"; Kraft, "Separating Parents from Their Kids at the Border."
2. Barnes, "US Officials Took Baby Daughter from Mother."
3. Hennessy-Fiske, "'Prison-Like' Migrant Youth Shelter."
4. Thompson, "Listen to Children Who've Just Been Separated from Their Parents."
5. U.S. Department of Homeland Security, "Next Steps for Families."
6. "NEW: I just spoke with the former head of US Immigration & Customs Enforcement (ICE)—He tells me that he expects hundreds of separated children will never be reunited with their parents. They will be lost in the system. Orphaned by the US Govt.'" Proskow, Twitter post.
7. Miroff, "A Family Was Separated at the Border."
8. Kraft, "Separating Parents from Their Kids at the Border."
9. Calderon et al., "Letter to DHS from Faculty."

10. Lanard, "UN Human Rights Chief." On June 19, the day commemorated in the United States for the abolition of the slavery of African Americans, the United States withdrew from the UN Council on Human Rights. Harris, "Trump Administration Withdraws U.S."
11. Amnesty International, "USA: Policy of Separating Children from Parents."
12. Klein and Liptak, "Trump Ramps Up Rhetoric."
13. van der Kolk, *The Body Keeps the Score*; Brand, "Healing and the Brain"; Ife, "Maktivist Literacies"; Vieira, "Writing's Potential to Heal"; Pennebaker and Evans, *Expressive Writing*.
14. Winn, *Girl Time*.
15. Galtung, "Tenemos un Potencial Enorme"; Ospina-Ramirez and Ospina-Alvarado, "Futuros Posibles."

*Introduction*

1. United Nations Department of Economic and Social Affairs, Population Division, "Change in World Migration Stock."
2. For example, on the effect of migration on left-behind families, primarily children, the authors of a UNICEF report on five countries in the Caribbean and Latin America note the impact of parental migration on remaining children (including psychological distress and risky behaviors) and in the reconfiguration of family structures. D'Emilio et al., "The Impact of International Migration."
3. Following economist Loïc Wacquant, I understand "globalization" as a global neoliberal regime characterized by social insecurity, a cultural trope of self-reliance that includes the mobility of labor, and the criminalization of poverty. Wacquant, *Punishing the Poor*.
4. On the net loss of skilled workers, see Gibson and McKenzie, "Eight Questions about Brain Drain." On the potential trauma of familial separation see Castañeda and Buck, "Remittances, Transnational Parenting, and the Children Left Behind" and D'Emilio et al., "The Impact of International Migration." It's important to note, however, that the psychological (and educational) impact of familial separation is contextual, as shown by Coe, *The Scattered Family*, Baldassar, "Missing Kin," Dreby, *Divided by Borders*, and Dreby and Stutz, "Making Something of Sacrifice."
5. For studies of how migrants' remittances can promote school success (depending on gender, legal status, and other factors), see Abrego, *Sacrificing Families*; Nobles, "Parenting from Abroad"; Dreby, *Divided by Borders*. For a rigorous ethnography of how migrants' social support can promote school success for homeland children (especially girls), see Oliveira, *Motherhood across Borders*.
6. For how potential migrants gain skills in anticipation of moving, see Beine, Docquier, and Rapoport, "Brain Drain"; Batista, Lacuesta, and Vicente,

"Testing the Brain Gain Hypothesis." For studies of brain grain and brain circulation, see Mayr and Peri, "Return Migration"; Tung and Lazarova, "Brain Drain." For an overview of how migration can promote the remittance of technological skills and scientific knowledge, see Docquier and Rapoport, "Globalization." Additionally, McKenzie, "Worrying Too Much about Brain Drain?," maintains that the detrimental effects of the emigration of skilled workers are overstated.

7. See the pathbreaking Guerra, *Close to Home* and Meyers, *Del Otro Lado*.
8. Vieira, *American by Paper*.
9. In *Motherhood across Borders,* Oliveira documents (and unpacks) similar stated reasons for migration—"a better education"—among Mexican mothers in New York City whose children have stayed in Mexico.
10. There is ample ethnographic evidence, however, that it does. See Coe, *The Scattered Family*; Zacharia and Rajan, *Researching International Migration;* Abrego, *Sacrificing Families*; Meyers, *Del Otro Lado*; Oliveira, *Motherhood across Borders*.
11. Out-of-school learning experiences can be productively leveraged in classrooms, as many studies have shown. For a more detailed discussion, particularly in relation to funds of knowledge, see chapter 5.
12. That is, they are participating in "co-constituting" globalization. Hart, "Geography and Development."
13. Vigouroux, "Rethinking (Un)skilled Migrants."
14. The labels "skilled" and "unskilled" as applied to migrants are, in the end, a social construction, terms that do not actually reflect the human or economic value of the knowledge migrants embody, gain, and deploy. These terms are instead often used to justify their marginalization. Hagan, Hernández-León, and Demonsant, *Skills of the Unskilled*.
15. Ibid.; Banks et al., *Learning in and out of School in Diverse Environments*, 12.
16. For more about writing on the move in relation to economic and other values, see Lorimer Leonard, "Traveling Literacies" and Lagman, "Moving Labor."
17. See Brandt, "Sponsors of Literacy," on changing literacy standards across the twentieth century in Wisconsin. See Prendergast, *Buying into English*, for ethnographic insight into the rising, and ultimately unattainable, standards of English faced by Slovakians during the country's transition to capitalism.
18. Lising, "Language in Skilled Migration"; Prendergast, *Buying into English*; Hurst, "Regional Flows and Language Resources"; Blommaert, *Grassroots Literacy*; Lagman, "Moving Labor."
19. Hurst, "Regional Flows and Language Resources"; Piller and Cho, "Neoliberalism as Language Policy"; Canagarajah, "Skilled Migration and Development."
20. Graff's *The Literacy Myth* provides a historical demographic study of how literacy attainment does not necessarily lead to upward social mobility (religion,

race, and gender play a more important role). The idea that literacy can be attained and then retrieved for use has been critiqued by critical pedagogue Paulo Freire as the banking model of education in "The Banking Model of Education." See also Allan and McElhinny, "Neoliberalism, Language and Migration." Finally, see chapter 2 for a more in-depth discussion of literacy's changing valuation across borders.

21. In *Literacy Work in the Reign of Human Capital*, Evan Watkins develops the concept of "just-in-time human capital" to describe how literacy must be adapted for people to use it as an economic resource, a concept the conclusion discusses in more depth.
22. For a discussion of literacy as a sociohistoric trend, see Vieira et al., "Literacy Is a Socio-Historic Phenomenon."
23. Brandt, "Writing over Reading," 63.
24. Bazerman's definition of "writing" is the following: "Writing is a complex social participatory performance in which the writer asserts meaning, goals, actions, affiliations, and identities with a constantly changing, contingently organized social world, relying on shared texts and knowledge. The projection of meaning and shared orientations at a distance requires making assumptions and predictions about who will be reading the texts, what their interest and knowledge are likely to be, and how they may be using this information" ("What Do Sociocultural Studies of Writing Tell Us," 18).
25. Brandt, "Writing over Reading."
26. Rosenblatt, "The Transactional Theory of Reading and Writing"; Nystrand, *Opening Dialogue*.
27. Brandt, "Writing over Reading"; Brandt, *The Rise of Writing*.
28. Lewis and Fabos, "Instant Messaging," point to how digital technology makes reading and writing more reciprocal practices, as do Smith and Hull, "Critical Literacies," which Alverman and Robinson build on to suggest that when confronted with the transnational potential of digital literacy, young people are "readers becoming writers becoming global citizens" ("Youths' Global Engagement," 170). Brandt, *Rise of Writing*, goes further to suggest that with the rise of writing, people are now reading as writers, such that the act of reading gets subsumed into writing. See also Lam, "Multiliteracies on Instant Messaging," who argues that "the value of the Internet and new technologies may lie less in their myriad arrays of searchable information and more in their potential to enable the (re)designing and (re)configuring of social relationships to facilitate new ways of producing and sharing knowledge" (395).
29. Brandt and Clinton, "Limits of the Local."
30. Vieira, *American by Paper*.
31. I follow Robert Courtney Smith to understand transnational life as including "those practices and relationships linking immigrants and their children with

the home country, where such practices have significant meaning and are regularly observed" (*Mexican New York,* 6).

32. Glick Schiller, Basch, and Blanc-Szanton, "Transnationalism."
33. Levitt, "Social Remittances"; Levitt and Lamba-Nieves, "Social Remittances Revisited"; Zelizer, "Circuits in Economic Life."
34. Burnett, Merchant, Pahl, and Rowsell, "The (Im)materiality of Literacy."
35. Bartlett and Vavrus, *Rethinking Case Study Research.*
36. Population Reference Bureau, "Population Data Set, 2012."
37. Bartlett and Vavrus, *Rethinking Case Study Research.*
38. Literacy's meanings "accumulate" in literacy materials and practices over time. Brandt, "Accumulating Literacy"; Prior, "Combining Phenomenological and Sociohistoric Frameworks."
39. Bartlett and Vavrus describe the advantages of a transversal analysis this way: "The study of change and constancy over time opens up alternative explanations for phenomena that may seem self-evident if only examined from a contemporary perspective" (*Rethinking Case Study Research,* 53). For the use of literacy history interviews in transnational research, see Vieira, "Doing Transnational Literacy."
40. United Nations Department of Economic and Social Affairs, Population Division, "Change in World Migration Stock."

*Chapter 1*

1. Abrego, *Sacrificing Families.*
2. Gerber, *Authors of Their Lives.*
3. Foner, *From Ellis Island to JFK.*
4. Brandt, "Accumulating Literacy."
5. Anthropologist Jack Goody introduced the notion of domains of literacy in *The Logic of Writing and the Organization of Society*. He identified religion, law, government, and economy as writing's central domains, united by the technology of writing.
6. Vieira et al., "Literacy Is a Socio-Historic Phenomenon."
7. United Nations Department of Economic and Social Affairs, Division for Social Policy and Development, "Inequality Matters."
8. There are a host of other reasons people choose to or do not migrate, including network migration (Massey et al., "Theories of International Migration"). Additionally, the poorest of the world's poor generally do not migrate, as migration demands some initial resources, which is likely why the majority of migrants move from middle-income countries to high-income countries (United Nations Department of Economic and Social Affairs, "Migration Report 2015").

9. Prendergast, *Buying into English*; Hernández-Zamora, *Decolonizing Literacy*; Blommaert, *Grassroots Literacies*; Lagman, "Moving Labor."
10. Lagman, "Moving Labor."
11. Prendergast, *Buying into English*.
12. Blommaert, *Grassroots Literacies*.
13. On Mexican migration, see Hernández-Zamora, *Decolonizing Literacy*. For Brazilian migration, see Vieira, *American by Paper*, chapter 1.
14. There are, however, examples of how migrants strategically use and adapt their often multilingual literacy skills for mobility in host countries. These examples will be discussed in more detail in chapter 4.
15. Goody, *The Logic of Writing*.
16. Schmandt-Besserat, "The Envelopes That Bear the First Writing."
17. Vee, *Coding Literacy*.
18. Clanchy, *From Memory to Written Record*.
19. Ibid.
20. Vincent, *The Rise of Mass Literacy*.
21. For more on the way the value of multilingual resources travels, see Allan and McElhinny's "Neoliberalism, Language and Migration," Hurst's "Regional Flows and Language Resources," Lising's "Language in Skilled Migration," and Lorimer Leonard's "Traveling Literacies."
22. Brandt, "Sponsors of Literacy."
23. Salomon and Niño-Murcia, *The Lettered Mountain*.
24. Cornelius, *When I Can Read My Title Clear*.
25. Laquintano, *Mass Authorship and the Rise of Self-Publishing*.
26. Literacy scholar Allan Luke notes in "Genres of Power?" that the value of literacy depends on its market value and individuals' access to institutions that can interpret or convert these literacy resources into material resources.
27. United Nations Department of Economic and Social Affairs, "Migration Report 2015"; International Organization for Migration, "Migrants Crossing U.S.-Mexico Border Dying."
28. See Abrego, *Sacrificing Families*, for a grounded examination of the results of border enforcement on children from transnational families in Mexico.
29. Nystrand, *The Structure of Written Communication*. Nystrand draws on Russian literary theorist Mikhail Bakhtin to adapt dialogism to understand the process of writing and how to best teach it.
30. Weinstein, *Feel These Words*.
31. Rosenblatt, "The Transactional Theory of Reading and Writing," 6. See also Micciche on "writing's economy of connectedness" in the dialogic genre of acknowledgements, "Writing Material," 499.
32. See Burkitt's "Social Relationships and Emotions" on the communicative nature of emotion (40). See Wetherell's *Affect and Emotion* on affective practices. Discussing dance, Wetherell explains, "It constituted an ordering of bodily

possibilities, narratives, sense-making, and local social relations" (20). On writing's embodiment, especially in handwriting, see Haas and McGrath, "Embodiment of Literacy."

33. Fitzgerald, "Exploring Transnational and Diasporic Families."
34. Besnier, *Literacy, Emotion, and Authority.*
35. For how families mediate emotions, see Skrbis, "Transnational Families." For letter-writing between families, see Gerber, *Authors of Their Lives.* Besnier also suggests that letter writing on Tuvalu island was motivated by labor migration—even though literacy had been brought there by Samoan missionaries for the very different purpose of missionary work. He calls this a "'spontaneous' transfer of consumption-oriented literacy skills in religious contexts to letter writing," an activity documented elsewhere (*Literacy, Emotion, and Authority,* 572). For "souls," see Vieira, *American by Paper.*
36. Barthes, *A Lover's Discourse,* 15.
37. Gerber, *Authors of Their Lives.*
38. Lyons, *The Writing Culture.*
39. Madianou and Miller, *Migration and New Media.*
40. Baldassar and Merla, "Introduction," define the circulation of care as "the reciprocal, multidirectional, and asymmetrical family networks subject to the political, economic, cultural, and social contexts of both sending and receiving societies" (13). They elsewhere argue that conceptions of families bounded by physical space are normative and restrictive, and that transnational family members often care for each other in ways that are "multidirectional, and can take place simultaneously and diachronically"—in other words, through literacy, across space, and over time. "Locating Transnational Care," 29.
41. Parreñas, *Children of Global Migration*; Hochschild, "Love and Gold."
42. Waldinger, *The Cross-Border Connection.*
43. Merla, "A Macro-Perspective on Transnational Families."
44. Lyons, *The Writing Culture.*
45. Gerber, *Authors of Their Lives.*
46. My current favorite is *An American Marriage* by Tayari Jones.
47. Henkin, *The Postal Age.*
48. Cushman, *The Cherokee Syllabary.*
49. See Schwartz, Noguerón-Liu, and Gonzalez, "The Compression of Time and Space," on how U.S. adult education students are motivated to learn digital literacy while sharing slide shows with family in Mexico. See Baldassar, "Transnational Families and Aged Care," on how digital communication among Italian families may increase intergenerational contact as family members help each other communicate with loved ones abroad. See Kang, "Online Spatialisation and Embodied Experience," on how there is a sense of embodied communication in synchronous online communication with transnational Chinese families in London.

50. Following literacy theorist Allan Luke, "Literacy was and remains a key technology for the expansion, manipulation, and reconstruction of temporal and spatial relations. . . . The effects and consequences of literacy depend upon both their spatial and their temporal contexts" ("On the Taming of Time and Space," xi–xii).
51. While love and money seem to belong to entirely different realms of human experience, economic sociologists have shown that they are interrelated. For economic sociologist Viviana Zelizer, financial remittances sent by migrants to family members in homelands are emotional and economic "circuits," through which people negotiate relationships. ("Circuits in Economic Life," 32–33).
52. Thomas and Znaniecki, *The Polish Peasant.*
53. Madianou and Miller, *Migration and New Media.*
54. Rebecca Lorimer Leonard has called such circulation of literacy among transnational family members "relays"—the "handoff, bestowal, or delivery of literate strategies, skills, and habits developed over the course of a lifetime on the move." *Writing on the Move*, 44.

*Chapter 2*

1. Bartlett and Vavrus, *Rethinking Case Study Research*, 19.
2. Ibid.
3. This is similar to what globalization ethnographer Anna Tsing calls "patchwork" (*Friction*, xi).
4. For more on life-span approaches to research on transnational literacy, see Falconer, Cushman, Juzwik, and Dunn, "Editors' Introduction."
5. Brandt, "Accumulating Literacy."
6. For the "macro-force of literacy" see Brandt, *Rise of Writing*. As Duffy points out, the subjectivity of this method is its strength, not its weakness, as it reveals how people understand their uses of literacy. If literacy is a sociocultural practice, as new literacy studies scholars have demonstrated since the 1980s, then these subjective experiences of literacy deserve sustained attention, particularly, as Duffy again argues, when those telling the stories are marginalized subjects, such as migrants or refugees, whose words may not be documented in archives ("Recalling the Letter"). For an argument on the utility of the literacy history interview in transnational research, also see Vieira, "Doing Transnational Literacy."
7. Frank, "Anthropology and Individual Lives."
8. I further develop these ideas in Vieira, "Writing about Others."
9. According to Tuck, "the danger in damage-centered research is that it is a pathologizing approach in which the oppression singularly defines a community. Here's a more applied definition of damage-centered research: research that

operates, even benevolently, from a theory of change that establishes harm or injury in order to achieve reparation" ("Suspending Damage," 413). She argues for a "desire-based framework" as an "antidote to damage-centered research" (416). For "humanizing" research agendas see Paris and Winn, *Humanizing Research*.

10. According to a 2017 estimate, 0.1 migrants leave for every 1,000 people in Brazil. That's a net loss counting both immigration and emigration. U.S. Central Intelligence Agency, "The World Factbook."
11. Instituto Brasileiro de Geografia e Estatística, "Brasil" and "São Paulo, Jaú, Infográficos, Frota."
12. Ivlevs, "Minorities on the Move?"
13. For Latvian overspending in the real estate boom, see Smith and Swain, "Economic Crisis." For the resulting inability of Latvians to pay their mortgages, see Apsite, Krisjane, and Berzins, "Emigration from Latvia."
14. Hazans, "The Changing Face of Latvian Emigration."
15. Latvia's net migration rate was –4 per 1,000—comparable to many places with long-standing conflict (Population Reference Bureau, "Population Data Set").
16. McGuinness, "Fears over Latvia Brain Drain."
17. Kalniņa-Lukaševica, "Demographic and Economic Changes."
18. Central Statistical Bureau of Latvia, "International Long-Term Emigration."
19. Daugavpils, "Society."
20. American Community Survey, "Educational Attainment" and "Place of Birth."
21. Annie E. Casey Foundation, "2017 Race for Results." For a qualitative critical race study of Wisconsin schools, see Lee, *Up Against Whiteness*.
22. American Community Survey, "Educational Attainment."
23. Ibarra, "Latin@ Wisconsin."

*Chapter 3*

1. Aguiar et al., "The Internet's New Billion."
2. Levitt, "Social Remittances."
3. Dick, "Diaspora and Discourse."
4. Zelizer, "Circuits in Economic Life," 32.
5. Ibid., 32–33.
6. To offer two examples: for low-wage transnational families from Vietnam, remittance money signals emotional investment, with implications for immigrants' social status back home (Thai, *Insufficient Funds*). Likewise, studies of transnational families across Ghana and the United States have shown that financial remittances signal care to such an extent that Ghanaian children whose parents are laboring abroad do not appear to experience psychological harm from lack of proximity to their parents; they experience

remittances as direct care (Coe, *The Scattered Family*; Poeze and Mazzucato, "Ghanaian Children in Transnational Families.") One can also consider, as sociologist Arlie Hochschild does, the directive for service workers, especially women, to smile. Emotions in this case are commercialized, becoming part of paid labor (Hochschild, *The Managed Heart*).

7. This realization came from an analytic process called "constant comparison," in which I built theory in relation to emergent findings (Glaser, "The Constant Comparative Method").
8. Lewis, "'We Txt 2 Sty Cnnectd.'" As Lankshear and Knobel write, digital literacies not only have new "technical stuff," but also new "ethos stuff," new values, sensibilities, norms, and relational potentials, that are "dynamically interrelated" ("Researching New Literacies," 225).
9. Pahl, *Materializing Literacies in Communities.*
10. Haas and Takayoshi, "Young People's Everyday Literacies."
11. Haas, *Writing Technology.*
12. Reddy, *Re-Entangling Literacy.*
13. Vieira, *American by Paper.*
14. Reddy, *Re-Entangling Literacy.*
15. Lorimer Leonard, "Writing through Bureaucracy."
16. Prendergast and Ličko, "The Ethos of Paper."
17. Vieira, *American by Paper.*
18. Cushman, *The Cherokee Syllabary.*
19. Mignolo, *The Darker Side of the Renaissance.*
20. Sebba, *Spelling and Society.*
21. Baca, *Mestiz@ Scripts.*
22. Leander, Phillips, and Taylor, for example, describe the potential of new media for considering mobilities in relation to place, networks, and trajectories, as both social systems and people move ("The Changing Social Spaces"). Stornaiuolo, Smith, and Phillips describe how a transliteracies framework "spotlights the activity of creating, maintaining, and disassembling associations across space-times," an approach which "invites attention to the material dimension of literacy" ("Developing a Transliteracies Framework," 73–74). Likewise, Christiansen describes "deterritorialization," the process by which Mexican transnationals create intimate spaces of communication, bringing time and space into the virtual spaces of a social media site ("Creating a Unique Transnational Place"). Here, the experience of "deterritorialization" is emplaced in the materiality of these virtual sites.
23. Brandt and Clinton, "Limits of the Local."
24. Brandt, *Literacy in American Lives.*
25. Moss and Lyons-Robinson point out that "sponsorship doesn't account for family bonds, professional identities and reciprocal relationships" ("Making Literacy Work," 138).

26. As Budach, Kell, and Patrick have articulated, as instantiations of literacy's materiality, literacy objects that move across space can be "invested with emotion and can structure affect" in ways that are material, embodied, and deeply felt. In this way, writing remittances can function as what the authors call a "bonding object," with the potential to make meaning across space in ways that emphasize, well, *bonding* among people—especially those separated by distance ("Objects and Language," 392).
27. Centro de Estudos sobre as Tecnologias da Informação e da Comunicação, "TIC domicílios e usuarios 2012." Additionally, a more recent study showed that as of 2015 in Brazil, there were 53.51 personal computers per 100 households and 59.08 with internet access per 100 people (Instituto Brasileiro de Geografia e Estatística, "Brasil").
28. Nishijima, Ivanauskas, and Sarti, "Evolution and Determinants of Digital Divide."
29. Warschauer, *Technology and Social Inclusion,* 46.
30. I include return migrants in this table to account for the experiences of families and individuals for whom writing remittances traveled not via post but with a migrant himself or herself.
31. Spyer, *Social Media in Emergent Brazil.* The study also suggests that social media use correlates to increased awareness of alphabetic literacy.
32. Such an agentive orientation to literacy is particularly important in countering deficit views of migrant and refugee literacy. For example, see MacDonald, "Emissaries of Literacy," and Shapiro and MacDonald, "From Deficit to Asset." Sociolinguist and educational researcher Gee describes this approach to learning as involving what he calls gut brain, heart brain, and head brain (*Teaching, Learning, Literacy*)—a humanizing orientation that, when married to technological views of literacy as "a set of practices with infrastructural communication technologies," as computer literacy scholar Vee has defined it (*Coding Literacy*, 216), helps position writing remittances as sites of individual literacy learning that are necessarily tied up in larger technological and historical shifts.
33. In what I have previously discussed as "socio-materiality," social relationships are often communicated in the very matter of literacy. Put another way, the computers, papers, or pens with which one writes leach meanings from the economic, political, and interpersonal contexts in which they are used (*American by Paper*).
34. In a sense, via his brother's letter, he began to develop what migration scholars call "bifocality," a dual perspective that often results from migration (Vertovec, "Migrant Transnationalism"). Felipe's brother's letter provided a new lens on his world.
35. See Gerber, *Authors of Their Lives,* on maintaining a stable narrative identity across borders via letters.

36. Madianou and Miller, *Migration and New Media.*
37. Graff, *The Literacy Myth*; Street, *Literacy in Theory and Practice*
38. Pegurer-Caprino and Martínez-Cerdá, "Media Literacy in Brazil."
39. Fantin, "Mídia-Educacão," 36.
40. This is what Brazilian scholar Divina Frau-Meigs calls "transletramento," involving reading, writing, and coding ("Transletramento").
41. Pegurer-Caprino and Martínez-Cerdá, "Media Literacy in Brazil"; Spyer, *Social Media in Emergent Brazil.*
42. Vertovec, "Migrant Transnationalism."
43. Aguiar et al., "The Internet's New Billion."

*Chapter 4*

1. Research by Wills et al. set in London, a popular destination for migrants from Latvia, points to "brain wastage," where immigrants are "de-professionalized" and "de-skilled" (*Global Cities at Work*, 158).
2. Hazans, "The Changing Face of Latvian Emigration."
3. While some studies in other locales have shown that education can be improved by emigration, via remittances for tuition (Abrego, *Sacrificing Families*; de Haas, "Remittances, Migration, and Social Development"; Nobles, "Parenting from Abroad"), others show how the psychological impact of parental emigration in particular can have negative or mixed results for educational aspirations (Castañeda and Buck, "Remittances, Transnational Parenting, and the Children Left Behind"; Dreby and Stutz, "Making Something of Sacrifice"). For a nuanced treatment of brain drain, literacy, and affect, see Lagman ("Moving Labor").
4. Hagan, Hernández-León, and Demonsant, *Skills of the Unskilled.*
5. Even the concepts of "brain gain" and "brain circulation" conceive of migration-driven educational possibilities in terms of formal education (Mayr and Peri, "Return Migration"; Tung and Lazarova, "Brain Drain").
6. Newman, Niemeyer, Seddon, and Devos, "Understanding Educational Work."
7. Valentin, "The Role of Education."
8. Kell, "Placing Practices"; Brandt and Clinton, "Limits of the Local"; Leander and Boldt, "Rereading 'A Pedagogy of Multiliteracies'"; Lorimer Leonard, *Writing on the Move*; Bartlett, López, Vasudevan, and Warriner, "The Anthropology of Literacy."
9. Keating and Solovova, "Multilingual Dynamics," 1252.
10. Holland and Lave, "History in Person," 5.
11. Latvia is not alone as a country undergoing political changes that result in migration—which subsequently has consequences for literacy learning. Linguist Jan Blommaert has shown how changing national borders in western

African can undercut the way that letter writers can make their meanings understood to interlocutors elsewhere. In this example, shifting borders and political instability stripped away the literate resources of an individual writer, whose writing, as a result, did not hit its mark. Blommaert, *Grassroots Literacies*. On the mobility of educational contexts (such as school buses crossing racial and class boundaries), see Nordquist, *Literacy and Mobility*.

12. It's important to note that "borders" in the Latvian context is a word with a painful history. For some, it recalls Soviet deportations. And for some, it is not relevant to the "borderless" EU context. For others, however, it is all too relevant, as financial or legal conditions complicate travel within the EU. Despite these differing and often charged perspectives, what most can agree on is that Latvia has undergone vast changes in its recent history—changes that have affected what counts as a "border" for whom and, for the purposes of this book, how loved ones communicate and learn across distance.
13. Tsing defines friction as "awkward, unequal, unstable, and creative qualities of interconnection across difference," which implicates learning (*Friction*, 4).
14. Skrbis, "Transnational Lives"; Gerber, *Authors of Their Lives*; Besnier, *Literacy, Emotion, and Authority*.
15. Baldassar, "Missing Kin."
16. To conceptualize how experiences of such learning were tied up in shifts in social context, I was helped by socio-cultural studies of digital literacy practices, such as instant messaging, social networking, and multimodal composing. Such studies demonstrate how technology practices are taken up within existing social structures and cultures, such as the culture of a college campus, a public school, a family, or a friendship group. For instant messaging, see Haas and Takayoshi, "Young People's Everyday Literacies." For social networking, see Lam and Rosario-Ramos, "Multilingual Literacies." For the use of multiple modes and objects, see Madianou and Miller, *Migration and New Media*. For self-sponsored practices, see Hull, "Youth Culture and Digital Media" and Berry, Selfe, and Hawisher, *Transnational Literate Lives*.
17. Kell, "Placing Practices."
18. Smith, "The Ethnic Democracy Thesis"; Ivlevs, "Minorities on the Move?"
19. Pavlenko, "Multilingualism in Post-Soviet Countries," 283.
20. For an informative and nuanced discussion of the history of linguistic Russification in Latvian educational spaces, see ibid. Additionally, for a beautiful and necessary read of Latvians' experiences during World War II and the Soviet Union, see Nesaule, *Woman in Amber*.
21. In making this case, Ivlevs's "Minorities on the Move?" builds from the theories of brain drain advanced by Docquier and Rapoport, "Ethnic Discrimination."
22. Prior, *Writing/Disciplinarity*.
23. Kaiser and Nikiforova, "Borderland Spaces."
24. Lorimer Leonard, *Writing on the Move*.

25. Baldassar, "Missing Kin."
26. This contextual uptake worked much like that of fishermen in Kalman's 2013 study, who adapted GPS technologies in ways consistent with existing practices ("GPS Technology"). In what writing studies scholars have called "semiotic remediation," readers and writers often take up materials present at the site of one literacy event into new sites and arenas, repurposing them, layering meaning-making over time and space (Prior and Hengst, "Introduction"). For example, one education researcher tracked how a college student used a poster board in an improv comedy skit to make jokes about the mathematical concept pi, and then took up the practice years later, as a math teacher, to pique his students' interest in the concept (Roozen, "The 'Poetry Slam'").
27. Family histories of migration also made migration more plausible (Ivlevs and King, "Family Migration Capital").
28. The idea of language investment was developed in response to overly individualistic ideas of how ordinary language learners were motivated to learn a language. The concept draws from Bourdieu to suggest that people learn language to amass social capital—that is, not because they are responding to individual stimuli but instead in response to social habitus (Norton, "Social Identity").
29. For the benefit of multilingualism in destination countries depending on class and ethnicity, see Vigouroux, "Informal Economy"; for the economic sector, see Grin, Sfreddo, and Vaillancourt, *The Economics of the Multilingual Workplace*; for scale of analysis, see Hurst, "Regional Flows and Language Resources." Despite the value of multilingualism, many host countries seek to enforce standardized monolingual policies (Piller and Cho, "Neoliberalism as Language Policy"). See also Dustmann, "Speaking Fluency," and Parella, Petroff, and Solé, "The Upward Occupational Mobility."
30. Street, *Literacy in Theory and Practice.* See also Bibb, "The African American Literacy Myth."
31. Prendergast, *Buying into English.*
32. Chu, *Cosmologies of Credit,*132.
33. As Latvian social scientists have suggested, Latvian Russian speakers' past experiences with migration from the Soviet republics to Latvia correlate with a high rate of their children's migration from Latvia under the European Union. Ivlevs and King, "Family Migration Capital."
34. Blommaert, *Grassroots Literacies*; Hernández-Zamora, *Decolonizing Literacy*; Lagman, "Moving Labor"; Prendergast, *Buying into English*; Vigouroux, "Rethinking (Un)skilled Migrants"; Block, *Multilingual Identities;* Wills et al., *Global Cities at Work.*
35. In attending to both "time" and "space," I follow linguists Blackledge and Creese's emphasis on both "history and location" ("Translanguaging in Mobility," 34), an emphasis echoed by Compton-Lilly, "Introduction." In looking at how time and space shape both material technologies and language

practices, I am helped by the concepts of literacy's "materiality" and "immateriality" developed in Burnett, Merchant, Pahl, and Rowsell, "The (Im)materiality of Literacy."

36. As scholars have shown of financial remittances, people sent writing remittances to improve not necessarily the nation as a whole but the lives of those near and dear: "Migrants are not necessarily interested in the macro development of their home countries, but rather the improvement of the lives of their children, parents, siblings, and wider extended families" (Wills et al., *Global Cities at Work*, 162).
37. While the learning gleaned in migratory contexts may in some cases promote broader national development, it nonetheless often participates in what scholars Kuznetsov and Sabel have called "the perennial problem of learning from abroad" while "being victimized by the foreign master" ("International Migration of Talent," 5).
38. As sociolinguist Pavlenko has written, to understand post-Soviet language and literacy shifts, one must look to "regional and global forces—including transnational cash, migration, education, and communication flows" ("Multilingualism in Post-Soviet Countries," 301).
39. Duchêne and Heller, *Language in Late Capitalism*, 10. Another example of a site of "new discursive production" involves a case in which the Spanish state tried to surveil family-based transnational communication among migrants, and in response migrant communities developed their own migrant-run communication centers; see Sabaté i Dalmau, "Fighting Exclusion."
40. Zygmunt, "Language Education"; on the importance of informal education in the Latvian context, see also Kravale-Pauliņa, Mārīte, and Irēna Kokina, "The Integration."

*Chapter 5*

1. For in-depth portraits of the intelligence of American workers, including servers, see Rose, *The Mind at Work*.
2. Levitt, "Social Remittances"; Menjivar, *Fragmented Ties*; Madianou and Miller, *Migration and New Media*; Thai, *Insufficient Funds*.
3. Dávila et al., "On Latin@s and the Immigration Debate."
4. Moll, Amanti, Neff, and González, "Funds of Knowledge for Teaching," 134.
5. Vélez-Ibañez and Greenberg, "Formation and Transformation," 48.
6. Amanti, "Beyond a Beads and Feathers Approach."
7. Delgado-Gaitan, *The Power of Community*; Valenzuela, *Subtractive Schooling*; Purcell-Gates, "Literacy Worlds"; Lorimer Leonard, "Traveling Literacies"; Alvarez, "Brokering the Immigrant Bargain."
8. González, Moll, and Amanti, *Funds of Knowledge*.

9. Lam, "Literacy and Capital."
10. Simon, "Forging a Path to Higher Education."
11. Rounsaville, "Genre Repertoires."
12. Vélez-Ibañez and Greenberg, "Formation and Transformation."
13. In this project, I join scholars who, though they don't call it migration-driven literacy learning, are working to examine the implications of transnational digital literacy for immigrant families. Some have shown how migrant families use digital tools to mediate relationships with homelands via the circulation of information (Noguerón-Liu and Hogan, "Remembering Michoacán"). Likewise, Lam, "Literacy and Capital," in a study in which she defines literacy as communicative practice used to generate capital, has shown how participation in transnational online digital communities can help young people develop capital both within their groups and in other social fields in which they want to succeed.
14. Migration Policy Institute, "Unauthorized Immigrant Population Profiles"; Gonzales, "Learning to Be Illegal." Oppressive immigration policies also wrought havoc on communities, and shaped their literacies, well before the Trump presidency (Vieira, *American by Paper*).
15. For a discussion of effects on children of the Trump presidency, see Southern Poverty Law Center, "The Trump Effect."
16. On skilled Latin American immigrants, see Batalova and Fix, "New Brain Gain." For more on Mexican educational achievement in the United States, see the Migration Policy Institute's 2011 report, which shows that while 36% of first-generation Mexicans do not have high school diplomas, the situation improves for the second generation, at 11%, but that intergenerational progress slows after the second generation (Brick, Challinor, and Rosenblum, "Mexican and Central American Immigrants").
17. To be clear, transnational communication is not an escape from the state, nor are families themselves apolitical entities.
18. In previous research I have conducted with undocumented Brazilian migrants in the United States, for example, engaging in Brazilian churches provided one way for people to tentatively transcend a hostile environment through spiritual connection with a homeland (Vieira, *American by Paper*).
19. This context made me feel my privilege keenly. Although I am from an immigrant community, I am generations removed from the experience of migrating, and have never faced the kinds of economic, educational, political, and racial injustices that families described. These differences were further highlighted by the fact that in other ways, we had much in common. Nadia's and Carolina's children were the same age as my daughter. During fieldwork with Nadia's family, my daughter and her son played happily in the yard or on computers. And my relationship with Carolina prior to recruiting her for this study had revolved around sharing notes on our daughters' schools and extracurricular

activities. All three of us were doing our level best for our children's educations, but under highly stratified circumstances.

20. Street, *Literacy in Theory and Practice.*
21. These educational efforts can be seen in light of what Steven Alvarez has described as "the immigrant bargain" ("Brokering the Immigrant Bargain").
22. José also knew that doing so too soon also posed the risk of falling flat. As part of Julia's ongoing involvement in the social life of her hometown, she sent her elderly parents Internet-connected devices to allow them to video-chat and even installed the Internet in her parents' rural house. But her parents, to whom in José's words, "electricity is like twenty years new!," did not learn to use the devices, and the writing remittance failed. Remitting literacy successfully took a particular kind of bicultural rhetorical savvy: Carolina, for example, knew the kinds of literacy remittances to which her sister would respond and had a sense of which apps to buy for her cousin's son's iPad. Seen in light of his solid transnational social position underwritten by his mother's investment in cattle, and in light of the lessons of his mother's and sister's failed and successful writing remittances, José could well afford to bide his pedagogical time.
23. In 2016, the time of my fieldwork, close to 1.5 million Ukrainians had fled to neighboring countries (United Nations High Commissioner for Refugees, "Ukraine Operational Update," 2016). By 2018, the number of official asylum seekers was close to 1.8 million (United Nations High Commissioner for Refugees, Ukraine Operational Update," 2018).
24. Block calls this "declassing" (*Multilingual Identities*), and Vigouroux describes the arbitrary process whereby migrants in new countries are deemed "skilled" or "unskilled" in "Rethinking (Un)skilled Migrants."
25. On how English's value is contingent on changing political and economic regimes, see You, *Writing in the Devil's Tongue,* and Prendergast, *Buying into English*; on legacies of colonization, see Phillipson, *Linguistic Imperialism,* and Canagarajah, *Resisting Linguistic Imperialism*; on assimilationist ideologies, see Vieira, *American by Paper*; and on racial ideologies specifically see Young, "Nah, We Straight."
26. Thai, *Insufficient Funds*; Menjivar, *Fragmented Ties.*
27. For more on how writing code is a literacy, see Vee, *Coding Literacy.*
28. Vertovec, "Migrant Transnationalism"; Valdés, *Learning and Not Learning English.*
29. This process calls to mind critical biliteracy scholar Mariana Pacheco's study of Latino community organizing against racist policies, in which learning results from the communal practice of confronting a "need-state," defined according to cultural historical activity theorists as a problem that must be resolved. In the case of the two families with whom I spoke in this chapter, the "need-state" consisted of familial separation and thwarted educational and professional

mobility in a context of cruel immigration policies, economic inequality, structural racism, and war. Pacheco, "Learning in/through Everyday Resistance."

30. Vieira, *American by Paper*.
31. I developed these ideas in light of proposed immigration policy changes that would include literacy tests in Vieira, "Literacy Tests, Love Letters, and Shifting Borders," an essay first published in the Youth Circulations blog.

*Conclusion*

1. See also Valdés, *Expanding Definitions of Giftedness*.
2. Kell, "Placing Practices"; Nordquist, *Literacy and Mobility*.
3. Prengamen, Dilorenzo, and Trielli, "Millions Return to Poverty."
4. For the power of *testimonio* in contexts of human rights abuses and violence, see Cervantes-Soon, *Juárez Girls Rising*. For work on writing for peace, see Rodas, *Voces en Flor*, poetry by children affected by Colombia's civil war.
5. In this way, it builds from the ethnographic tradition in literacy studies (Street, *Literacy in Theory and Practice*), specifically drawing from work examining literacy in sites of community learning (Besnier, *Literacy, Emotion, and Authority*; Delgado-Gaitan, *The Power of Community*; Heath, *Ways with Words*).
6. Glick Schiller, Basch, and Blanc-Szanton, "Transnationalism"; Levitt, *Transnational Villagers*.
7. See also Guerra (*Close to Home*) and Meyers (*Del Otro Lado*) for studies of the transnational movement of literacy and literacy ideologies.
8. Moje et al., "Working toward Third Space." For earlier iterations of the relationship between community and school learning see Moll, Amanti, Neff, and González, "Funds of Knowledge for Teaching," and Heath, *Ways with Words*.
9. Gutiérrez, "Developing a Sociocritical Literacy."
10. Some of this learning would likely include digital and/or multimodal literacy learning, arguments for the importance of which have been made by Kress, *Literacy in the New Media Age*, Rowsell, "Artifactual English," and Shipka, *Toward a Composition Made Whole*. Such learning, when employed in classrooms in culturally relevant ways, can promote learning gains in content areas (Jewitt, "A Multimodal Perspective"), as well as critical consciousness (Vasudevan, "Education Remix" and "Multimodal Cosmopolitanism"; Lam and Rosario-Ramos, "Multilingual Literacies").
11. On emotional regimes of school, see Boler, *Feeling Power*. See also Ginwright, *Hope and Healing*; and Orellana, *Immigrant Children*.
12. hooks, *Teaching to Transgress*.
13. Sandoval, *Methodology of the Oppressed*, 183. For another qualitative study of literacy that takes up Sandoval's theories of love, see Pritchard, *Fashioning Lives*.

14. As compositionist Peter Elbow once remarked on the importance of teaching writing beyond academic purposes, "Life is long. College is short."
15. Watkins, *Literacy Work in the Reign of Human Capital.*
16. On the increasing debt of U.S. college students in light of defunding, see Goldrick Rab, *Paying the Price*; Brody, "I Didn't Even Have an Address"; Contino, "UW-Milwaukee Student Turns to Egg Donation to Pay Loans."
17. Brandt, *The Rise of Writing.*
18. Vieira, *American by Paper.*
19. Royster, *Traces of a Stream.* Another example of how literacy is used as a tool of political liberation is the invention of the Cherokee syllabary in the nineteenth century. See Cushman, *The Cherokee Syllabary.*
20. For example, Mary Antin, *The Promised Land.*

*Afterword*

1. Oliveira, *Motherhood across Borders.*

*Appendix A*

1. Koven, *Interviewing.*
2. Charmaz, *Constructing Grounded Theory.*
3. For the educational impact of financial remittances, see de Haas, "Remittances, Migration, and Social Development"; Nobles, "Parenting from Abroad." For social remittances, see Levitt, "Social Remittances"; Levitt, *Transnational Villagers*; Levitt and Lamba-Nieves, "Social Remittances Revisited."
4. Glaser, "The Constant Comparative Method."
5. Zelizer, "Circuits in Economic Life," 32.

# BIBLIOGRAPHY

Abrego, Leisy Janet. *Sacrificing Families: Navigating Laws, Labor, and Love across Borders*. Stanford, CA: Stanford University Press, 2014.

Aguiar, Marcos, Vladislav Boutenko, David Michael, Vaishali Rastogi, Arvind Subramanian, and Yvonne Zhou. "The Internet's New Billion: Digital Consumers in Brazil, Russia, India, China, and Indonesia." Boston Consulting Group, September 2010. https://www.bcg.com/documents/file58645.pdf.

Ahmed, Sara. *The Cultural Politics of Emotion*. New York: Routledge, 2004.

Allan, Kori, and Bonnie McElhinny. "Neoliberalism, Language, and Migration." In *The Routledge Handbook of Migration and Language*, edited by Suresh Canagarajah, 79–101. London: Routledge, 2017.

Alvarez, Steven. "Brokering the Immigrant Bargain: Second-Generation Immigrant Youth Negotiating Orientations to Literacy." *Literacy in Composition Studies* 3, no. 3 (2015): 25–47.

Alverman, Donna E., and Bradley Robinson. "Youths' Global Engagement in Digital Writing Ecologies." In *Handbook of Writing, Literacies, and Education in Digital Cultures*, edited by Kathy A. Mills, Amy Stornaiuolo, Anna Smith, and Jessica Zacher Pandya, 161–172. New York: Routledge, 2018.

Amanti, Cathy. "Beyond a Beads and Feathers Approach." In *Funds of Knowledge: Theorizing Practices in Households, Communities, and Classrooms*, edited by Norma Gonzalez, Luis C. Moll, and Cathy Amanti, 131–142. New York: Routledge, 2005.

American Community Survey. "Educational Attainment: 2012–2016 American Community Survey Estimates." https://factfinder.census.gov/faces/tableservices/jsf/pages/productview.xhtml?src=CF.

———. "Place of Birth by Nativity and Citizenship Status: 2012–2016 American Community Survey Estimates." https://factfinder.census.gov/faces/nav/jsf/pages/community_facts.xhtml?src=bkmk.

Amnesty International. "USA: Policy of Separating Children from Parents Is Nothing Short of Torture." Last modified June 18, 2018. https://www.amnesty.org/en/latest/news/2018/06/usa-family-separation-torture/.

Annie E. Casey Foundation. "2017 Race for Results: Building a Path to Opportunity for All Children." 2017. http://www.aecf.org/resources/2017-race-for-results/.

Antin, Mary. *The Promised Land.* Boston: Houghton Mifflin, 1912.

Apsite, Elina, Zaiga Krisjane, and Maris Berzins. "Emigration from Latvia under Economic Crisis Conditions." 2nd International Conference on Social Science and Humanity. *International Proceedings of Economics Development and Research* 31 (2012): 134–138.

Baca, Damián. *Mestiz@ Scripts, Digital Migrations, and the Territories of Writing.* New York: Palgrave Macmillan, 2008.

Baldassar, Loretta. "Missing Kin and Longing to Be Together: Emotions and the Construction of Co-Presence in Longing to Be Together." *Journal of Intercultural Studies* 29 (2008): 247–266.

———. "Transnational Families and Aged Care: "The Mobility of Care and the Migrancy of Ageing." *Journal of Ethnic and Migration Studies* 33 (2007): 275–295.

Baldassar, Loretta, and Laura Merla. "Introduction: Transnational Family Caregiving through the Lens of Circulation." In *Transnational Families, Migration, and the Circulation of Care,* edited by Loretta Baldassar and Laura Merla, 3–24. New York: Routledge, 2014.

Baldassar, Loretta, and Laura Merla. "Locating Transnational Care Circulation in Migration and Family Studies." In *Transnational Families, Migration, and the Circulation of Care,* edited by Loretta Baldassar and Laura Merla, 25–60. New York: Routledge, 2014.

Banks, James A., Kathryn H. Au, Arnetha F. Ball, Philip Bell, Edmund W. Gordon, Kris D. Gutiérrez, Shirley Brice Heath, et al. *Learning in and out of School in Diverse Environments: Life-Long, Life-Wide, Life-Deep.* Seattle: LIFE Center, 2007. http://life-slc.org/docs/Banks_etal-LIFE-Diversity-Report.pdf.

Barnes, Tom. "US Officials Took Baby Daughter from Mother While She Breastfed in Immigration Detention Centre, Says Attorney." *The Independent,* last modified June 14, 2018. https://www.independent.co.uk/news/world/americas/us-immigration-center-mother-child-breastfeeding-mexico-border-patrol-ice-a8398186.html.

Barthes, Roland. *A Lover's Discourse: Fragments.* Translated by Richard Howard. New York: Hill and Wang, 2010.

Bartlett, Lesley, Dina López, Lalitha Vasudevan, and Dorris Warriner. "The Anthropology of Literacy." In *Blackwell Companion to Anthropology of Education,* edited by Mica Pollock and Bradley Levinson, 154–176. Malden, MA: Blackwell, 2011.

Bartlett, Lesley, and Frances Katherine Vavrus. *Rethinking Case Study Research: A Comparative Approach*. New York: Routledge, 2017.

Batalova, Jeanne, and Michael Fix. "New Brain Gain: Rising Human Capital among Recent Immigrants to the United States." Migration Policy Institute, June 2017. https://www.migrationpolicy.org/research/new-brain-gain-rising-human-capital-among-recent-immigrants-united-states.

Batista, Catia, Aitor Lacuesta, and Pedro C. Vicente. "Testing the Brain Gain Hypothesis: Micro Evidence from Cape Verde." *Journal of Developmental Economics* 97 (2012): 32–45.

Bazerman, Charles. "What Do Sociocultural Studies of Writing Tell Us about Learning to Write?" In *Handbook of Writing Research*, edited by Charles A. MacArthur, Steve Graham, and Jill Fitzgerald, 11–23. New York: Guilford Press, 2016.

Beine, Michel, Fréderic Docquier, and Hillel Rapoport. "Brain Drain and Human Capital Formation in Developing Countries: Winners and Losers." *Economic Journal* 118 (2008): 631–652.

Berry, Patrick W., Gail E. Hawisher, and Cynthia L. Selfe. *Transnational Literate Lives in Digital Times*. Logan: Computers and Composition Digital Press/Utah State University Press, 2012. http://ccdigitalpress.org/transnational.

Besnier, Niko. *Literacy, Emotion, and Authority: Reading and Writing on a Polynesian Atoll*. Studies in the Social and Cultural Foundations of Language 16. Cambridge, UK: Cambridge University Press, 1995.

Bibb, Maria. "The African American Literacy Myth: Literacy's Ethical Objective during the Progressive Era, 1890–1919." PhD diss., University of Wisconsin–Madison, 2011.

Blackledge, Adrian, and Angela Creese. "Translanguaging in Mobility." In *The Routledge Handbook of Migration and Language*, edited by Suresh Canagarajah, 31–46. London: Routledge, 2017.

Block, David. *Multilingual Identities in a Global City: London Stories*. London: Palgrave, 2006.

Blommaert, Jan. *Grassroots Literacies: Identity and Voice in South Central Africa*. New York: Routledge, 2008.

Boler, Megan. *Feeling Power: Emotions and Education*. New York: Routledge, 1999.

Brand, Alice. "Healing and the Brain." In *Writing and Healing: Toward an Informed Practice*, edited by Charles M. Anderson and Marian Mesrobian Maccurdy, 201–221. Urbana, IL: National Council of Teachers of English, 2000.

Brandt, Deborah. "Accumulating Literacy: Writing and Learning to Write in the Twentieth Century." *College English* 57, no. 6 (1995): 649–668.

———. *Literacy in American Lives*. New York: Cambridge University Press, 2001.

———. *The Rise of Writing: Redefining Mass Literacy*. Cambridge, UK: Cambridge University Press, 2015.

———. "Sponsors of Literacy." *College Composition and Communication* 49, no. 2 (1998): 165–185.

———. "Writing over Reading: New Directions in Mass Literacy." In *The Future of Literacy Studies*, edited by Mike Baynham and Mastin Prinsloo, 54–74. London: Palgrave Macmillan, 2009.

Brandt, Deborah, and Kate Clinton. "Limits of the Local: Expanding Perspectives on Literacy as a Social Practice." *Journal of Literacy Research* 34, no. 3 (2002): 337–356.

Brick, Kate, A. E. Challinor, and Marc R. Rosenblum. "Mexican and Central American Immigrants in the United States." Migration Policy Institute, June 2011. https://www.migrationpolicy.org/pubs/MexCentAmimmigrants.pdf.

Brody, Liz. "I Didn't Even Have an Address." *Glamour*, August 9, 2016. https://www.glamour.com/story/i-didnt-even-have-an-address.

Budach, Gabriele, Catherine Kell, and Donna Patrick. "Objects and Language in Transcontextual Communication." *Social Semiotics* 25, no. 4 (2015): 387–400.

Burke, Garance, and Martha Mendoza. "At Least 3 Tender Age Shelters Set Up for Child Migrants." Associated Press, last modified June 20, 2018. https://apnews.com/dc0c9a5134d14862ba7c7ad9a811160e.

Burkitt, Ian. "Social Relationships and Emotions." *Sociology* 31, no. 1 (1997): 37–55.

Burnett, Cathy, Guy Merchant, Kate Pahl, and Jennifer Rowsell. "The (Im)materiality of Literacy: The Significance of Subjectivity to New Literacies Research." *Discourse: Studies in the Cultural Politics of Education* 35, no. 1 (2014): 90–103.

Calderon, Dolores, Anna Lees, Tracy Lachica Buenavista, Maria C. Ledesma, Lourdes Alberto, Lauren Araiza, Eliza Noh, et al. "Letter to DHS from Faculty." Accessed September 2, 2018. https://docs.google.com/document/d/1B3pLkGl0TYWgLU9FcDLdzT49vMcp7MDAielgKW7ddSg/edit.

Canagarajah, Suresh. *Resisting Linguistic Imperialism in English Teaching.* Oxford: Oxford University Press, 1999.

———. "Skilled Migration and Development: Portable Communicative Resources for Transnational Work." *Multilingual Education* 3, no. 8 (2013).

Castañeda, Ernesto, and Lesley Buck. "Remittances, Transnational Parenting, and the Children Left Behind: Economic and Psychological Implications." *Latin Americanist* 55, no. 4 (2011): 85–110.

Central Statistical Bureau of Latvia. "International Long-Term Emigration Indicates Reduction, While Immigration-Rise." Accessed July 30, 2013. http://www.baltic-course.com/eng/analytics/?doc=77919.

Centro de Estudos sobre as Tecnologias da Informação e da Comunicação. "TIC domicílios e usuarios 2012, período outubro de 2012 / fevereiro de 2013, AI Proporção de domicílios com computador, C1—Proporção de indivíduos que já acessaram a Internet" [Household users of information and communication technologies, 2012, period of October 2012 to February 2013, AI proportion of 40 houses with computers, C1 proportion of individuals who have accessed the internet]. 2013. Accessed August 28, 2013. http://www.cetic.br/usuarios/tic/2012/.

Cervantes-Soon, Claudia G. *Juárez Girls Rising: Transformative Education in Times of Dystopia.* Minneapolis: University of Minnesota Press, 2017.

Charmaz, Kathy. *Constructing Grounded Theory: A Practical Guide through Qualitative Analysis.* London: Sage, 2006.

Christiansen, M. Sidury. "Creating a Unique Transnational Place: Deterritorialized Discourse and the Blending of Time and Space in Online Social Media." *Written Communication* 34, no. 2 (2017): 135–164.

Chu, Julie Y. *Cosmologies of Credit: Transnational Mobility and the Politics of Destination in China.* Durham, NC: Duke University Press, 2010.

Clanchy, Michael. *From Memory to Written Record: England 1066–1307.* Chichester, UK: Wiley-Blackwell, 2013.

Coe, Cati. *The Scattered Family: Parenting, African Migrants, and Global Inequality.* Chicago: University of Chicago Press, 2013.

Compton-Lilly, Catherine. "Introduction: Conceptualizing Past, Present, and Future Timespaces." In *Time and Space in Literacy Research,* edited by Catherine Compton-Lily and Erica Halverson, 1–16. New York: Routledge, 2014.

Contino, Mary Jo. "UW-Milwaukee Student Turns to Egg Donation to Pay Loans." *Media Milwaukee,* last modified November 30, 2015. http://mediamilwaukee.com/features/uw-milwaukee-student-turns-to-egg-donation-to-pay-loans.

Cornelius, Janet Duitsman. *When I Can Read My Title Clear: Literacy, Slavery, and Religion in the Antebellum South.* Columbia: University of South Carolina Press, 1991.

Cushman, Ellen. *The Cherokee Syllabary: Writing the People's Perseverance.* Norman: University of Oklahoma Press, 2011.

Daugavpils. "Society." Accessed July 30, 2013. http://www.daugavpils.lv/en/society.

Dávila, Arlene, Leith Mullings, Renato Rosaldo, Luis F. B. Plascencia, Leo R. Chavez, Rocío Magaña, Gilberto Rosas, et al. "On Latin@s and the Immigration Debate." *American Anthropologist* 116, no. 1 (2014): 1–14.

de Haas, Hein. "Remittances, Migration, and Social Development: A Conceptual Review of the Literature." United Nations Research Institute for Social Development, 2007. Accessed September 8, 2018. https://www.ssrc.org/publications/view/F2D42ACD-F751-DE11-AFAC-001CC477EC70/.

Delgado-Gaitan, Concha. *The Power of Community: Mobilizing for Family and Schooling.* New York: Rowman and Littlefield, 2001.

D'Emilio, Anna Lucia, Berenice Cordero, Bertrand Bainvel, Christian Skoog, Debora Comini, Jean Gough, Monica Dias, et al. "The Impact of International Migration: Children Left Behind in Selected Countries of Latin America and the Caribbean." United Nations Children's Fund, 2007. https://www.unicef.org/socialpolicy/files/The_Impact_of_International_Migration_LAC.pdf.

Dick, Hilary Parsons. "Diaspora and Discourse: The Contrapuntal Lives of Mexican Non-Migrants." In *A Companion to Diaspora and Transnationalism*, edited by Ato Quayson and Girish Daswani, 412–427. West Sussex, UK: Wiley-Blackwell, 2013.

Docquier, Frédéric, and Hillel Rapoport. "Ethnic Discrimination and the Migration of Skilled Labor." *Journal of Development Economics* 70, no. 1 (2003): 159–172.

———. "Globalization, Brain Drain, and Development." *Journal of Economic Literature* 50, no. 3 (2012): 681–730.

Dreby, Joanna. *Divided by Borders: Mexican Migrants and Their Children*. Berkeley: University of California Press, 2010.

Dreby, Joanna, and Lindsay Stutz. "Making Something of Sacrifice: Gender, Migration, and Mexican Children's Educational Aspirations." *Global Networks* 12 (2012): 71–90.

Duchêne, Alexandre, and Monica Heller, eds. *Language in Late Capitalism: Pride and Profit*. Routledge Critical Studies in Multilingualism 1. New York: Routledge, 2013.

Duffy, John. "Recalling the Letter: The Uses of Oral Testimony in Historical Studies of Literacy." *Written Communication* 24, no. 1 (2007): 84–107.

Dustmann, Christian. "Speaking Fluency, Writing Fluency and Earnings of Migrants." *Journal of Population Economics* 7, no. 2 (1994): 133–156.

Falconer, Heather, Ellen Cushman, Mary M. Juzwik, and Mandie B. Dunn. "Editors' Introduction: Writing and Its Development across Lifespans and in Transnational Contexts." *Research in the Teaching of English* 51, no. 3 (2017): 261–266.

Fantin, Monica. "Mídia-Educacão: Aspectos Históricos e Teórico-Metodológicos." [Media education: Historical and theoretical-methodological aspects.]. *Olhar de Professor* 14, no. 1 (2011): 27–40.

Fitzgerald, Patrick. "Exploring Transnational and Diasporic Families through the Irish Emigration Database." *Journal of Intercultural Studies* 19, no. 3 (2008): 247–266.

Foner, Nancy. *From Ellis Island to JFK: New York's Two Great Waves of Immigration*. New Haven, CT: Yale University Press, 2002.

Frank, Geyla. "Anthropology and Individual Lives: The Story of the Life History and the History of the Life Story." *American Anthropologist* 97, no. 1 (1995): 145–148.

Frau-Meigs, Divina. "Transletramento: Operar a Transição Digital e o Domínio das Culturas da Informação" [Transliteracy: Operating the digital transition and the field of information cultures]. *Comunicação & Educação* 19, no. 2 (2014): 61–73.

Freire, Paulo. "The Banking Model of Education." In *Critical Issues in Education: An Anthology of Readings*, edited by Eugene F. Provenzo, 106–119. Thousand Oaks, CA: Sage, 2006.

Galtung, Johan. "Tenemos un Potencial Enorme para la Construcción de Paz" [We have an enormous potential for the building of peace]. Centro de Estudios Avanzados en Niñez y Juventud. Accessed August 31, 2018. http://ceanj.cinde.org.co/index.php/ct-menu-item-97/ct-menu-item-99/ct-menu-item-101.

Gee, James Paul. *Teaching, Learning, Literacy in Our High-Risk High-Tech World: A Framework for Becoming Human*. New York: Teachers College Press, 2017.

Gerber, David A. *Authors of Their Lives: Personal Correspondence in the Lives of Nineteenth Century British Immigrants to the United States*. New York: New York University Press, 2006.

Gibson, John, and David McKenzie. "Eight Questions about Brain Drain." *Journal of Economic Perspectives* 25, no. 3 (2011): 107–128.

Ginwright, Shawn. *Hope and Healing in Urban Education: How Urban Activists and Teachers Are Reclaiming Matters of the Heart*. New York: Routledge, 2016.

Glaser, Barney. "The Constant Comparative Method of Qualitative Analysis." *Social Problems* 12, no. 4 (1965): 436–445.

Glick Schiller, Nina, Linda Basch, and Christina Blanc-Szanton. "Transnationalism: A New Analytic Framework for Understanding Migration." *Annals of the New York Academy of Sciences* 645, no. 1 (1992): 1–24.

Goldrick-Rab, Sarah. *Paying the Price: College Costs, Financial Aid, and the Betrayal of the American Dream*. Chicago: University of Chicago Press, 2016.

Gonzales, Roberto G. "Learning to Be Illegal: Undocumented Youth and Shifting Legal Contexts in the Transition to Adulthood." *American Sociological Review* 76, no. 4 (2011): 602–619.

Gonzalez, Norma, Luis C. Moll, and Cathy Amanti, eds. *Funds of Knowledge: Theorizing Practices in Households, Communities, and Classrooms*. New York: Routledge, 2005.

Goody, Jack. *The Logic of Writing and the Organization of Society*. Cambridge, UK: Cambridge University Press, 2001.

Graff, Harvey. *The Literacy Myth: Cultural Integration and Social Structure in the Nineteenth Century*. New York: Routledge, 1991.

Grin, François, Claudio Sfreddo, and François Vaillancourt. *The Economics of the Multilingual Workplace*. New York: Routledge, 2010.

Guerra, Juan. *Close to Home: Oral and Literate Practices in a Transnational Mexicano Community*. New York: Teachers College Press, 1998.

Gutiérrez, Kris. "Developing a Sociocritical Literacy in the Third Space." *Reading Research Quarterly* 43, no. 2 (2008): 148–164.

Haas, Christina. *Writing Technology: Studies on the Materiality of Literacy*. Mahwah, NJ: Lawrence Erlbaum Associates, 1996.

Haas, Christina, and Megan McGrath. "Embodiment of Literacy in a Digital Age: The Case of Handwriting." In *Handbook of Writing, Literacies, and Education in Digital Cultures,* edited by Kathy A. Mills, Amy Stornaiuolo, Anna Smith, and Jessica Zacher Pandya, 125–135. New York: Routledge, 2018.

Haas, Christina, and Pamela Takayoshi. "Young People's Everyday Literacies: The Language Features of Instant Messaging." *Research in the Teaching of English* 45, no. 4 (2011): 378–404.

Hagan, Jacqueline, Rubén Hernández-León, and Jean-Luc Demonsant. *Skills of the Unskilled: Work and Mobility among Mexican Migrants.* Oakland: University of California Press, 2015.

Harris, Gardiner. "Trump Administration Withdraws U.S. from U.N. Human Rights Council." *New York Times,* last modified June 19, 2018. https://www.nytimes.com/2018/06/19/us/politics/trump-israel-palestinians-human-rights.html.

Hart, Gillian. "Geography and Development: Development/s beyond Neoliberalism? Power, Culture, Political Economy." *Progress in Human Geography* 26, no. 6 (2002): 812–822.

Hazans, Mihails. "The Changing Face of Latvian Emigration, 2000–2010." In *Latvia Human Development Report 2010–2011: National Identity, Mobility and Capability,* edited by Brigita Zepa and Evija Kave, 77–101. Riga: Advanced Social and Political Research Institute of University of Latvia, 2011.

Heath, Shirley Brice. *Ways with Words: Language, Life, and Work in Communities and Classrooms.* Cambridge, UK: Cambridge University Press, 1983.

Henkin, David M. *The Postal Age: The Emergence of Modern Communications in Nineteenth-Century America.* Chicago: University of Chicago Press, 2008.

Hennessy-Fiske, Molly. "'Prison-Like' Migrant Youth Shelter Is Understaffed, Unequipped for Trump's 'Zero Tolerance' Policy, Insider Says." *Los Angeles Times,* last modified June 14, 2018. http://www.latimes.com/nation/la-na-border-migrant-shelter-20180614-story.html.

Hernández-Zamora, Gregorio. *Decolonizing Literacy: Mexican Lives in the Era of Global Capitalism.* Bristol, UK: Multilingual Matters, 2010.

Hochschild, Arlene Russell. "Love and Gold." In *Global Woman: Nannies, Maids, and Sex Workers in the New Economy,* edited by Barbara Ehrenreich and Arlie Russell Hochschild, 15–30. London: Granta Books, 2003.

Hochschild, Arlene Russell. *The Managed Heart: Commercialization of Human Feeling.* Berkeley: University of California Press, 1983.

Holland, Dorothy, and Jean Lave. "History in Person: An Introduction." In *History in Person: Enduring Struggles, Contentious Practice, Intimate Identities,* edited by Dorothy Holland and Jean Lave, 3–36. Santa Fe, NM: School of American Research Press, 2001.

hooks, bell. *Teaching to Transgress: Education as the Practice of Freedom.* New York: Routledge, 1994.

Hull, Glynda. "Youth Culture and Digital Media: New Literacies for New Times." *Research in the Teaching of English* 38, no. 2 (2003): 229–233.

Hurst, Ellen. "Regional Flows and Language Resources." In *The Routledge Handbook of Migration and Language,* edited by Suresh Canagarajah, 171–186. London: Routledge, 2017.

Ibarra, Armando. "Latin@ Wisconsin: Needs Assessment and Family Integration." Talk for Wisconsin Center for the Advancement of Postsecondary Education. Madison, Wisconsin, October 24, 2017.

Ife, Fahima. "Maktivist Literacies: Black Women's Making, Activism, and Writing in DIY Spaces." PhD diss., University of Wisconsin–Madison, 2015.

Instituto Brasileiro de Geografia e Estatística. "Brasil." Accessed September 4, 2018. https://paises.ibge.gov.br/#/en/pais/brasil/info/redes.

———. "São Paulo, Jaú, Infográficos, Frota" [São Paulo, Jaú, infographics, fleet]. Accessed on September 8, 2013. https://cidades.ibge.gov.br/brasil/sp/jau/pesquisa/22/28120.

International Organization for Migration. "Migrants Crossing U.S.-Mexico Border Dying at Faster Rates in 2017: UN Migration Agency." August 4, 2017. https://www.iom.int/news/migrants-crossing-us-mexico-border-dying-faster-rate-2017-un-migration-agency.

Ivlevs, Artjoms. "Minorities on the Move? Assessing Post-Enlargement Emigration Intentions of Latvia's Russian Speaking Minority." *Annals of Regional Science* 51, no. 1 (2012): 33–52.

Ivlevs, Artjoms and Roswitha King. "Family Migration Capital and Migration Intentions." *Journal of Family and Economic Issues* 33, no. 1 (2012): 118–129.

Jewitt, Carey. "A Multimodal Perspective on Textuality and Contexts." *Pedagogy, Culture, and Society* 15 (2007): 275–289.

Jones, Tayari. *An American Marriage: A Novel.* Chapel Hill, NC: Algonquin Books, 2018.

Kaiser, Robert, and Elena Nikiforova. "Borderland Spaces of Identification and Dis/location: Multiscalar Narratives and Enactments of Seto Identity and Place in the Estonian-Russian Borderlands." *Ethnic and Racial Studies* 29, no. 5 (2006): 928–958.

Kalman, Judy. "GPS Technology, Map Reading, and Everyday Location Practices in a Fishing Community." In *Literacy and Numeracy in Latin America,* edited by Judy Kalman and Brian V. Street, 69–80. New York: Routledge, 2013.

Kalniņa-Lukaševica, Zanda. "Demographic and Economic Changes of Latgale Region, Latvia." In *Demographic Change and Local Development: Shrinkage, Regeneration, and Social Dynamics,* edited by Cristina Martinez-Fernandez, Naoko Kubo, Antonella Noya, and Tamara Weyman, 149–158. Paris: OECD Programme on Local Economic and Employment Development, 2012.

Kang, Tingyu. "Online Spatialisation and Embodied Experience: The London-Based Chinese Community." *Journal of Intercultural Studies* 32, no. 5 (2011): 465–477.

Keating, Maria Clara, and Olga Solovova. "Multilingual Dynamics among Portuguese-Based Migrant Contexts in Europe." *Journal of Pragmatics* 43 (2011): 1251–1263.

Kell, Catherine. "Placing Practices: Literacy and Meaning Making across Space and Time." In *The Future of Literacy Studies*, edited by Mike Baynham and Mastin Prinsloo, 75–99. London: Palgrave, 2009.

Klein, Betsy, and Kevin Liptak. "Trump Ramps Up Rhetoric: Dems Want 'Illegal Immigrants' to 'Infest Our Country.'" *CNN Politics*, last modified June 19, 2018. https://www.cnn.com/2018/06/19/politics/trump-illegal-immigrants-infest/index.html.

Koven, Michéle. "Interviewing: Practice, Ideology, Genre, and Intertextuality." *Annual Review of Anthropology* 43 (2014): 499–520.

Kraft, Colleen. "Separating Parents from Their Kids at the Border Contradicts Everything We Know about Children's Welfare." *Los Angeles Times*, last modified May 3, 2018. http://www.latimes.com/opinion/op-ed/la-oe-kraft-border-separation-suit-20180503-story.html.

Kravale-Pauliņa, Mārīte, and Irēna Kokina. "The Integration of Formal and Non-Formal Education in the Context of Sustainable Development: Views of Latvian Educators." *Discourse and Communication for Sustainable Education* 1, no. 1 (2010): 68–78.

Kress, Gunther. *Literacy in the New Media Age*. New York: Routledge, 2004.

Kuznetsov, Yevgeny, and Charles Sabel. "International Migration of Talent, Diaspora Networks, and Development: Overview of Main Issues." In *Diaspora Networks and the International Migration of Skills: How Countries Can Draw on Their Talent Abroad*, edited by Yevgeny Kuznetsov, 3–20. Washington, DC: World Bank, 2006.

Lagman, Eileen. "Moving Labor: Transnational Migrant Workers and Affective Literacies of Care." *Literacy in Composition Studies* 3, no. 5 (2015): 1–24.

Lam, Wan Shun Eva. "Literacy and Capital in Immigrant Youths' Online Networks across Countries." *Learning, Media and Technology* 39, no. 4 (2014): 488–506.

———. "Multiliteracies on Instant Messaging in Negotiating Local, Translocal, and Transnational Affiliations: A Case of an Adolescent Immigrant." *Reading Research Quarterly* 44, no. 4 (2009): 377–397.

Lam, Wan Shun Eva, and Enid Rosario-Ramos. "Multilingual Literacies in Transnational Digitally Mediated Contexts: An Exploratory Study of Immigrant Teens in the United States." *Language and Education* 23, no. 2 (2009): 171–190.

Lanard, Noah. "UN Human Rights Chief: Family Separations Forced by Trump Administration Are Child Abuse." *Mother Jones*, last modified June 18, 2018. https://www.motherjones.com/politics/2018/06/

un-human-rights-chief-family-separations-forced-by-trump-administration-are-child-abuse/.

Lankshear, Colin, and Michele Knobel. "Researching New Literacies: Web 2.0 Practices and Insider Perspectives." *E-Learning and Digital Media* 4, no. 3 (2007): 224–240.

Laquintano, Timothy. *Mass Authorship and the Rise of Self-Publishing.* Iowa City: University of Iowa Press, 2016.

Leander, Kevin, and Gail Boldt. "Rereading 'A Pedagogy of Multiliteracies': Bodies, Texts, and Emergence." *Journal of Literacy Research* 45, no. 1 (2013): 22–46.

Leander, Kevin M., Nathan C. Phillips, and Katherine Headrick Taylor. "The Changing Social Spaces of Learning: Mapping New Mobilities." *Review of Research in Education* 34 (2010): 329–365.

Lee, Stacey. *Up Against Whiteness: Race, School, and Immigrant Youth.* New York: Colombia Teachers College Press, 2005.

Levitt, Peggy. "Social Remittances: Migration Driven Local-Level Forms of Cultural Diffusion." *International Migration Review* 32, no. 4 (1998): 926–948.

———. *The Transnational Villagers.* Berkeley: University of California Press, 2001.

Levitt, Peggy, and Deepak Lamba-Nieves. "Social Remittances Revisited." *Journal of Ethnic and Migration Studies* 37, no. 1 (2010): 1–22.

Lewis, Cynthia, and Bettina Fabos. "Instant Messaging, Literacies, and Social Identities." *Reading Research Quarterly* 40, no. 4 (2005): 470–501.

Lewis, Tisha Y. "'We Txt 2 Sty Cnnectd': An African American Mother and Son Communicate. Digital Literacies, Meaning-Making, and Activity Theory Systems." *Journal of Education* 193, no. 2 (2013): 1–13.

Lising, Loy. "Language in Skilled Migration." In *The Routledge Handbook of Migration and Language,* edited by Suresh Canagarajah, 296–311. London: Routledge, 2017.

Lorimer Leonard, Rebecca. "Traveling Literacies: Multilingual Writing on the Move." *Research in the Teaching of English* 18, no. 3 (2013): 13–39.

———. *Writing on the Move: Migrant Women and the Value of Literacy.* Pittsburgh: University of Pittsburgh Press, 2017.

———. "Writing through Bureaucracy: Migrant Correspondence and Managed Mobility." *Written Communication* 32, no. 1 (2015): 87–113.

Luke, Allan. "Genres of Power? Literacy Education and the Production of Capital." In *Literacy in Society: Language Description and Language Education,* edited by Rugalya Hasan and Geoffrey Williams, 308–338. New York: Longman, 1996.

———. "On the Taming of Time and Space." In *Time and Space in Literacy Research,* edited by Catherine Compton-Lily and Erica Halverson, ix–xiv. New York: Routledge, 2014.

Lyons, Martyn. *The Writing Culture of Ordinary People in Europe, 1860–1920.* Cambridge, UK: Cambridge University Press, 2013.

MacDonald, Michael T. "Emissaries of Literacy: Representations of Sponsorship and Refugee Experience in the Stories of the Lost Boys of Sudan." *College English* 77, no. 5 (2015): 408–428.

Madianou, Mirca, and Daniel Miller. *Migration and New Media: Transnational Families and Polymedia*. London: Routledge, 2012.

Massey, Douglas S., Joaquin Arango, Graeme Hugo, Ali Kouaouci, Adela Pellegrino, and J. Edward Taylor. "Theories of International Migration: A Review and Appraisal." *Population and Development Review* 19, no. 3 (1993): 431–446.

Mayr, Karin, and Giovanni Peri. "Return Migration as a Channel of Brain Gain." National Bureau of Economic Research, May 2008. http://www.nber.org/papers/w14039.pdf.

McGuinness, Damien. "Fears over Latvia Brain Drain as Economy Struggles." BBC News, Riga, last modified August 20, 2010. http://www.bbc.com/news/world-europe-10913098.

McKenzie, David. "Worrying Too Much about Brain Drain?" *All about Finance* (blog), World Bank, last modified May 2011. http://blogs.worldbank.org/allaboutfinance/worrying-too-much-about-brain-drain.

Menjivar, Cecilia. *Fragmented Ties: Salvadoran Immigrant Networks in America*. Berkeley: University of California Press, 2000.

Merla, Laura. "A Macro-Perspective on Transnational Families and Care Circulation: Situating Capacity, Obligation, and Family Commitments." In *Transnational Families, Migration, and the Circulation of Care*, edited by Loretta Baldassar and Laura Merla, 115–132. New York: Routledge, 2014.

Meyers, Susan V. *Del Otro Lado: Literacy and Migration across the U.S.-Mexico Border*. Carbondale: Southern Illinois University Press, 2014.

Micciche, Laura. "Writing Material." *College English* 76, no. 6 (2014): 488–505.

Mignolo, Walter. *The Darker Side of the Renaissance: Literacy, Territoriality, and Colonization*. Ann Arbor: University of Michigan Press, 1995.

Migration Policy Institute. "Unauthorized Immigrant Population Profiles." Accessed September 8, 2018. https://www.migrationpolicy.org/programs/us-immigration-policy-program-data-hub/unauthorized-immigrant-population-profiles.

Miroff, Nick. "A Family Was Separated at the Border, and This Distraught Father Took His Own Life." *Washington Post*, last modified June 9, 2018. https://www.washingtonpost.com/world/national-security/a-family-was-separated-at-the-border-and-this-distraught-father-took-his-own-life/2018/06/08/24e40b70-6b5d-11e8-9e38-24e693b38637_story.html?utm_term=.54d2f11a07d1.

Moje, Elizabeth Birr, Kathryn McIntosh Ciechanowski, Katherine Kramer, Lindsay Ellis, Rosario Carrillo, and Tehani Collazo. "Working toward Third Space in Content Area Literacy: An Examination of Everyday Funds of Knowledge and Discourse." *Reading Research Quarterly* 39, no. 1 (2004): 38–70.

Moll, Luis, Cathy Amanti, Deborah Neff, and Norma González. "Funds of Knowledge for Teaching: Using a Qualitative Approach to Connect Homes and Classrooms." *Theory into Practice* 31, no. 2 (1992): 132–141.

Moll, Luis, and Norma Gonzalez. "Critical Issues: Lessons from Working with Minority-Language Children." *Journal of Reading Behavior* 26 (1994): 439–456.

Moss, Beverly J., and Robyn Lyons-Robinson. "Making Literacy Work: A 'Phenomenal Woman' Negotiating Her Literacy Identity in and for an African American Women's Club." In *Literacy, Economy, and Power: Writing and Research after Literacy in American Lives,* edited by John Duffy, Julie Nelson Christoph, Eli Goldblatt, Nelson Graff, Rebecca S. Nowacek, and Bryan Trabold, 136–154. Carbondale: Southern Illinois University Press, 2014.

Nesaule, Agate. *Woman in Amber: Healing the Trauma of War and Exile.* New York: Penguin Books, 1995.

Newman, Sally, Beatrix Niemeyer, Terri Seddon, and Anita Devos. "Understanding Educational Work: Exploring the Analytic Borderlands around the Labour That Enables Learning." *Globalisation, Societies, and Education* 12, no. 3 (2014): 321–335.

Ngai, Mae. *Impossible Subjects: Illegal Aliens and the Making of Modern America.* Princeton, NJ: Princeton University Press, 2004.

Nishijima, Marislei, Terry Macedo Ivanauskas, and Flavia Mori Sarti. "Evolution and Determinants of Digital Divide in Brazil (2005–2013)." *Telecommunications Policy* 41, no. 1 (2017): 12–24.

Nobles, Jenna. "Parenting from Abroad: Migration, Nonresident Father Involvement, and Children's Education in Mexico." *Journal of Marriage and Family* 73, no. 4 (2011): 729–746.

Noguerón-Liu, Silvia, and Jamie Jordan Hogan. "Remembering Michoacán: Digital Representations of the Homeland by Immigrant Adults and Adolescents." *Research in the Teaching of English* 51, no. 3 (2017): 267–289.

Nordquist, Brice. *Literacy and Mobility: Complexity, Uncertainty, and Agency at the Nexus of High School and College.* New York: Routledge, 2017.

Norton, Bonnie. "Social Identity, Investment, and Language Learning." *TESOL Quarterly* 29, no. 1 (1995): 9–31.

Nystrand, Martin. *Opening Dialogue: Understanding the Dynamics of Language and Learning in the English Classroom.* New York: Teachers College, Columbia University, 1997.

———. *The Structure of Written Communication: Studies in Reciprocity between Writers and Readers.* Bingley, UK: Emerald Group, 1986.

Oliveira, Gabrielle. *Motherhood across Borders: Immigrants and Their Children in Mexico and New York.* New York: NYU Press, 2018.

Ong, Aihwa. *Flexible Citizenship: The Cultural Logics of Transnationality.* Durham, NC: Duke University Press, 1999.

Orellana, Marjorie Faulstich. *Immigrant Children in Transcultural Spaces: Language, Learning, and Love.* New York: Routledge, 2016.

Ospina-Ramirez, David Arturo, and Maria Camila Ospina-Alvarado. "Futuros Posibles, el Potencial Creativo de Niñas y Niños para la Construccion de Paz" [Possible futures, the creative potential of boys and girls for the construction of peace]. *Revista Latinoamericana de Ciencias Socialies, Niñez y Juventud* 15, no. 1 (2017): 175–192.

Pacheco, Mariana. "Learning in/through Everyday Resistance: A Cultural-Historical Perspective on Community Resources and Curriculum." *Educational Researcher* 41, no. 4 (2012): 121–132.

Pahl, Kate. *Materializing Literacies in Communities: The Uses of Literacy Revisited.* London: Bloomsbury Academic, 2014.

Parella, Sònia, Alisa Petroff, and Carlota Solé. "The Upward Occupational Mobility of Immigrant Women in Spain." *Journal of Ethnic and Migration Studies* 39, no. 9 (2013): 1365–1382.

Paris, Django, and Maisha Winn. *Humanizing Research: Decolonizing Qualitative Inquiry with Youth and Communities.* Los Angeles: Sage, 2014.

Parreñas, Rhacel. *Children of Global Migration: Transnational Families and Gendered Woes.* Palo Alto, CA: Stanford University Press, 2005.

Pavlenko, Aneta. "Multilingualism in Post-Soviet Countries: Language Revival, Language Removal, and Sociolinguistic Theory." *International Journal of Bilingual Education and Bilingualism* 11, nos. 3–4 (2008): 275–314.

Pegurer-Caprino, Mônica, and Juan-Francisco Martínez-Cerdá. "Media Literacy in Brazil: Experiences and Models in Non-formal Education." *Media Education Research Journal* 24, no. 49 (2016): 39–48.

Pennebaker, James, and John Evans. *Expressive Writing: Words That Heal.* Enumclaw, WA: Idyll Arbor, 2014.

Phillipson, Robert. *Linguistic Imperialism.* Oxford: Oxford University Press, 1992.

Piller, Ingrid, and Jinhyun Cho. "Neoliberalism as Language Policy." *Language in Society* 42, no. 1 (2013): B 23–44.

Poeze, Miranda, and Valentine Mazzucato. "Ghanaian Children in Transnational Families." In *Transnational Families, Migration, and the Circulation of Care,* edited by Loretta Baldassar and Laura Merla, 149–169. New York: Routledge, 2014.

Population Reference Bureau. "Population Data Set, 2012." Accessed August 30, 2014. http://www.prb.org/pdf12/2012.

Prendergast, Catherine. *Buying into English: Language and Investment in the New Capitalist World.* Pittsburgh: University of Pittsburgh Press, 2008.

Prendergast, Catherine, and Roman Ličko. "The Ethos of Paper: Here and There." *Journal of Advanced Composition* 29, nos. 1–2 (2009): 199–228.

Prengamen, Peter, Sarah Dilorenzo, and Daniel Trielli. "Millions Return to Poverty in Brazil, Eroding 'Boom' Decade." *Washington Post,* October 23, 2017. https://

www.washingtonpost.com/world/the_americas/millions-return-to-poverty-in-brazil-eroding-boom-decade/2017/10/23/.

Prior, Paul. "Combining Phenomenological and Sociohistoric Frameworks for Studying Literate Practices: Some Implications of Deborah Brandt's Methodological Trajectory." In *Literacy, Economy, and Power: Writing and Research after Literacy in American Lives,* edited by John Duffy, Julie Nelson Christoph, Eli Goldblatt, Nelson Graff, Rebecca S. Nowacek, and Bryan Trabold, 166–184. Carbondale: Southern Illinois University Press, 2014.

———. *Writing/Disciplinarity: A Sociohistoric Account of Literate Activity in the Academy.* Mahwah, NJ: Lawrence Erlbaum Associates, 1998.

Prior, Paul, and Julie Hengst. "Introduction: Exploring Semiotic Remediation." In *Exploring Semiotic Remediation as Discourse Practice,* edited by Paul Prior and Julie Hengst, 1–23. New York: Palgrave Macmillan, 2010.

Pritchard, Eric. *Fashioning Lives:Black Queers and the Politics of Literacy.* Carbondale: Southern Illinois University Press, 2017.

Proskow, Jackson (@JProskowGlobal). Twitter post. June 19, 2018. Accessed August 31, 2018. https://twitter.com/JProskowGlobal/status/1009119915348021249.

Purcell-Gates, Victoria. "Literacy Worlds of Children of Migrant Farmworker Communities: Participating in a Migrant Head Start Program." *Research in the Teaching of English* 48, no. 1 (2013): 68–97.

Reddy, Nancy. "Re-Entangling Literacy: A Historical Study of Extra-Curricular Writing Practices." PhD diss., University of Wisconsin, Madison, 2015.

Rodas, Martín, ed. *Voces en Flor: Poesía para la Paz.* Manizales, Colombia: Ojo con la gota de (TIN)ta.

Roozen, Kevin. "The 'Poetry Slam,' Mathemagicians, and Middle School Math: Tracing Trajectories of Actors and Artifacts." In *Exploring Semiotic Remediation as Discourse Practice,* edited by Paul Prior and Julie Hengst, 24–51. New York: Palgrave Macmillan, 2010.

Rose, Mike. *The Mind at Work: Valuing the Intelligence of the American Worker.* New York: Penguin, 2004.

Rosenblatt, Louise. "The Transactional Theory of Reading and Writing." In *Making Meaning with Texts,* edited by Louise Rosenblatt, 1–37. Portsmouth, NH: Heinemann, 2005.

Rounsaville, Angela. "Genre Repertoires from Below: How One Writer Built and Moved a Writing Life across Generations, Borders, and Communities." *Research in the Teaching of English* 51, no. 3 (2017): 317–340.

Rowsell, Jennifer. "Artifactual English." In *Language, Ethnography, and Education: Bridging New Literacy Studies and Bourdieu,* edited by Michael Grenfell, David Bloome, Cheryl Hardy, Kate Pahl, Jennifer Rowsell, and Brian Street, 110–113. New York: Routledge, 2012.

Royster, Jacqueline Jones. *Traces of a Stream: Literacy and Social Change among African American Women.* Pittsburgh: University of Pittsburgh Press, 2001.

Sabaté i Dalmau, Maria. "Fighting Exclusion from the Margins: *Locutorios* as Sites of Social Agency and Resistance for Migrants." In *Language, Migration and Social Inequalities: A Critical Sociolinguistic Perspective on Institutions and Work,* edited by Alexandre Duchene, Melissa Moyer, and Celia Roberts, 248–271. Bristol, UK: Multilingual Matters, 2013.

Salomon, Frank, and Niño-Murcia, Mercedes. *The Lettered Mountain: A Peruvian Village's Ways with Writing.* Durham, NC: Duke University Press, 2011.

Sandoval, Chela. *Methodology of the Oppressed.* Minneapolis: University of Minnesota Press, 2000.

Schmandt-Besserat, Denise. "The Envelopes That Bear the First Writing." *Technology and Culture* 21, no. 3 (1980): 357–385.

Schwartz, Lisa, Silvia Noguerón-Liu, and Norma Gonzalez. "The Compression of Time and Space in Transnational Social Fields: Mobilizing the Affordances of Digital Media with Latina Students." In *Time and Space in Literacy Research,* edited by Catherine Compton-Lily and Erica Halverson, 183–195. New York: Routledge, 2014.

Sebba, Mark. *Spelling and Society: The Culture and Politics of Orthography around the World.* Cambridge, UK: Cambridge University Press, 2007.

Shapiro, Shawna, and Michael T. MacDonald. "From Deficit to Asset: Locating Discursive Resistance in a Refugee-Background Student's Written and Oral Narrative." *Journal of Language, Identity, and Education* 15, no. 2 (2017): 80–93.

Shipka, Jody. *Toward a Composition Made Whole.* Pittsburgh: University of Pittsburgh Press, 2011.

Simon, Kaia. "Translating a Path to College: Literate and Resonances of Child Language Brokering." *College Composition and Communication* (forthcoming, 2019).

Skrbis, Zlato. "Transnational Families: Theorizing Migration, Emotions, and Belonging." *Journal of Intercultural Studies* 29, no. 3 (2008): 231–246.

Smith, Adrian, and Adam Swain. "Economic Crisis in the East of the European Union: Models of Development and the Contradictions of Internationalization." *Eurasian Geography and Economics* 51, no. 1 (2010): 1–34.

Smith, Anna, and Glynda Hull. "Critical Literacies and Social Media: Fostering Ethical Engagement with Global Youth." In *Critical Digital Literacies as Social Praxis: Intersections and Challenges,* edited by JuliAnna Ávila and Jessica Zacher Pandya, 63–84. New York: Peter Lang, 2012.

Smith, Graham. "The Ethnic Democracy Thesis and the Citizenship Question in Estonia and Latvia." *Nationalities Papers* 24, no. 2 (1996): 199–216.

Smith, Robert Courtney. *Mexican New York: Transnational Lives of New Immigrants.* Berkeley: University of California Press, 2006.

Southern Poverty Law Center. "The Trump Effect: The Impact of the 2016 Presidential Election on Our Nation's Schools." 2016. https://www.splcenter.org/sites/default/files/the_trump_effect.pdf.

Spyer, Juliano. *Social Media in Emergent Brazil: How the Internet Affects Social Mobility*. London: UCL Press, 2018.

Stornaiuolo, Amy, Anna Smith, and Nathan C. Phillips. "Developing a Transliteracies Framework for a Connected World." *Journal of Literacy Research* 49, no. 1 (2017): 68–91.

Street, Brian. *Literacy in Theory and Practice*. Cambridge, UK: Cambridge University Press, 1984.

Thai, Hung Cam. *Insufficient Funds: The Culture of Money in Low-Wage Transnational Families*. Redwood City, CA: Stanford University Press, 2014.

Thomas, William, and Florian Znaniecki. *The Polish Peasant in Europe and America: A Classic Work in Immigration History* (1918). Edited by Eli Zaretsky. Champaign-Urbana: University of Illinois Press, 1996.

Thompson, Ginger. "Listen to Children Who've Just Been Separated from Their Parents at the Border." *ProPublica*, last modified June 18, 2018. https://www.propublica.org/article/children-separated-from-parents-border-patrol-cbp-trump-immigration-policy.

Tsing, Anna Lowenhaupt. *Friction: An Ethnography of Global Connection*. Princeton, NJ: Princeton University Press, 2004.

Tuck, Eve. "Suspending Damage: A Letter to Communities." *Harvard Educational Review* 79, no. 3 (2009): 409–427.

Tung, Rosalie L., and Mila Lazarova. "Brain Drain versus Brain Gain: An Exploratory Study of Ex–Host Country Nationals in Central and East Europe." *International Journal of Human Resource Management* 17, no. 11 (2006): 1853–1872.

United Nations Department of Economic and Social Affairs. "Migration Report 2015." http://www.un.org/en/development/desa/population/migration/publications/migrationreport/docs/MigrationReport2015_Highlights.pdf.

United Nations Department of Economic and Social Affairs, Division for Social Policy and Development. "Inequality Matters: Report on the World Social Situation 2013." 2013. http://www.un.org/esa/socdev/documents/reports/InequalityMatters.pdf.

United Nations Department of Economic and Social Affairs, Population Division. "Change in World Migration Stock from 1990–2013." Accessed August 30, 2014. http://esa.un.org/unmigration/migrantstocks2013.

United Nations High Commissioner for Refugees. "Ukraine Operational Update." December 2016. http://www.refworld.org/docid/5887592f4.html.

———. "Ukraine Operational Update." June 2018. unhcr.org/ua/wp-content/upload/sites/38/2018/7/2018-06-UNHCR-Ukraine/operational-update-final-eng-1.pdf.

U.S. Central Intelligence Agency. "The World Factbook." Accessed September 3, 2018. https://www.cia.gov/library/publications/the-world-factbook/fields/2112.html.

Valdés, Guadalupe. *Expanding Definitions of Giftedness: The Case of Young Interpreters from Immigrant Communities*. New York: Routledge, 2003.

———. *Learning and Not Learning English: Latino Students in American Schools.* Edited by James A. Banks. New York: Teachers College Press, 2001.

Valentin, Karen. "The Role of Education in Mobile Livelihoods: Social and Geographical Routes of Young Nepalese Migrants in India." *Anthropology and Education Quarterly* 43, no. 4 (2012): 429–442.

Valenzuela, Angela. *Subtractive Schooling: U.S.-Mexican Youth and the Politics of Caring*. Albany: State University of New York Press, 1999.

van der Kolk, Bessel. *The Body Keeps the Score: Brain, Mind, and Body in the Healing of Trauma*. London: Penguin, 2014.

Vasudevan, Lalitha. "Education Remix: New Media, Literacies, and Emerging Digital Geographies." *Digital Culture and Education* 2, no. 1 (2010): 62–82.

———. "Multimodal Cosmopolitanism: Cultivating Belonging in Everyday Moments with Youth." *Curriculum Inquiry* 44, no. 1 (2014): 45–67.

Vee, Annette. *Coding Literacy: How Computer Programming Is Changing Writing.* Boston: MIT Press, 2017.

Vélez-Ibañez, Carlos, and James Greenberg. "Formation and Transformation of Funds of Knowledge." In *Funds of Knowledge: Theorizing Practices in Households, Communities, and Classrooms*, edited by Norma Gonzalez, Luis C. Moll, and Cathy Amanti, 47–70. New York: Routledge, 2005.

Vertovec, Steven. "Migrant Transnationalism and Modes of Transformation." *International Migration Review* 38, no. 3 (2004): 970–1001.

Vieira, Kate. *American by Paper: How Documents Matter in Immigrant Literacy.* Minneapolis: University of Minnesota Press, 2016.

———. "Doing Transnational Literacy: The Case for the Literacy History Interview." *Composition Studies* 44, no. 1 (2016): 138–140.

———. "Literacy Tests, Love Letters, and Shifting Borders." *Youth Circulations* (blog), April 18, 2018. http://www.youthcirculations.com/blog/2018/4/18/literacy-tests-love-letters-and-shifting-borders.

———. "Writing about Others: Some Fieldnotes." In *Rhetorics Elsewhere and Otherwise: Contested Modernities, Decolonial Visions*, edited by Damián Baca and Romeo Garcia, 49–61. Urbana: NCTE, 2019.

———. "Writing's Potential to Heal: Women Writing from their Bodies." *Community Literacy Journal* (forthcoming, 2019).

Vieira, Kate, Chris Castillo, Sandra Descourtis, Margaret Bertucci Hamper, Lauren Heap, Jonathan Isaac, Ann Meejung Kim, et al.. "Literacy Is a Socio-Historic Phenomenon with the Potential to Liberate and Oppress." In *(Re)considering*

*What We Know*, edited by Elizabeth Wardle and Linda Adler-Kassner. Utah State University Press, forthcoming 2019.

Vigouroux, Cécile B. "Informal Economy and Language Practice in the Context of Migrations." In *Language, Migration and Social Inequalities: A Critical Sociolinguistic Perspective on Institutions and Work*, edited by Alexandre Duchene, Melissa Moyer, and Celia Roberts, 225–247. Bristol, UK: Multilingual Matters, 2013.

———. "Rethinking (Un)skilled Migrants: Whose Skills, What Skills, for What, and for Whom?" In *The Routledge Handbook of Migration and Language*, edited by Suresh Canagarajah, 312–329. London: Routledge, 2017.

Vincent, David. *The Rise of Mass Literacy: Reading and Writing in Modern Europe*. Cambridge, UK: Polity Press, 2000.

Wacquant, Loïc. *Punishing the Poor: The Neoliberal Government of Social Insecurity*. Durham, NC: Duke University Press, 2009.

Waldinger, Roger. *The Cross-Border Connection: Immigrants, Emigrants, and Their Homelands*. Cambridge, MA: Harvard University Press, 2015.

Warschauer, Mark. *Technology and Social Inclusion: Rethinking the Digital Divide*. Cambridge, MA: MIT Press, 2004.

Watkins, Evan. *Literacy Work in the Reign of Human Capital*. New York: Fordham University Press, 2015.

Weinstein, Susan. *Feel These Words: Writing in the Lives of Urban Youth*. Albany, NY: SUNY Press, 2009.

Wetherell, Margaret. *Affect and Emotion: A New Social Science Understanding*. London: Sage, 2014.

Wills, Jane, Kavita Datta, Yara Evans, Joanna Herbert, Jon June, and Cathy McIlwaine. *Global Cities at Work: New Migrant Divisions of Labour*. London: Pluto Press, 2010.

Winn, Maisha T. *Girl Time: Literacy, Justice, and the School-to-Prison Pipeline*. New York: Teachers College Press, 2011.

You, Xiaoye. *Writing in the Devil's Tongue: A History of English Composition in China*. Carbondale: Southern Illinois University Press, 2010.

Young, Vershawn. "Nah, We Straight: An Argument against Code-Switching." *Journal of Advanced Composition* 29, nos. 1–2 (2009): 49–76.

Zacharia, K. C., and S. Irudaya Rajan. *Researching International Migration: Lessons from the Kerala Experience*. New Delhi: Routledge, 2015.

Zelizer, Viviana A. "Circuits in Economic Life." *Economic Sociology* 8, no. 1 (2006): 30–35.

Zygmunt, Tomasz. "Language Education for Sustainable Development." *Discourse and Communication for Sustainable Education* 7, no. 1 (2016): 112–124.

[illegible] University Press, [illegible], 2018.

[illegible] "[illegible] in the [illegible] of Migrations." In [illegible] and [illegible], edited by [illegible] and [illegible] Roberts, 225–[illegible]. Bristol, UK: Multilingual Matters, [illegible].

———. "[illegible] Migrants [illegible]: What Skills for What and for Whom?" [illegible] of Migration and Language, [illegible] 311–[illegible]. London: Routledge, [illegible].

[illegible] David. [illegible] Reading and Writing [illegible]. Cambridge, [illegible] Press, [illegible].

[illegible] of Social [illegible]. Durham, NC: Duke University Press, 2009.

[illegible] Cambridge, MA: Harvard University Press, [illegible].

[illegible] Cambridge, MA: MIT Press, [illegible].

[illegible] New York: [illegible] University Press, 201[illegible].

[illegible] SUNY Press, 20[illegible].

[illegible] London: Sage, 2014.

[illegible] London: [illegible] Press, 2016.

[illegible] New York: Teachers College Press, 2011.

[illegible] Illinois University Press, 20[illegible].

[illegible] "[illegible] Code Switching." Journal of [illegible] 2[illegible] 49–[illegible].

[illegible] New York: Routledge, 20[illegible].

[illegible] 2009.

[illegible] 11–12[illegible].

# INDEX

# INDEX

# INDEX